FINANCIAL SERVICES

For Warren A. Law
Edmund Cogswell Converse Professor of
Finance and Banking
Emeritus

In honor of his distinguished career
as teacher and scholar at the
Harvard Business School

FINANCIAL SERVICES

Perspectives and Challenges
Edited by Samuel L. Hayes, III

Harvard Business School Press
Boston, Massachusetts

97   96   95   94   5 4 3 2

Library of Congress Cataloging-in-Publication Data
Financial services: perspectives and challenges / edited by Samuel L. Hayes, III.
        p. cm.
    Includes bibliographical references and index.
    ISBN 0-87584-402-2 (acid free paper)
    1. Financial services industry—Management—Case studies.
I. Hayes, Samuel L.
HG174.F526 1993
332.1'068—dc20
93-16967
CIP

The paper used in this publication meets the requirements of the American National Standard for Permanence of Paper for Printed Library Materials Z39.49-1984.

CONTENTS

FINANCIAL SERVICES

INTRODUCTION

Samuel L. Hayes, III

"Globalization" has become a leading buzzword of the 1990s, conjuring up images of mammoth enterprises on whose outposts the sun (literally) never sets. Professor Theodore Levitt heralded the formation of global markets for goods and services in a seminal 1983 *Harvard Business Review* article.[1] Levitt was roundly criticized by other members of the academic community who maintained that many product and service markets would remain highly segmented by region or by country because of lifestyle and cultural idiosyncracies. Not only would products have to be tailored to these varied tastes, they insisted, but the marketing and advertising used to sell them would likewise require customization.

A decade later, the speed and complexion of the product market integration remains a subject of spirited debate. Nevertheless, Professor Levitt's prediction that money and capital markets would be among the first to achieve true global status turned out to be remarkably close to the mark.

Politicians and regulators of the postwar era spent decades building barriers to entry and exit around their national financial markets, which many viewed as important to national independence and well-being as defense and air transport. They actively precluded foreign interloping with a thicket of currency restrictions, ownership prohibitions, and sundry other controls. But even as governments labored to build fences around their national financial turfs, other forces were at work knocking holes in them.

The growth of international trade in the postwar era created a demand for trade financing and off-shore capital investment. As multinational firms set up offices, subsidiaries, and production centers

---

1. Theodore Levitt, "The Globalization of Markets," *Harvard Business Review,* May–June 1983, pp. 92–102.

abroad, their requirements for capital and financial services challenged both the existing national markets and the resourcefulness of the existing community of financial services firms. Even the corporations that stayed at home hoped to reach across borders—if only to tap cheaper or more accessible pools of capital than those to which regulation had restricted them. But neither the globe-trotting multinationals nor the domestic enterprises were capable of satisfying their new financing needs without the assistance of market-wise specialists. As always, they needed the intervention of financial advisers who had the two things that financiers of every era have possessed: the most up-to-date information and the ability to use it for the benefit of their clients.

Financial intermediaries are, at their core, "vendors of information," and the advances they have made in gathering and exploiting information have been dramatic. At each stage in history, the banker-financier earned a place at the table by being the first to acquire information that in one way or another related to the availability and pricing of capital. In the eighteenth century the Rothschilds placed semaphores on strategic hilltops to speed the transmission of information across long distances for the benefit of themselves and their clients. Other financiers utilized carrier pigeons and fast ships for the same purpose.

As we head into the twenty-first century, the modern equivalent of semaphores and pigeons are fiber-optic cables and satellite relay systems connecting computers to massive data bases. Information in these data bases is constantly updated to reflect the latest information on developments in a myriad of financial and product markets. Technological advances, especially the development of the microcomputer and associated software, have fostered financial market revolution where evolution had once sufficed. Indeed, the emphasis today with financial market information is on its manipulation: market participants now routinely massage data in real time against historic patterns and possible future trends, using both proprietary and third-party software and systems.

The revolution has extended beyond information to products. The traditional financial market products—bank credits and "plain vanilla" debt and equity underwritings—have been overshadowed by financial instruments of greater complexity. To enable them to act more effectively on the implications of massive rapid information flows, players in the world's capital markets have devised financial packaging techniques and routines, some designed specifically to reduce the friction that has historically encumbered movements of money. A good example is the "swap" transaction, a financial innovation of the early 1980s. This vehicle, by which borrowers can trade contractual features of their financings among themselves, has greatly aided the integration of money and capital markets by providing an efficient way to move from one currency to another. The swap also makes it possible to alter the terms of a financial instrument so as to play to the strengths of the parties to the transaction, while shielding them from their respective vulnerabilities. Derivatives, options, index products, asset-backed securities, and myriad other innovations have found much of their inspiration in laying off risk and enhancing liquidity.

Lively debate continues about the extent to which capital markets in major industrial countries are, in fact, effectively integrated. Some economists have argued that the ultimate measure of integrated capital markets is complete lack of correlation between national savings rates and investment rates. Since they *do* remain correlated, these researchers conclude that the markets are not completely global.[2]

There has been a substantial alteration in both the composition and the attitudes of the competitors in these interrelated financial markets. Investment funds are coalescing into large professionally managed pools, and this process of "institutionalization" continues to move forward in various parts of the world. Financial services vendors increasingly direct their product-marketing efforts *toward* these sophisticated investor-buyers and *away* from the once-dominant individual investor. Indeed, as we march toward the year 2000, the individual investor has become like a VW Beetle on a superhighway filled with eighteen-wheelers!

There are hazards aplenty in the fast lane of finance, but the individual investor is not the only one at risk. Financial intermediaries have begun emphasizing principal transactions for their own account over agency work for clients. These actions hold forth potential for profits, but have raised questions about the degree to which bona fide arm's-length advice and execution are being provided to institutional and corporate clients of these intermediaries. At times, tension has colored the relations between intermediary and customer—where a surprising gulf of perception and communication can prevail.

Capital-raising corporations and governmental units also have undergone substantial evolution. Many have increased the sophistication of their in-house financial capabilities and at the same time have grown wary of the motives and priorities of the financial vendors. This process has been greatly assisted by the development of cheap and effective computer hardware and software, which has made some level of "financial engineering" accessible to nearly all parties.

The proliferation of product offerings and the trend toward principal activities (transactions for the vendor's own account) have placed a

---

2. Martin Feldstein and Charles Harioka, "Domestic Saving and International Capital Flows," *The Economic Journal*, June 1980.

special focus on the capital requirements of various financial intermediaries. The Bank of International Settlements (BIS) has already set guidelines for capital adequacy as it relates to commercial banks. But it can be argued that no such single rule of thumb can prescribe an adequate cushion of risk capital to deal with the complexion of assets and liabilities of a particular financial intermediary. The complex interrelationships among various asset classes, firm activities, and commitments may yield an overall portfolio effect which is quite different.

All of this highlights the importance of an appropriate regulatory response to the transformed financial services sector. National regulation has historically been inward-looking and heavily overlaid with political agendas often at odds with financial market imperatives. It goes without saying that in the interdependent global capital markets described earlier, these practices must end; regulation must be fine-tuned to the new reality. Governments, having acquiesced to the development of off-shore markets, found that they were able to exercise less and less control over actions of financial intermediaries and their clients. Capital controls in many cases had to be relaxed. Today we appear to be moving inexorably toward a condition in which all of the participants in the financial markets around the world will be in one boat. If capital is to become fully fungible across national boundaries, then an advanced degree of regulatory harmonization is unavoidable. While the BIS guidelines, the various "Groups" (of Five, Seven, and Eleven), and European Community (EC) initiatives are steps down this road, much uniformity of regulation remains to be accomplished. Not only must national regulators row together, but they must avoid the partisan bickering that has the effect of chopping holes in the bottom of the boat.

A variety of research into the managerial and strategic challenges facing various financial service vendors has been ongoing at the Harvard Business School. As part of the celebration of the career of HBS Professor Warren A. Law, a pioneering teacher and scholar in the field of financial services, his faculty colleagues decided to bring the fruits of some of that research together in a colloquium, which was held in May 1992 and attended by a number of financial services sector leaders from the United States and abroad. A series of papers by members of the Harvard Business School faculty was therefore commissioned on topics relating to various aspects of the rapidly evolving financial services sector. The chapters that follow delve into the diverse issues and developments with which managers of financial intermediaries have had to come to grips.

In Chapter 1, Richard Vietor addresses the U.S. commercial banking sector as a prototype for a variety of deposit-taking and lending institutions in various national settings. The case of the Bank of America (BOA) provides a gripping tale of the bank management's response to changing market and environmental circumstances. After decades of dramatic growth in assets, people, profits, and market presence, BOA was caught in the crosswinds of early 1980s deregulation and shifting market conditions. The bank's stubborn inefficiencies, poor credit management, outmoded technology, and high fixed costs were rudely exposed, and its operations produced horrendous losses. The initial decline and subsequent rebuilding of Bank of America highlights both the capricious effects of regulation and the new imperatives of financial market competition that should concern management as we approach the turn of the century.

The unfortunate results of the efforts by politicians and regulators in the United States to transform the once-staid savings and loan business into something resembling full-service commercial banking are chronicled by Carliss Baldwin and Benjamin Esty in Chapter 2. The authors show how the practice of "securitizing" assets, when combined with a more uninhibited approach to liabilities, influenced a financial vendor group that had previously been forced to hold its mortgage investments until maturity. It also raises questions about capital adequacy in a vendor group with liabilities guaranteed by the state at minimal cost to the vendors themselves. Moral hazard, adverse selection, and almost inevitable abuse are suggested; with a government safety net in place, managers and stockholders in recently privatized savings and loans had every incentive to push into higher-risk, higher-reward investments. Sadly for taxpayers, this chapter demonstrates why national policy makers must thoroughly understand the operating and competitive dynamics of the industry sector for which they have responsibility before they start pushing any action buttons.

In Chapter 3, Carl Kester extends the discussion of regulatory impact to a country analysis of the behavior of an important class of financial institutions—commercial banks. Kester points out that Japanese and German bankers maintain close and active relationships with their industrial clients and that their involvement in matters of corporate governance is substantial. Concluding that this involvement has had a positive effect on corporate performance in those countries, he argues that the United States should reconsider the current restrictive policies on the involvement of financial institutions in corporate governance.

The apparent free-for-all of competitive scrambling that characterizes some of the largest public capital markets is not replicated in certain other sectors of the cross-national financial market spectrum. In Chapter 4, John Goodman contrasts the competitive environments in the non-life and reinsurance segments of the global insurance market. They have radically different characteristics and therefore have responded to the push toward globalization of financial markets in quite different ways.

The managerial implications of relationships between clients and their banking intermediaries are addressed by Dwight Crane and Robert Eccles in Chapter 5. The 1980s witnessed an attenuation in client-banker relationships on Wall Street as easy credit and an active market for corporate control introduced a more mercenary tone to the financial marketplace. After a period of movement away from "relationship" banking to "transactional" encounters between vendors and clients, the pendulum in the 1990s has begun to swing back toward more of a relationship orientation, aided by a shift toward equity and equity-linked products. Both investment bankers and their corporate customers confirm the importance of relationships, but neither understands or appreciates the term "banking relationship" in the same way. Crane and Eccles, using an interdisciplinary approach based in finance and organizational behavior, describe this client-vendor perception gap.

In Chapter 6, Samuel Hayes and Andrew Regan pick up this line of thought in looking at the evolving state of competition in the securities underwriting area. Using the recently introduced "shelf" registrations as an organizing focus, they chronicle the impact of this increasingly competitive public capital market on both clients and their bankers. Competition in the markets as a whole is seen as intensifying despite evergreater vendor concentration. This is attributed to client sophistication, technological complexity, and convergence among financial markets along all dimensions—product, geographic, regulatory, and so forth.

In Chapter 7, still another market sector—professionally managed mutual funds—is observed to have its own particular set of competitive characteristics. Erik Sirri and Peter Tufano examine the attraction of money to specific professional money management groups, the persistence of loyalty to that money manager, and the likely sources of competitive threat to dominant fund groups in the future.

In Chapter 8, Robert Merton and André Perold tackle the important question of measuring and then managing the capital positions of financial firms operating in an increasingly complex financial world. The authors develop a framework for analyzing these positions based on a clear distinction between what is really "risk" capital and what is riskless capital borrowed in order to finance asset positions. A need to examine firm needs on an aggregated as well as disaggregated (e.g., along business lines) basis is emphasized.

Some of the implications of the studies are examined in the conclusion, Chapter 9.

Basically, all the chapters in this volume are about financial sector change: in regulation and markets; in the attitudes and sophistication of customers; in the technology underlying new products and services; in competition; and even in the internal financing of the financial services firm. Change is the hot forge that tempers the substance of this industry and gives it its sharp edge. Change is the wolf that culls the herd, leaving the stronger and more agile ones to carry on.

For managers in this industry, the pace of change has never been more rapid; keeping ahead of it, and finding new and better ways to serve clients profitably is the essential managerial challenge. It is our hope that these chapters will provide some guidance in this important task.

CHAPTER 1

BANK OF AMERICA AND DEREGULATION: THE GREAT TURNAROUND

Richard H.K. Vietor

Introduction

For most of this century, government has played an immense role in American financial markets, as lender, borrower, intermediary, and regulator.* But the government's role as regulator—all but eliminating competition in price, product, and geographic scope—appears now to have been an anomaly, an emergency departure from more integrated and competitive markets. By the end of the 1980s, these controls had been largely superseded by the forces of economic and technological change.

For commercial banks in particular, a new and asymmetrical form of supervised competition has replaced a comfortable era of riskless stability. Although still closely regulated, banks and thrifts alike have been exposed to price and product competition from similar institutions, from nonbank financial firms, from foreign banks with relatively protected home markets, from securitized substitutes, and from disintermediation by large customers.

Bank of America's historical rise to pre-eminence exemplifies in microcosm the ebb and flow of regulation and competition in financial services. Its relatively late founding, early growth, and diversification occurred in an era of "free banking," when entrepreneurship mattered. Bank of America experienced phenomenal growth after World War II in an unusually prosperous macroeconomic environment, thoroughly shielded from competition by the elaborate New Deal structure of banking regulation installed in the 1930s. But in the early 1980s, its late

---

* This chapter is a substantially revised portion of a chapter in *Contrived Competition* by Richard H.K. Vietor, forthcoming from the Harvard University Press.

exposure to risk and competition with little prior preparation nearly caused its demise. "Since Bank of America had benefited more from regulation than anybody else," as one executive observed, "it was going to get hurt more than anybody else from deregulation."[1]

With the onset of deregulation in the early 1980s, Bank of America's profits declined and its assets deteriorated for the first time in more than a decade. Efforts at strategic redirection, although well-intentioned, were too little and too late. By 1986, the bank stood at the brink of collapse, with losses of nearly $1 billion.

This chapter analyzes Bank of America's adjustment to partial deregulation. It examines the forces behind regulatory reform— macroeconomic change, technology, entrepreneurship, and regulatory failure—the peculiar conditions that insulated Bank of America from change during the Clausen era (1970–1981), the bank's traumatic struggle to adjust during the Armacost years (1981–1986), and its final turnaround after Clausen's return (1986–1989). The conclusions generalized from this case have a number of implications for commercial banks as they plan strategies for adjusting to regulatory change.

Giannini's Bank

When Tom Clausen was appointed its president in 1970, Bank of America had already been in business for 64 years. It looked like a money-center bank by size of assets, but the resemblance ended there. This bank was created "to serve the little fellow," and it had. Its founder, A. P. Giannini, a second-generation Italian immigrant, had built a branch system throughout California, and had consolidated his banking interests in that state and in New York under a holding company—the Transamerica Corporation. Giannini championed nationwide branch banking,[2] opposed the principal restrictive provisions of the McFadden Act, and supported Franklin Roosevelt.[3] He endorsed the banking holiday and

---

1. Interview with Steve McLin, March 1990.
2. A.P. Giannini was an extraordinarily colorful as well as successful individual, whose biography can hardly be separated from the history of the bank. There are two biographies of Giannini: Julian Dana, *A.P. Giannini: Giant in the West* (New York: Prentice-Hall, 1947), and Fred Yeates, *The Gentle Giant* (San Francisco: Bank of America, 1954). However, for a history of the bank itself, there is a very good scholarly book: Marquis James and Bessie Rowland James, *Biography of a Bank: The Story of Bank of America* (New York: Harper Brothers, 1954).
3. James and James, *Biography of a Bank,* pp. 187–192, 262–292.

was influential in the debate over the Banking Act of 1933. "No other banking group," wrote the bank's chief lobbyist at the time, "gains from this act as many advantages as does Transamerica."[4]

Under this elaborate system of regulatory stabilization, Bank of America had indeed prospered. As early as 1945, it surpassed Chase National in deposits and assets ($5 billion), making it the largest bank in the world.[5] This distinction was maintained well into the 1980s by Giannini's three successors—S. Clark Beise (1954–1962), Rudolph Peterson (1962–1969), and Alden W. Clausen (1970–1981). After the Justice Department ordered the divestment of Giannini's Transamerica Corporation, the Bank of America refocused on growth within California and outside the United States.[6] Deposits tripled, from $8 billion to $25 billion; loans, from $4 billion to $15 billion; and earnings, from $68 million to $163 million. In California the branch system more than doubled in size, from 453 to 977 branches. There was almost no community in California where a customer could not conveniently make a deposit in or apply for a mortgage from the Bank of America. In 1950, Beise automated documents handling and bookkeeping at least a decade before his competitors.[7] During this same period, the BankAmericard was

---

4. C.W. Collins, quoted in James and James, *Biography of a Bank,* pp. 374–376. Giannini's efforts helped ensure the Banking Act's provision of branching parity for national banks with state banks. The act allowed Giannini to merge his state- and national-chartered banks in California, creating Bank of America N.T. & S.A., with 423 branches. It also allowed Transamerica to buy multibranch banks in Oregon and Nevada, adding to Bank of America's overwhelming regional dominance. The 1935 amendments, which increased deposit insurance and raised the ceiling on real estate investments for national banks to 60% of deposits, were also of greater benefit to the Bank of America than any other bank. In fact, Federal Reserve Chairman Marriner Eccles wired Giannini to thank him for supporting these amendments, which the New York banks had adamantly opposed; M.S. Eccles to A.P. Giannini, August 25, 1935, quoted on pp. 389.

5. James and James, *Biography of a Bank,* p. 477.

6. Antitrust actions, initiated by Treasury Secretary Henry Morganthau in 1937, and carried on during the 1940s by Marriner Eccles, chairman of the Federal Reserve Board, eventually forced the divestment of Transamerica in the early 1950s. The Bank of America in California was separated from the bank in New York and from the insurance and diversified financial assets of Transamerica; see Marriner S. Eccles, *Beckoning Frontiers: Public and Personal Recollections* (New York: Alfred A. Knopf, 1951), pp. 443–453; and *Transamerica Corporation vs. Board of Governors of the Federal Reserve System,* "Findings as to the Facts," in U.S. Congress, Senate, Select Committee on Small Business, Subcommittee on Monopoly, *Concentration of Banking in the United States,* Staff Report of the Board of Governors of the Federal Reserve System (82d Cong., 2d Sess.), Committee Print No. 7 (Washington, D.C., 1952), pp. 28–50.

7. "A History of the Electronic Recording Machine (ERM)," Engineering Division, Stanford Research Institute, June 1, 1955, in BankAmerica Archives, file 752.6.

introduced, eventually to become the first bank credit card offered nationwide.[8]

The Bank of America's international activities, begun by Giannini during the late 1930s, expanded rapidly during this period. In the 1950s, the bank opened several offices in Southeast Asia and Latin America and expanded the corporate lending activities of its London office. A large step was taken in 1956 with the purchase of Banca d'America e d'Italia—a multibranch, retail and commercial bank in Italy. In the eight years of Peterson's presidency, the number of overseas branches grew from 22 to 100, with 61 subsidiaries in 77 countries. International assets increased to $8 billion—approximately one-fourth of the bank's total assets.[9]

The Unraveling of Regulation

Fundamental changes in basic economic conditions during the late 1960s triggered the process of regulatory reform. Inflationary pressures from rapid investment growth and heavy government borrowing pushed short-term interest rates above long-term rates *and* the interest-rate ceilings set by the Fed under Regulation Q.[10] Disintermediation (financial transactions that circumvent banks) was the result. Potential depositors diverted their savings to more attractive financial instruments, and commercial customers turned to foreign capital markets and a greater reliance on commercial paper, new equity, or bonds. For most banks and thrifts, this meant a slowing of growth, starting with deposits.[11]

After 1968, persistent inflation, oil price shocks in 1973 and 1979, slower productivity growth, and still large fiscal deficits combined to drive nominal interest rates to new heights. Further and more serious

8. J. Williams to S.C. Beise, "Report on Charge Account Banking," October 1957; Bank of America Archives, file no. 923.15. The bank expanded the card nationwide through a licensing arrangement with other banks. In less than two years, it had enrolled 6.4 million cardholders and 165,000 merchants. BankAmericard Fact Sheet, March 11, 1968; Bank of America Archives, file no. 1454.20.
9. Bank of America, *Annual Report for 1970*, pp. 12, 28–29.
10. Albert H. Cox, *Regulation of Interest Rates on Bank Deposits* (Ann Arbor: University of Michigan, 1966), p. 121.
11. Charles F. Haywood and Charles M. Linke, *Regulation of Deposit Interest Rates* (Chicago: Association of Reserve City Bankers, 1968), pp. 38–41; and Lewis J. Spellman, *The Depository Firm and Industry* (New York: Academic Press, 1982), pp. 141–142. Meanwhile, long-term corporate borrowing, led by the bond issues of rapidly expanding utilities, accelerated. The yield on corporate bonds increased sharply, from 5% to 9% between 1965 and 1970. The volume of new public bond issues, which had grown at a rate of about 3% (1960–1965), also accelerated to 35% (1965–1970). In equity markets, the volume of trading increased dramatically as new institutional investors sought to maximize their returns; Herbert Dougall and Jack Gaumnitz, *Capital Markets and Institutions*, 3d ed. (Englewood Cliffs, N.J.: Prentice-Hall, 1975), p. 173.

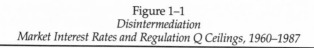

Figure 1–1
Disintermediation
Market Interest Rates and Regulation Q Ceilings, 1960–1987

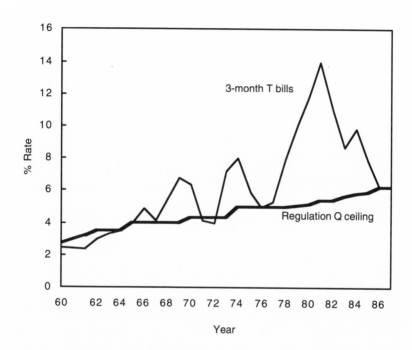

Source: Economic Report of the President, 1989.

bouts of disintermediation followed, in 1969–1970, 1974, 1979, and 1981 (Figures 1–1 and 1–2). These dramatic macroeconomic developments changed the balance sheets of financial intermediaries for the worse. On the liability side, noninterest-sensitive deposits—especially demand deposits—contracted dramatically as a source of funds (from 70% in 1950 to 20% by 1980). These were gradually replaced by time deposits and then interest-sensitive deposits and purchased funds. On the asset side, however, competition threatened interest-sensitive business— especially commercial lending. So loan portfolios gradually shifted toward less competitive markets such as mortgages and agricultural and consumer loans, where interest rates were typically fixed (and where credit worthiness was substantially inferior).

This was an historic reversal for financial intermediaries, and to the extent that banks held more fixed-rate loans than fixed-rate deposits,

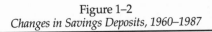

Figure 1–2
Changes in Savings Deposits, 1960–1987

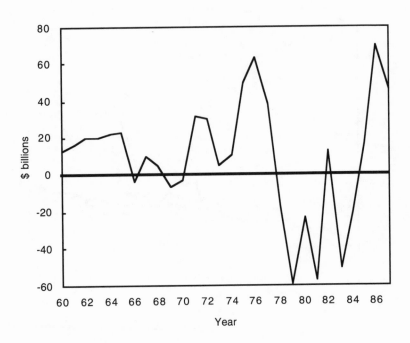

Source: Economic Report of the President, 1989.

they would suffer a negative "mismatch" of funds. In other words, in periods of rising interest rates, the banks' stable revenues (on fixed-rate mortgages) would be outstripped by the rising interest costs of attracting new deposits. The new and dramatic volatility of both interest rates and economic growth during the 1970s increased banks' exposure to "interest-rate risk" as well as credit risk. Bank of America, as we will see, fell victim to just this problem.

Developments in international finance were part of this change. The breakdown of the Bretton Woods system of fixed exchange rates after 1973 facilitated international transmission of inflation and cross-border capital flows. These market pressures undermined the artificial segmentation of previously closed domestic capital markets, allowed access to unregulated sources of funds, and encouraged competitive entry. Foreign banks, usually operating with less liquidity and greater leverage, entered the U.S. market in large numbers during the 1970s.[12] In California, for example, 74 foreign banks had claimed 30% of the commercial loan market by 1979 (up from 7% in 1970).

The oil crisis of 1973–1974 unleashed even longer-term forces that would contribute further to the destabilization of financial markets. In addition to firing domestic inflation, the sudden fourfold increase in oil prices caused large new flows of revenues across national borders, from oil-consuming countries to oil-producing countries, especially in the Middle East. When these immense revenues could not immediately be absorbed by the small and underdeveloped populations of producing countries, they were recycled into American banks. But since the stagnant U.S. economy had reduced loan demand, big banks—including BOA—eagerly lent these funds to developing countries, which were desperate to leverage their own economic growth. Eight years later, when these seemingly lucrative sovereign loans went bad, money-center banks like Bank of America would face massive international credit problems at the very moment of deregulatory adjustment.

Financial innovation flowed from these various disequilibria. The process was characterized by market-driven initiatives and technological innovations that literally forced regulators and legislators to make changes in public policy. As John Heimann, a former Comptroller of the Currency, wrote with only some exaggeration, "No such thing as government deregulation of the financial services industry exists today. Rather, it is the market that has deregulated the industry and continues to do so."[13]

By creating gaps between cost and price, outmoded regulation sowed "the seeds of its own destruction."[14] Where regulatory con-

---

12. The assets of foreign banks in the United States increased by 310% between 1973 ($63 billion) and 1982 ($275 billion), more than three times as fast as the growth of domestic banks. The number of offices increased sixfold, from approximately 100 to 600 during this period; David A. Walker, "U.S. Banking Regulations and Foreign Banks' Entry into the United States," *Journal of Banking and Finance* 7 (1983), pp. 569–580.

13. John Heimann, "Market-Driven Deregulation of Financial Services," a speech to the Atlanta Fed Directors, reprinted in Federal Reserve Bank of Atlanta, *Economic Review*, December 1984, p. 37.

14. See Thomas F. Huertas, "The Regulation of Financial Institutions: A Historical Perspective on Current Issues," in American Assembly, *Financial Services: The Changing Institutions and Government Policy* (Englewood Cliffs, N.J.: Prentice Hall, 1983), p. 23. For similar models of this self-adjusting tension, see Richard Vietor, *Energy Policy in America Since 1945* (New York: Cambridge University Press, 1984), pp. 1–12; and Edward J. Kane, "Accelerating Inflation, Technological Innovation, and the Decreasing Effectiveness of Banking Regulation," *Journal of Finance* 36 (May 1981), pp. 355–367.

straints were especially binding, or where loopholes opened opportunities to breach geographic or functional segmentation, entrepreneurs
seized "regulatory rents" through product and organizational innovation.[15] Prominent examples include negotiable certificates of deposit
(CDs), commercial paper, negotiable order of withdrawal (NOW)
accounts, and eventually money market mutual funds (MMMFs).[16] To
circumvent the constraints of the McFadden Act and Glass-Steagall,
banks used holding companies to enter "closely related areas"—leasing,
mortgage banking, trusts, investment advice, insurance brokerage, general finance, data processing, community development, and so forth.[17]
The number of one-bank holding companies (exempted from regulation
under the 1956 Bank Holding Company Act) increased from 550 to 2,200
between 1965 and 1978.[18]

New technology also worked to destabilize the regulated financial
system. Especially during the 1970s and early 1980s, information-pro-
cessing and telecommunications capabilities dramatically affected the
supply and demand for financial services and transaction products, as
well as industry operations and structure.[19] Computers revolutionized
account management and control, while automated teller machines
reduced costs while expanding market presence. Besides their obvious
impact on retail distribution and new-product definition, these technological developments created some limited economies of scale and even
more significant economies of multiproduct scope.[20] The effect of these

15. Spellman uses the term "regulatory rents" to describe the windfall income that a bank
    receives from the depressed deposit costs due to Regulation Q; see Spellman, *The
    Depository Firm and Industry,* pp. 148–151.
16. For an analysis and more complete chronology of these innovations, see Robert A.
    Eisenbeis, "Inflation and Regulation: The Effects on Financial Institutions and Struc-
    ture," in R.C. Aspinwall and R.A. Eisenbeis, *Handbook for Banking Strategy* (New York:
    Wiley, 1985), pp. 65–123.
17. C.A. Glassman and R.A. Eisenbeis, "Bank Holding Companies and Concentration of
    Banking and Financial Resources," in *The Bank Holding Company Movement to 1978: A
    Compendium* (Washington, D.C.: Board of Governors of the Federal Reserve System,
    1978), p. 255.
18. Donald T. Savage, "A History of the Bank Holding Company Movement, 1900–1978,"
    in *The Bank Holding Company Movement to 1978,* pp. 56, 62–65.
19. Office of Technology Assessment, *Effects of Information Technology on Financial Service
    Systems* (Washington, D.C., 1984), especially Chapters 3 and 4.
20. Richard W. Nelson, "Branching, Scale Economies, and Banking Costs," *Journal of Bank-
    ing and Finance* 9, 1985, pp. 177–191. Internal studies at Bank of America confirmed that
    the scale effects of transaction processing were insignificant, at least as of 1980; Bank of
    America consultant study, "Strategy Audit: Retail Delivery Systems" (September 1980),
    p. 37. On the economies of scope, see Collin Lawrence and Robert P. Shay, "Technology
    and Financial Intermediation in Multiproduct Banking Firms: An Econometric Study of
    U.S. Banks, 1979–1982," in Lawrence and Shay, *Technological Innovation, Regulation, and
    the Monetary Economy* (Cambridge, Mass.: Ballinger Books, 1986), pp. 53–92.

economies was to lower the barriers to arbitrage across the two key regulatory boundaries—product and geographic segmentation.[21]

Tom Clausen: Business as Usual, 1970–1981

In 1970, a relatively unknown, 46-year-old executive named Alden (Tom) Clausen, succeeded Rudolph Peterson as president of Bank of America. Clausen, a credit expert with experience in international lending, inherited a growing, multinational bank with the strongest domestic base of any bank in America. Under Clausen, Bank of America's business strategy remained essentially unchanged until 1981. Clausen focused on two targets, one explicit and the other implicit: a 15% growth in return on equity and surpassing Citicorp in profitability. Convinced that a global economy was emerging, Clausen used free cash from the California Division to help Bank of America catch up with the money-center banks in Europe and Latin America. The swirl of new competitive forces, deteriorating regulation, and technological innovation scarcely touched Bank of America. There were several reasons for this.

Foremost was Bank of America's unique competitive advantage—a statewide system of more than 1,000 branches. This distribution system gave Bank of America a broader and deeper access to low-cost funds and a degree of market dominance that no other bank could match. It meant that Bank of America did not experience a squeeze on net interest margins in the mid-1970s, when most other banks did. It meant that disintermediation was not a significant problem in the mid-1970s, when it first hit other banks. Bank of America's demand deposits and passbook savings accounts continued to grow at a healthy rate even in the 1980s. It meant that Bank of America's market saturation and first-mover locational advantages could preempt much of the new competition from S&Ls and nonbank financial companies. In fact, it meant that Bank of America did not *have* to adjust its cost structure, at least not yet.

This very strength in distribution reinforced another element of inertia—Bank of America's failure to effectively modernize its electronic processing and distribution capabilities. Part of the problem was the

---

21. Laurie S. Goodman, "The Interface between Technology and Regulation in Banking," in Anthony Saunders and Lawrence J. White, *Technology and the Regulation of Financial Markets* (Lexington, Mass.: D.C. Heath, 1986), pp. 181–193; Edward J. Kane, "Technological and Regulatory Forces in the Developing Fusion of Financial-Services Competition," *Journal of Finance* 39 (June 1984), pp. 759–772. Franklin Edwards adds the point that technological innovation drives regulatory change in part by lowering the cost of circumventing it; Franklin Edwards, "Commentary on Chapters 3 and 4," in Collins and Shay, *Technological Innovation*, pp. 144–145.

absence of any compelling short-term need. With a branch in every town, and demand growing on every side, it was hard to see a need to be first with unproven technology. The rest, according to Sam Armacost looking back at this period, was because of short-term cost containment and a void in technical management.[22] After developing a position of technology leadership in the 1960s, Bank of America seemed merely to let things go in the 1970s.[23] Even after an early pilot program with automated teller machines in 1975, top management decided that the economics didn't warrant a full-scale roll-out. According to a technology audit performed in 1980, this technological stasis resulted in "a lack of significant productivity gains in the branches," smaller competitors catching up with Bank of America's cost advantage, service problems associated with inflexible batch-oriented systems, and a continued reliance on mainframe computers and paper-based transactions right into the 1980s.[24]

A third factor that reinforced the status quo was the incredible strength of the California market, which seemed impervious to the economic shocks that plagued the rest of the nation. California's huge economy, already larger than that of most countries, scarcely missed a beat during the recession of 1974–1975. Agriculture, construction, aerospace, computers, entertainment, and increasing trade-related activity with Asia all contributed to strong loan demand and deposit growth for Bank of America. And the California housing market was the most vigorous of all. In the late 1970s, the real estate market grew at 30% a year. In 1978, for example, Bank of America's single-family mortgage portfolio jumped 37%.

California's extraordinary growth uniquely shielded Bank of America from some early reverberations of deregulation. When the recession of 1974–1975 undermined real estate values in the East, money-center banks suffered significant losses.[25] While they were forced to slow growth, revamp their credit-policy systems, and "internally rebuild their

---

22. Interview with Samuel Armacost, April 1990.
23. Tom Clausen attributed the problem to a lack of good technical management after the retirement of Al Ziff, the bank's computer innovator, in the mid-1970s; interview with Tom Clausen, April 1990.
24. The Boston Consulting Group, "Strategy Audit: Retail Delivery Systems," prepared for Bank of America Corporation, September 1980, pp. 13–16, 37–38.
25. New York banks had invested heavily in real estate investment trusts (REITS); Bank of America, with many other sources of growth, had not. The Wells Fargo Bank also experienced serious credit problems in the recession of 1974–1975, and was forced to reform its credit-control policies. The manager who dealt with those problems, and thus gained valuable experience with credit control, was Glenhall Taylor. He was subsequently hired by Seafirst to clean up its bad loans and then brought to Bank of America in 1985 to deal with its deepening crisis.

houses," Bank of America remained unscathed, and simply continued to grow. As Armacost put it from the perspective of a decade later, "They had done what the Bank of America had to do in the early 1980s," but then without the benefit of double-digit inflation.[26]

Still another reason for Bank of America's strategic inertia was its decentralized organizational structure, characterized by a tradition of autonomous branch managers operating what were effectively full-service banks, and a corporate culture oriented to loyalty, lifetime employment, low salaries (without incentive compensation), and promotions from within. There was a growth tradition and a service tradition, but nothing that could be called a competitive experience. The flip side of its strengths—the statewide branch network and presence in more than 100 countries—was also a weakness. This huge organization was like an oil tanker—it had great momentum, but it could scarcely slow down, much less "turn on a dime."[27]

Even the changes that were made during this period scarcely prepared Bank of America for deregulation. Budgetary coordination was strengthened with the implementation of a "building block system" designed to calculate "the contribution of individual units to overall profit." But there was no strategic planning, and credit authority was shifted increasingly from headquarters to line organizations.[28] Loan authority in the field was increased from $5 million to $20 million. Responsibility for larger loans was more or less divided between the General Loan Committee, the comptroller, and the cashier.[29]

Although the California Retail Banking Division grew steadily in the 1970s, it gradually lost market share to smaller banks and S&Ls.[30] (See Figure 1-3.) With little new investment in processing technology, and a compensation system based on seniority, it was no wonder that service quality deteriorated and customers switched banks.[31] Still, by controlling noninterest costs and growing steadily, Bank of America realized Tom Clausen's goals in 1978. Return on equity had surpassed Citicorp's in

26. Armacost interview.
27. In Bank of America, *Annual Report for 1977*, Clausen approvingly cites the use of this metaphor by a bank analyst; p. 3.
28. When it did adopt strategic planning in 1979, the Managing Committee qualified its decision in several respects. Two of these foretold part of the problem that Armacost and McLin would subsequently have in selling their ideas to line management: (1) "the process should be line management driven," and (2) "most of the staff resources devoted to planning should be domiciled in the line units;" Managing Committee, "Summary of Transactions," March 28, 1979.
29. Interview with Leland Prussia, March 1990.
30. Bank of America, *Annual Report for 1978*, p. 13.
31. Bank of America Market Research, 1979 CUSFIRB Study.

Figure 1–3
BOA's Share of California Commercial Banking Market

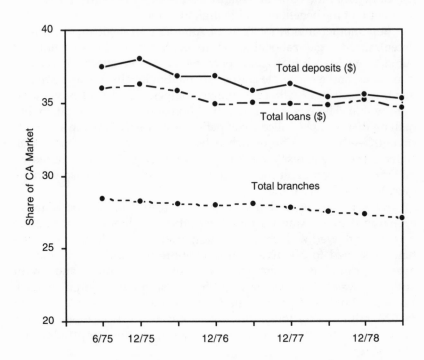

Source: Bank of America Corporation Market Research Data.

1977, and return on total assets in 1978.[32] Bank of America's operating income of $514 million that year also exceeded Citicorp's by $32 million. "When I became president," observed Clausen, "one of my goals was to make our bank profit-conscious. I thought it could be done in three years or so. Well, it took more time than I expected, but nevertheless, we have achieved that goal. Now, profitability is a working idea that we find wherever we go in this bank. We're thinking *profits,* and that's one key to success."[33] Bank of America could rightfully claim to be the world's biggest bank—in earnings as well as assets.[34] (See Table 1-1.)

32. Charles H. Lott, "B of A vs. CITI: A Perspective," in Keefe, Bruyette & Woods, *Keefe Bankreview,* November 14, 1980.
33. Tom Clausen, speech at Bank of America's Management Conference, February 1977.
34. The Boston Consulting Group, "Comparative Competitive Position: Bank of America Corporation versus Citicorp," prepared for Bank of America Corporation, February 1980.

Table 1-1
Bank of America Growth and Performance
1975–1980

	1975	1976	1977	1978	1979	1980	CAGR* 1975– 1980
Domestic							(%)
Assets ($bil)	36.6	38.0	38.5	44.7	55.0	59.2	10.1
Income ($mil)	158	201	229	338	375	358	17.8
No. Branches	1,057	1,074	1,092	1,095	1,096	1,104	
Foreign							
Assets ($bil)	23.7	26.5	33.1	36.8	39.3	44.9	13.6
Income ($mil)	135	144	167	177	225	287	16.3
No. Branches	107	114	114	114	110	113	
No. Employees	67,229	69,182	79,922	76,666	80,959	83,713	4.5
Noninterest costs ($mil)	1,163	1,294	1,495	1,784	2,001	2,313	14.7
							[5-yr. average]
ROA (%)	0.50	0.52	0.55	0.63	0.64	0.57	0.57
ROE (%)	16.0	15.5	15.5	18.0	18.4	17.5	16.8

* Compound annual growth rate.
   Source: Bank of America, *Annual Reports,* various years.

Now the unbroken string of increases in quarterly earnings, especially after market analysts had come to expect it, dominated decision making. So the push for profits continued, increasing annually for an eighteenth consecutive year through 1980—Clausen's last full year as CEO.[35]

One of the decisions taken in this environment—to lend long and mismatch the bank's interest exposure—would cause a huge problem for Clausen's successor, just at the juncture of deregulation. With the approval of the Money and Loan Policy Committee, the bank intentionally mismatched its fixed-rate assets and variable-rate liabilities; the pressure to grow profits was enormous. But the lower anticipated rates failed to materialize, as Paul Volcker, the new chairman of the Federal Reserve, squeezed the nation's money supply to curb inflation. During 1979, despite a negative interest-rate exposure greater than most other

35. Sam Armacost, as cashier, reportedly had to deplete every available source of hidden accounting profit (euphemistically referred to as "Baumhefner's cookiejar") to show positive growth; Gary Hector, *Breaking the Bank: The Decline of Bank of America* (Boston: Little, Brown, 1988), pp. 117–124.

banks, the Money and Loan Policy Committee allowed Bank of America's negative mismatch to reach $7 billion—about 8% of total assets.[36]

In January 1980, when Sam Armacost took over the committee, he realized that "the existing excess of fixed-rate assets was near the maximum desirable."[37] But then, as Armacost tried to slow the flow of fixed-rate assets, he discovered just how difficult it was for headquarters staff to affect the institutional momentum of so large an organization. Even after the Money and Loan Policy Committee decided to curb real estate lending, recalled Armacost, "it took seven or nine months to shut this off." With experienced loan officers in the bank's 1,100 autonomous branches motivated by a transfer pricing system that decoupled loan rates from the cost of funds, "the stuff just kept flying out of the branch system."[38] Over the next two years, Bank of America's annual losses on net interest reached $500 million.[39]

Regulatory Reform

As John Heimann's observation suggested, regulatory reform in the banking sector was little more than the political acknowledgment of de facto competition. Piecemeal efforts by the Fed to extend Regulation Q to S&Ls and raise large-deposit interest ceilings had done little to stem the tide.[40] Only when disintermediation reached crisis proportions in 1980, and the return on equity for S&Ls approached zero, did Congress finally act. Combining the piecemeal interests of a dozen bills introduced in 1979, the Carter administration succeeded in forging a coalition.[41] In March 1980,

36. The Boston Consulting Group, "Alternative Funding Strategies: Influence on Level and Stability of Profits," prepared for Bank of America Corporation, June 1980, pp. 63–66, 119. The 38 large banks analyzed in this study showed a wide range of mismatch positions at the end of 1979—from Bank of America's extreme of negative 8%, to 0.3% for Citibank, to positive 10.8 % for Irving Trust. Of the 15 largest banks, the five in California and two in Chicago were the most negatively exposed; the New York banks were the least negatively exposed. During 1979, the group of 38 banks shifted from an average positive exposure of 2.9% to -0.3%; pp. 48–49.
37. Money and Loan Policy Committee, "Report," January 4, 1980.
38. Armacost interview.
39. In September 1982, for example, the Managing Committee approved a mismatch target of $6.1 billion by the end of 1983. To accomplish this, fixed-rate loans would be limited to $4.3 billion, with fixed-rate liability growth budgeted for $1.7 billion; Managing Committee, "Summary of Transactions," September 16, 1982.
40. Haywood and Linke, *Regulation of Deposit Interest Rates*, pp. 41–43.
41. In a message to Congress dated May 22, 1979, President Carter proposed legislation that included NOW account equalization, adjustable rate mortgages, a phaseout of Reg. Q, and provision for consumer lending by S&Ls (up to 10% of their assets). Evidently, without provision for greater Fed authority and a sizable increase in federal deposit insurance, this proposal did not attract adequate political support; U.S. Congress, House, Committee on Banking, Finance and Urban Affairs, H.R. Doc. No. 96-129, 96th Cong., 1st Sess., (1979) pp. 1–3.

Congress enacted the Depository Institutions Deregulation and Monetary Control Act (DIDMCA). This bill, according to one senator, looked like a cross between "a Christmas tree" and "a forest primeval."[42]

Reflecting its diverse origins, DIDMCA did many different things.[43] It created a six-member Depository Institutions Deregulation Committee (DIDC), composed of banking regulators and the secretary of the Treasury, charged with implementing a phaseout of Reg Q. It extended the Federal Reserve's authority over reserve requirements to all depository institutions that used its payments systems. It allowed commercial banks and S&Ls to offer interest-bearing checking accounts (to individuals, but not to businesses), and raised deposit insurance ceilings from $40,000 to $100,000. This little-debated measure provided banks and thrifts with a perverse incentive to take undue risks. Federally chartered thrifts received several new powers: an expansion of geographic scope for residential mortgage lending, parity with commercial banks on consumer finance, and broader authority to make construction and development loans. Investment authority was increased to 20% of total assets in consumer loans, commercial paper, and corporate debt securities. Finally, state usury ceilings on residential mortgage and certain agricultural loans were preempted.[44]

Despite all this, DIDMCA proved to be just another stage in the decomposition of the regulatory tar baby. It may have mitigated disintermediation, but the S&L sector was still stuck with a portfolio of long-term fixed-rate mortgages. Thus higher short-term rates only aggravated their mismatch, pushing net income into the red by 16.5%, and tangible net worth close to zero.[45] Although commercial banks also suffered, they could more easily raise funds to staunch the disintermediation.

In something of a panic, Congress passed the Garn-St. Germain Depository Institutions Act of 1982.[46] This law, like the DIDMCA before it, was a collage of pending bills that represented disparate, particularistic interests. It was clearly an emergency measure, designed to relieve the thrift industry from disintermediation. Both S&Ls and commercial

---

42. Senator Donald Stewart, *Congressional Record*, March 27, 1980, p. 6910.
43. Pub. L. No. 96-221, 94 Stat. 132 (1980).
44. For analysis of these provisions, see H. Helmut Loring and James M. Brundy, "The Deregulation of Banks," *Washington and Lee Law Review* 42, 2 (Spring 1985), pp. 347–354; also, Peter I. Berman and Alfred A. Olbrycht, "Another Look at the Deregulation and Monetary Control Act of 1980," *The Bankers Magazine*, July–August 1981, pp. 16–21.
45. Norman Strunk and Fred Case, *Where Deregulation Went Wrong* (Washington, D.C.: United States League of Savings Institutions, 1988), p. 37.
46. Pub. L. No. 97-320, 96 Stat. 1501 (1982); for analysis of legislative origins, see Richard Fischer et al., *The Garn-St. Germain Depository Institutions Act of 1982: What's in It for You?* (Arlington, Va.: The Consumer Bankers Association, 1982).

banks were authorized to offer Super NOW accounts to a wider range of customers, and money market deposit accounts (MMDAs) with unrestricted interest and minimum balance of $2,500 (thus in direct competition with MMMFs). On the asset side of their business, thrifts were granted new freedoms as to how to use their funds. They could now buy state and local securities and corporate bonds (up to 20% of assets), and could expand their lending into previously restricted markets, including nonresidential real estate, education, and commercial loans.[47] The act also vested the FDIC (and the Federal Savings and Loan Insurance Corporation) with broader authority to bail out ailing institutions. These powers included making loans, purchasing assets or liabilities, and arranging mergers and acquisitions between failing thrifts and other financial institutions, including bank holding companies across state lines.[48]

Although the DIDMCA and the Garn-St. Germain Act fostered increased competition within the banking sector, neither law explicitly addressed restrictions on interstate banking or the Glass-Steagall separation of commercial and investment banking.

Sam Armacost: Strategic Response to Deregulation, 1981–1986

As he prepared to leave the bank, Clausen reshuffled his two top executives: Leland Prussia, the cashier, was moved to head the World Bank Division, and Sam Armacost, then head of European operations, was appointed cashier. Both executives joined the Managing Committee and the Money and Loan Policy Committee, which Armacost chaired. Prussia, an economist known as "the professor," had spent his entire career at the bank's headquarters. Armacost, a 39-year-old MBA from Stanford, had risen through a spectacular series of commercial-lending assignments. Neither man, however, had any firsthand experience with the California Retail Division. In 1981, when Clausen left Bank of America to head the World Bank Division, he chose Armacost to be president and

---

47. An important provision of the act, for both thrifts and commercial banks, was the pre-emption of state restrictions on the execution of due-on-sale clauses in mortgage contracts. A dozen states, including California, had passed laws of this sort during the 1970s so that homeowners could pass on an old, low-interest fixed-rate mortgage to the buyer, despite the fact that mortgage contracts typically contained provision for due-on-sale. For thrifts and banks generally, and for Bank of America in particular, this restriction of due-on-sale conversion had severely exacerbated mismatch problems. In *Wellingkamp vs. Bank of America, the* U.S. Supreme Court had upheld the state's restriction.

48. Gillian Garcia et al., "The Garn-St. Germain Depository Institutions Act of 1982," in Federal Reserve Board of Chicago, *Economic Perspectives,* March/April 1983, pp. 1–31.

chief executive officer; Prussia would hold the titular position of chairman.[49]

No sooner did Armacost take over as president of Bank of America than net income declined—for the first time in a decade—from $643 to $445 million. Armacost diplomatically attributed this 31% drop to the deregulation of deposits, to high and volatile interest rates, to unavoidable capital investments in electronic banking, and to competition from nonbank financial institutions. While all of these mattered, they were scarcely the root causes. Losses from mismatch, catch-up expenditures on ATMs, and a sharp increase in loan-loss reserves (from $241 to $322 million) all reflected prior policy.

Although wary now of the risks associated with deregulation, Armacost saw great opportunities:

> We can look on change as a threat, or we can seize on it as an opportunity. We can resign ourselves to it, or we can creatively adapt to change and manage it. My bias is to be on the offensive, on the positive side of the equation. . .We have no intention of pulling in our strategic planning horizons. . .[50]

Steve McLin, a young strategic planner who Armacost elevated to executive vice president in 1981, very much agreed with this approach. McLin was responsible for bringing in The Boston Consulting Group to help Armacost formulate a new strategy for Bank of America. Together they set out to make "a clear distinction," as one analyst put it, "between the 'old bank,' which had operated effectively under Tom Clausen in the pre-deregulation period, and the 'new bank' which was restructuring for this more competitive environment of the 1980s."[51]

This positive vision of deregulation eventually crystallized around four strategic initiatives: (1) acquisitions designed to strengthen Bank of America's West Coast dominance and to breach regulatory barriers to geographic and product expansion; (2) reorganization of the California Retail Division to cut costs and strengthen the core business; (3) an effort to catch up in electronic distribution and processing, converting the latter into a profit center; and (4) a cultural change within the bank to encourage risk taking, cost consciousness, and competitiveness. All of these policies were implemented over the next few years, but slowly and with mixed results.

49. At Bank of America, the position of chairman was more of an honorary position, secondary to the role of president and CEO.
50. Samuel Armacost, remarks before the Annual Meeting of Shareholders, San Francisco, April 21, 1981.
51. Keefe, Bruyette & Woods, "Bank America Corporation: How Bad Is It?" *Keefe Bankreview*, July 3, 1985.

Acquisitions

Both Armacost and McLin believed that success in the 1980s would require, in McLin's words, "finding synergies between merged institutions and, for banks, moving from a world of government-regulated monopoly privileges into a deregulated world." But for the moment, Bank of America continued to suffer from serious competitive disadvantages:

> Even though the bank had operations throughout the United States and could offer the full range of "legal" bank products, we face[d] significant limitations on product types due to the Glass-Steagall and limitations on geography because of the McFadden Act. We [we]re missing several key financial services (money market funds, underwriting, securities brokerage, and insurance) that make it difficult for us to bundle our existing assortment of products and services.

> [Even within California], our home market was particularly vulnerable—better products (Cash Management Accounts), from more competitors (Sears), and from familiar faces (Citibank). If we c[ould] offer our customers a wider choice of products, our banking relationship would be more secure.[52]

Acquisition of a full-line securities company such as Dean Witter would be problematic, since its underwriting activities exceeded 10% of revenues—the threshold allowed by Glass-Steagall. But it occurred to McLin that a discount brokerage that did no underwriting might work. Moreover, with its emphasis on retail transactions, it might complement Bank of America's huge branch network. McLin promptly called Peter Moss, his counterpart at Charles Schwab & Company, to set up a meeting.

The Schwab company, a creation of brokerage deregulation in 1975, had grown to become the nation's largest discount brokerage. With 37 retail offices in 22 states, Charles Schwab & Company had 250,000 accounts (of which 40% were in California) and sales of $41 million, a 9% share of the discount segment of the brokerage business. As a discount broker, Schwab specialized in transactions—processing sales and purchases of stocks that customers requested. By not offering any analytical, advisory, or other specialized services, and by developing large volumes, firms such as Schwab kept costs below those of their full-line com-

---

52. Steve McLin, interview with Dekkers Davidson, 1985, quoted in Dekkers Davidson and Richard Vietor, *Bank of America Corporation: "Project Charles"* (Boston: HBS Case Services, No. 9-385-246), pp. 7–8.

petitors. Charles Schwab, the company's young founder, was a one-man marketing department who delighted in undercutting the overpriced, cross-subsidized business of the full-line brokerage firms.[53] But with average growth of 70% per year, Schwab was continuously cash short, and had twice been turned down for loans by Bank of America.

In less than three months, Armacost and Schwab met and struck a deal—$53 million and a position for Charles Schwab on Bank of America's board of directors.[54] By 1986, Schwab's revenues reached $256 million, with a customer base of 1.2 million. Net income was $32 million, on $1.5 billion in assets. From a financial perspective, it was a great acquisition. Yet operationally, few of the synergies were actually achieved, and cultural fusion never occurred. To the contrary, Charles Schwab and many of his managers felt increasingly stifled by the hierarchy and formality of Bank of America.

The second prong of Armacost's acquisition strategy was the purchase of the Seafirst Corporation in 1983. With $8.2 billion in assets, Seafirst was the parent of the largest bank in the state of Washington—the Seattle First National Bank. It had a strong franchise, a dominant position in the consumer market, and a good reputation for service. Its management, however, had foolishly bought oil and gas loans from the Penn Square Bank of Oklahoma. When Penn Square went broke, Seafirst checked into its assets, and like Continental Illinois and Chase Manhattan, discovered a lot of worthless paper. McLin and Armacost saw Seafirst as a unique opportunity to circumvent restrictions on interstate banking and build a regional dominance *before* federal barriers were removed. (The Garn-St. Germain Act, liberalizing interstate bailouts, had just been passed but had yet to be tested before federal regulators.) McLin negotiated a price of $250 million for Seafirst, with a clever purchase mechanism that limited Bank of America's cash contribution to $132 million.[55]

Seafirst held the potential for strategic, but not economic, synergy. Profitable national expansion, Armacost believed, should occur in large chunks of local market dominance, rather than branded outlets (a "Texaco strategy") in all 50 states.[56] In fact, to preserve customer loyalty and name recognition, Armacost promised "there would be no

---

53. In fact, Schwab's advertising often contained an inflammatory "P.S.," suggesting that "many of our customers have found it highly profitable to maintain *two accounts*, one at Schwab and one with a full-commission broker"; ibid., p. 18.

54. Ibid., pp. 11–19.

55. For a detailed account of the Seafirst acquisition, see Hope Lampert, *Behind Closed Doors* (New York: Atheneum, 1986), pp. 8–55.

56. This analysis was reported in the Armacost interview from a perspective of seven years.

loss or blurring of Seafirst's identity." It would "operate as an independent bank, with its own management and own board of directors."[57] After a very difficult start, Seafirst appeared to have recovered by 1986. By 1989, when Seafirst reported profits of $120 million, its market value was estimated at $1 billion.

The California Retail Division

The Boston Consulting Group (BCG) began its strategic audit of Bank of America in 1980. Although this review examined the "middle market" (commercial lending to medium and small business) and the wholesale market (large corporations and institutions worldwide), it concentrated on the branch system, technology, and the retail market. This, after all, was Bank of America's cash cow.

In its study of pricing and deposit structure, BCG showed that net operating income as a percentage of deposits increased with the size of deposits in the branch system. Large balances and large transactions yielded relatively high earnings. Yet Bank of America used average-cost pricing; thus earnings from large and generally profitable accounts subsidized small and unprofitable ones, and some competitors had begun to take advantage of this "price umbrella" by lowering prices for larger accounts.[58] The BCG studies also revealed Bank of America's cost disadvantage in processing. Its continued reliance on paper-based, batch-oriented operations, still mostly located in the individual branches, had undermined productivity and hurt customer service.[59]

"The BCG work," explained Armacost, "made clear that you had to be a low-cost provider of services if you're gonna survive."[60] The Managing Committee approved plans to overhaul the full-service, full-function branch system both to reduce costs and improve service. Consolidation would be achieved by reconfiguring small branches in clusters around regional centers. At first, Armacost recalled with some frustration, "You couldn't get the retail branch structure to even think about doing anything differently, because they would say, 'Gee, it's been successful—look at our growth.'"[61]

Eventually, though, area management groups were designated to operate on a sort of hub-and-spoke basis. Convenience banking centers,

57. Quoted in Keefe, Bruyette & Woods, "The Bank of America-Seafirst Merger," *Keefe Bankreview*, April 29, 1983, p. 5.
58. The Boston Consulting Group, "Strategy Audit: California Retail," prepared for Bank of America Corporation, April 1980.
59. The Boston Consulting Group, "Retail Delivery Systems," September 1980, p. 45.
60. Armacost interview.
61. Ibid.

with ATMs and few tellers, were opened in shopping centers and office buildings; there were 35 such centers by 1985. Proof processing for 700 branches was consolidated into 42 centers. Real estate applications were processed in 48 home loan centers, while servicing the mortgages was concentrated in a single center. Consumer loan applications, credit checks, and collateral agreements, formerly handled by more than 1,000 branches, were now handled by 150. In 1984, this consolidation elimi- nated 130 branches and 9,000 jobs.[62] And finally, corporate lending within California ("the middle market") was removed from its tradi- tional dispersion in the branches and concentrated in 46 corporate bank- ing centers.

Technology

In 1981, Armacost approved the installation of ATMs at a rate of one per day—an investment of more than $100 million. Feasibility studies had estimated benefits from rapid ATM deployment of $626 million over 10 years.[63] By 1984, Bank of America already operated 1,300 ATMs, more than any bank in the country. Bank of America cardholders could even- tually perform banking transactions at 10,000 locations in 47 states.

Meanwhile, Armacost had hired Max Hopper, the man who had overseen American Airlines' development of its SABRE computerized reservation system. Hopper envisaged a computer system at Bank of America that could serve all the bank's various needs. But development of the proposed transaction processing facility proved overwhelming. Even after development expenditures of more than $1 billion, it still could not embrace the diversity of transactions and information needs represented in Bank of America.[64]

Organizational Structure and Culture.

Although Armacost acknowledged that Bank of America "needed a good kick in the fanny," he seemed constrained from doing so during his first year or two as CEO. This was due in part to holdovers among top

62. Bank of America, *Annual Reports*, 1984–1985; also Steve McLin, "BAC Corporate Strat- egy," February 14, 1985, p. 30.
63. The original planning documents, which suggested annual investments of about $14 million per year for a decade, estimated a break-even by 1984, not including sizable estimated benefits from market retention; Bank of America, Financial Planning & Con- trol, "ATM Strategic Plan," July 18, 1980, p. 2.
64. A piece of this effort, called International Banking Systems (IBS), was completed by 1988 to synchronize the World Bank Division (WBD) processing needs. This, in turn, helped the WBD serve global customers better and reduce the number of personnel in many of its foreign offices; interview with Lewis Teel, senior vice president, World Bank Division, January 1990.

management. Armacost complained that they were used to taking orders rather than initiating change: "They were all waiting to see which way the wind blew."[65] As one manager put it rather more bluntly, "Sam had no control over his direct reports. . ."[66] Two of the executives who resisted rapid change, the heads of the California Retail Division and the World Bank Division, finally retired in 1982.[67] Eventually, Armacost was able to replace more than half of the bank's 80 top executives.

Still, change within the ranks of the remaining management took time. For all its strengths, the Giannini legacy of a family-like institution had metastasized into a tradition of lifetime employment, low noncompetitive wages, and a culture of undemanding organizational slack. Top management could plan all sorts of dynamic changes, but these initiatives were simply swallowed up by a lethargic culture.

To facilitate the process of change, "to involve multiple levels of management in the change process," and "to get people comfortable with each other in terms of active disagreement over business issues," Armacost hired a consultant named Ichak Adizes,[68] a relatively unknown entrepreneur from Santa Monica, who had impressed Armacost with his unusual approach to organizational change. Adizes deployed a time-consuming process of change at the bank—fostering confrontation within small groups of managers, forcing them to bare frustrations and share deep-seated criticism with one another. The seminars continued for two and a half years.[69]

While Armacost and Prussia felt strongly that the Adizes process fostered team spirit and was necessary to force changes in the culture, many other executives were less sanguine. Some simply felt that it distracted top executives at a time when they could ill afford it; others felt that it misdirected the focus of change, and they simply declined to participate.[70] Whatever its costs or benefits, the Adizes process appeared to facilitate some important organizational changes needed to implement the profit-center approach suggested by BCG. Three so-called umbrella organizations were established: Bank of America Systems Engineering (BASE), Bank of America Real Estate (BARE), and Bank of America Payment Systems (BAPS). Under BASE, the bank's computer-based systems for telecommunications, data processing, and operations were consolidated. BARE brought together real estate experts from across the firm, presumably to realize on the synergies. And BAPS, the most important

65. Quoted in *The Wall Street Journal*, July 18, 1985.
66. Bank of America, interviews with middle management, January 1990.
67. Hector, *Breaking the Bank*, pp. 145–146, 148–149.
68. Armacost interview.
69. Moira Johnston, *Roller Coaster: The Bank of America and the Future of American Banking* (New York: Ticknor & Fields, 1990), pp. 189–204.
70. Bank of America, middle management interviews.

of these, combined all of Bank of America's transactions businesses—from check and currency services to card products, converting a huge center of costs to a profit-driven organization.

In 1984, Sam Armacost tried to crystallize these changes in organizational culture and purpose by personally articulating a sort of credo he called "Vision, Values and Strategies." The vision was one of worldwide leadership in financial services, based on values that emphasized customer service, technology, and the recognition and reward of employees.[71] Cynics in the bank whispered that "if Sam had a vision that had any value, then we'd have a strategy."

But a cogent strategy did evolve. It was summarized as follows by Steve McLin, and endorsed by the Managing Committee in January 1986:

> Expand our western regional dominance of the consumer and middle markets. Aggressively manage the global network [for large U.S. corporations and for multinational companies]. Integrate the delivery of services to U.S. commercial customers. And, linking all of these, become dominant in the payments business.[72]

Unfortunately, this positive vision of deregulation had come together and been implemented too slowly and without *first* making the harsh adjustments that the transition to competition required. So now the Armacost vision was all but extinguished by the dark sides of deregulation—noncompetitive costs and devalued assets—compounded by deflation. No sooner had Congress finished deregulating liabilities than the domestic economy plunged into recession, and debt crisis swept Latin America.

Bank of America's problems came in successive waves: mismatch gave way to disintermediation, then came a domestic credit crisis, and then the failure of its sovereign loans. As Armacost's management struggled to cope with these problems, regulators reasserted their authority over credit and reserves.

Disintermediation

Until 1982, Bank of America had moved cautiously with its pricing, minimum deposit requirements, and withdrawal penalties in order to minimize the costs of internal disintermediation (the shift by its own customers to the bank's higher-yield products). Armacost and others were hesitant to push the deregulatory process, since the bank had not

71. Bank of America, *Annual Report for 1984*, pp. 14–15, 61.
72. McLin, "Corporate Strategy Presentation," January 1985, p. 58; and Managing Committee, "Summary of Transactions," January 29, 1986.

prepared for the costs.[73] And since much of Bank of America's huge deposit base represented loyal and relatively unsophisticated savers, disintermediation affected it less than some other banks.[74]

But when Congress authorized money market demand accounts (MMDAs), the California Retail Division saw its chance to grab a dominant share of the market for this new product—if it moved fast and priced aggressively. Although the cashier's division worried about costs, analysis indicated that introduction of MMDAs might affect the account patterns of 30% of California's savers, who controlled 83% of the deposits. This realignment had first-mover attributes given the switching costs for depositors.

So Bank of America went for it—pricing its Cash Maximizer Account (CMA) at 50 basis points above its nine major competitors and holding it there for six months.[75] By the end of 1983, Bank of America's CMA had attracted $11 billion, representing a 55% market share in this new-product segment. Although most of these funds simply came out of lower-yielding Bank of America accounts, CMAs prevented the loss of deposits to competitors and the necessity to rely on even more expensive CDs.[76] And with the recession ending at this same time, interest rates declined and the bank's net interest revenue improved dramatically.

Credit Crisis

Despite this important victory, the Reagan recession—six quarters of negative GNP growth—was taking its toll. The booming California real estate market crashed; so did agriculture, shipping, and oil. Yet only after the recovery had begun did Bank of America's real problems become evident. The years of rapid growth with decentralized credit authority had produced billions of dollars of risky loans—in shipping, in commercial real estate, and in consumer credit. In agriculture and residential real estate, deflation decimated asset values. When mortgages suddenly exceeded the market value of properties, defaults escalated.

Figures 1-4 and 1-5 tell the story. In 1983, charge-offs jumped 61% to $707 million, then to $907 million in 1984, $1,599 million in 1985, and $1,419 million in 1986. Late in 1984, the Comptroller of the Currency

73. Armacost interview.
74. In fact, the bank decided to take a neutral position on the issue of a legislated, money-fund alternative. Money and Loan Policy Committee, Minutes, March 18, 1982.
75. Consumer Branch Service-Marketing, Memo to Money and Loan Policy Committee, Sub.: Garn Consumer Deposit Product, November 11, 1983 (file #3670).
76. As a proportion of liabilities, the new MMDAs grew from 1.8% to 12%; however, individual savings and time deposits decreased from 19% to 15.2%, and business deposits decreased 4%. So it would appear that internal disintermediation accounted for two-thirds of the gain from the new product; Bank of America, *Annual Report for 1983*, p. 23.

Figure 1–4
Bank of America Loan Loss Charge-Offs and Nonperforming Assets, 1980–1986

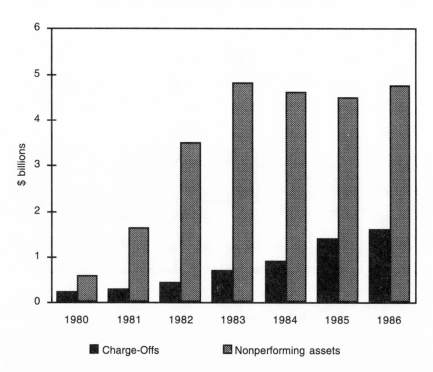

■ Charge-Offs   ▨ Nonperforming assets

Source: Bank of America, *Annual Reports.*

reviewed Bank of America's books and ordered it to increase reserves. The next year an even more critical Comptroller ordered an increase in primary capital to 6% by 1986. "How," asked Armacost rhetorically, "could Bank of America, which was highly levered, double its capital while it's not growing? That's a pretty deft trick."[77]

As the bank's domestic loan portfolio disintegrated, the debt crisis in Latin America worsened. In the two years after Mexico announced its moratorium on interest payments, there was plausible hope that "restructuring," supervised by the International Monetary Fund, would put debtor countries back on track. U.S. banks, including Bank of America, delayed making significant increases to loan-loss reserves. But by 1985, after oil prices turned down, it became clear that Mexico and most

77. Armacost interview.

Figure 1–5
Bank of America Loans and Loan Losses by Segment, 1983–1986

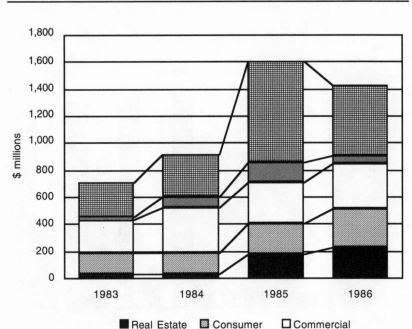

■ Real Estate   ▨ Consumer   ☐ Commercial

▨ Agricultural   ▦ Foreign

Source: Bank of America, *Annual Reports*.

of the other Latin American countries could not service their debt. Thus in 1985, foreign loans kept on a "nonaccrual" basis had to be shifted into loan-loss reserves, and some of that, charged off.

When Bank of America increased loan-loss reserves by $892 million and reported a loss of $388 million for the second quarter of 1985, the credit-rating agency of Keefe, Bruyette & Woods called it "horrendous," and promptly dropped the bank's rating to C/D.[78] By year's end, Bank of America's loan-loss reserves had reached $2.1 billion. "Our diversity," explained Armacost rather lamely to stockholders, "made us uniquely vulnerable."[79]

78. Keefe, Bruyette & Woods, "Bank of America Corporation: How Bad Is it?" *Keefe Bankreview,* July 3, 1985.
79. Bank of America, *Annual Report for 1985*, p. 2.

Belatedly now, Armacost undertook the really painful adjustments to deregulation. He brought in several top executives from outside Bank of America to take over and restructure key areas of the business. Among these were Glenhall Taylor, from Wells Fargo by way of Seafirst, who took charge of credit policy, and Thomas Cooper, from Mellon, to head the Payments System.

A "new and very tough credit approval system," with increased individual accountability as well as centralized control and oversight by a Credit Policy Committee, was instituted.[80] One analyst described Glenhall Taylor as "the quintessential credit officer . . . experienced at overhauling the credit process at a large banking organization."[81] Taylor conducted a thorough audit to identify and isolate bad assets. Agribusiness centers staffed by industry experts took charge of the bank's agricultural loans, and a specialized London-based task force took over the shipping portfolio. Loan officers were retrained in credit evaluation and given new incentives to reflect credit quality in their additions to the bank's portfolio. Managers who resisted these reforms saw their credit authority diminished or withdrawn altogether. Charge-offs in Taylor's first quarter reached $527 million. They continued at a gradually declining rate through the first quarter of 1986, when the bank reported another loss of $640 million.

Tom Cooper, meanwhile, was assigned the task of cutting costs and turning around the bank's newly organized Payments System. Among the ten largest banks, Bank of America ranked last in productivity (assets to employee). Even as assets were being sold, Cooper intended to increase the bank's efficiency by lowering noninterest costs and increasing market share. Some of his colleagues described Cooper as "Atilla the Hun," others as "John the Baptist."[82] The number of full-time employees decreased by 18,000 between 1983 and 1986; asset efficiency increased 27%.

To meet the Comptroller's new guidelines for primary capital, nonproductive and nonstrategic assets, including the headquarters building in San Francisco, FinanceAmerica, Decimus Corporation, and Banca d' America e d'Italia were sold. Securitization of mortgages was accelerated, and even automobile and credit card loans were packaged for sale.[83]

Even as this was happening, a great drama began to unfold in Bank of America's executive suite. The bank's weakened condition attracted the attention of Sanford Weill, an investment banker who had recently

80. Interview with Glenhall Taylor, March 1990.
81. Smith Barney, "Bank of America Corporation," June 14, 1988, p. 8.
82. Middle management interviews.
83. Bank of America, *Annual Report for 1985* and *Annual Report for 1986*.

sold his share of Shearson Lehman Brothers to American Express. Weill offered $1 billion in financial backing if Armacost would step aside and let him take over. Bank of America's board of directors rejected this offer out of hand, but began pressing Armacost for signs of a turnaround. Armacost set a goal of $1 billion in pre-tax profits for 1990 and appointed Tom Cooper president and chief operating officer of the bank.

But for Armacost, it was too late. Bank of America's stock plummeted and institutional investors began withdrawing funds. Joe Pinola, the head of First Interstate, made an offer to buy Bank of America for $18 per share. With $45 billion in assets, First Interstate, a spinoff from the Transamerica Corporation in the 1950s, had become a major West Coast rival to Bank of America.[84] This offer was also rejected, but something clearly had to give. On October 7, 1986, Bank of America's board of directors relieved Sam Armacost and Lee Prussia of their duties and voted to bring back Tom Clausen as Bank of America's chief executive officer.

The Transition to Regulated Competition

Just eleven months later, in September 1987, the investment bank of Smith Barney issued a "four-thump" (i.e., table-pounding) recommendation to buy Bank of America stock.[85] This was the first public recognition of what was soon touted as "the greatest turnaround in the history of U.S. banking."

When he returned to the bank in October 1986, "credibility was a big problem," recalled Tom Clausen. He immediately reassured institutional investors that drastic cost reductions and asset sales were in order. First Interstate dropped its takeover bid and the run on deposits stopped.[86]

Clausen quickly formed a new management team around four senior executives with prior experience at the Wells Fargo Bank; of these, three had been recruited by Armacost. Glenhall Taylor was retained as vice chairman for credit policy, and Frank Newman, deemed "the best banking CFO in the country," was made cashier.[87] Lewis Coleman, from the bank's Capital Markets Division, was promoted to head the World Bank Division. And finally, Richard Rosenberg, whom Armacost had recruited to Seafirst, was brought in to head the California Banking

---

84. The interpersonal details of these machinations are described at length in Hector, *Breaking the Bank*, pp. 250–316.
85. Smith Barney, "Bank Notes," September 10, 1987, p. 1.
86. This section draws heavily on *Bank of America Corporation (B)*, a case written by John M. Lynch and Richard Vietor (Boston: HBS Case Services, No. 9-390-177, 1990).
87. "BofA Chief to Step Down," *San Francisco Examiner,* January 1, 1990, p. A-14.

Group. Analysts were pleased by this visible empowerment of outsiders.[88]

This group went to work to implement the bank's modified strategic goals:

The two objectives are to be the major provider of premier retail and wholesale banking services in the western United States and to be a preeminent wholesale bank offering a focused package of credit, capital market, investment banking, and payment services in the U.S. and world markets.[89]

Divestiture of "nonessential" assets and the enhancement of core markets were crucial tenets of this new strategy. In the first 78 days of Clausen's second tenure, Bank of America reduced its assets by $9.6 billion. Besides selling loan portfolios and buildings, it completed the sale of Banca d'America e d'Italia, and a few months later, Charles Schwab & Company. Capital ratios improved markedly. The primary capital ratio increased from 6.9% in 1986 to 9.4% by 1989. Risk-based capital, under the new international guidelines, stood at 11%.[90] (See Figure 1-6.)

Operating costs were cut immediately. "It took me two nights," recalled Clausen, "to figure out what the hell was wrong with this organization—just by looking at simple, lousy expense-to-revenue ratios."[91] Over the next 30 months, head count was further reduced by 20,000. The bank's efficiency ratio (operating expenses/total income) dropped from 79% in 1986 to 63% in 1990. (See Figure 1-7.) This was in line with costs at Bank of America's competitors—First Interstate (80%), Security Pacific (71%), and Wells Fargo (61%).[92]

The California Banking Group targeted the retail deposit market with innovative consumer services and built on the payment services business that Tom Cooper had reorganized. Under Rosenberg, it enlarged its portfolio of credit card loans, home equity loans, and consumer lines of credit. By the end of 1989, Bank of America once again made more real estate loans than any other California bank.

The World Banking Group similarly rationalized its business by withdrawing from retail and middle markets in various international locations and concentrating on major international clients. Its integrated data base was completed and extended to Asia, Latin America, and the

---

88. Thomas K. Brown, "Bank of America Corporation," Smith Barney Research, June 14, 1988, p. 4.
89. Bank of America Corporation, *Annual Report for 1987*, p. 2.
90. Bank of America Corporation, *Annual Report for 1989*, p. 18.
91. Clausen interview.
92. Bernstein Research, "Banking Industry Outlook: Financial Forecast," March 1989, pp. 89, 93, 99, 10?

Figure 1–6
Bank of America Corporation Equity and Capital Ratios, 1986–1989

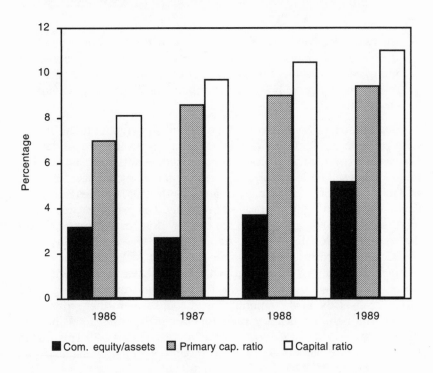

■ Com. equity/assets   ▨ Primary cap. ratio   □ Capital ratio

Source: Bank of America, *Annual Reports*.

United States. Staff levels were reduced in dozens of international offices.

At the heart of Bank of America's turnaround was the transformation in its credit practices. By 1988, according to one analyst, "Bank of America ha[d] moved from being among the most liberal of the major banks to being among the most conservative."[93] With help from credit experts he recruited, Taylor introduced new statistical practices for measuring the adequacy of loan-loss reserves and conservative adjustments to the accounting treatment of nonperforming loans. Credit losses were reduced from $1.4 billion in 1986 to $425 million in 1989. Although the bank still had $7.5 billion in loans to developing countries, it had increased reserves to cover 47% of them.

93. Brown, "Bank of America Corporation," pp. 9–10.

Figure 1–7
Bank of America's Efficiency Ratio
Noninterest Expenses/Income, 1970–1990

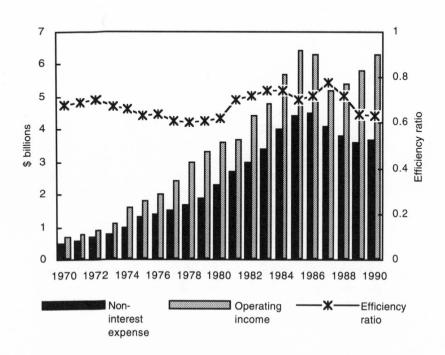

Source: Bank of America, *Annual Reports*.

In 1989, after its earnings had recovered, a resurgent Bank of America launched a program called Investment Network of America, through which an unaffiliated life insurance firm and securities brokers sold mutual funds, life insurance, and tax-deferred annuities in most California branches. Bank of America next purchased a Nevada bank with 14 branches, while Seafirst bought banks in Washington and Oregon.

In the spring of 1990, Tom Clausen asserted, "The turnaround has been accomplished. The recovery is a fact. My job is done."[94] Bank of America had indeed recovered from a net loss of $519 million in 1986, to a positive net earnings of $726 million by 1987, and eventually a record net income of $1.1 billion in 1989. Return on assets recovered to 1.14%. The bank's stock, which had bottomed out at $7 per share in the winter

94. Bank of America Corporation, *Annual Report for 1989*, p. 2.

of 1986, was back up to $30 by 1990. Tom Clausen announced his retirement and appointed Richard Rosenberg to succeed him.

Competitive Markets, Structural Adjustment, and Leadership

By the late 1980s, even limited deregulation had fundamentally altered financial services markets. Bank of America, like all other firms, had been forced to either adjust or disappear. Product-market boundaries and entry restrictions created by New Deal legislation had faded or vanished altogether. A wave of new financial products on both sides of the balance sheet engulfed the regulatory boundaries that remained. Geographic barriers were similarly eroded through market failure and interstate rationalization. Distribution channels such as ATMs and regional loan-service centers became more important than ever. Pricing—to the extent that regulation allowed—moved dramatically toward marginal cost. Average-cost pricing of deposits, free or bundled services, and fixed-rate mortgages became less common; variable rates, price packages, and options proliferated. And across the board, costs were forced down as a necessity of price competition.

Although Armacost saw that a "new bank" would be necessary, he underestimated the magnitude of necessary cost reductions, the importance of first-mover adjustments, and the difficulties of implementation. He had gotten the cart before the horse; he had implemented a positive vision of acquisitions, modernization, and cultural reorientation *before* undertaking the dirty work of shrinking excess capacity and reducing costs. He simply took too long to streamline the branch network (in California and worldwide), downsize the work force, sell bad assets, and centralize managerial control. Only in 1986, when faced with calamity, did Armacost abandon uncompetitive markets and refocus on Bank of America's strengths: regional dominance in retail banking and global service for multinational customers. The data in Figure 1-7 were Armacost's undoing. Ironically, Tom Clausen's strengths *after his return* complemented Armacost's failings. Working by the numbers, Clausen disposed of assets, reduced head count, and restored the bank to profitability.

Bank of America's near-disastrous transition to less-regulated markets fairly represents both the successes and failures experienced by other incumbent firms faced with deregulation in the transport, communications, and energy sectors. Successful adjustment generally entailed immediate shrinkage, cost reduction and asset consolidation, employee re-education, productivity incentives, and strategic focus. Failure most often came from premature expansion and diversification, excessive leverage, bureaucratic and uncompetitive behavior within middle management, and delay—all of which failed to generate the cash flow necessary to modernize and eventually expand.

The Bank of America experience would seem to indicate that big institutions must go through a rapid and thorough shakeout as a precondition to the positive changes that will prepare them for competition in deregulated markets. Excess capacity and high costs have to be shed *before* meaningful reforms can be implemented. As Armacost discovered, institutional reform is not feasible when you are drowning in red ink. The first job is to stem the losses, even if draconian measures are required.

American financial institutions have already experienced one round of deregulation. If a second round gains political momentum in the 1990s, commercial banks will again come face to face with the need for competitive adjustment. Bank of America's recent experience is a reminder of how painful that adjustment may be, and a useful guide to managers in creating strategies of competitive reform.

CHAPTER 2

LESSONS FROM THE THRIFT CRISIS

Carliss Y. Baldwin and Benjamin C. Esty

Introduction

Since 1980, over 1,400 thrifts have failed. Because the U.S. government insures over 90% of the money deposited in thrifts, these failures have caused massive losses to the government deposit insurance funds. In response, Congress has passed several laws designed to prevent future losses and to modernize the banking system. However, existing and proposed legislation (U.S. Congress, 1989; U.S. Treasury Department, 1991) tends to focus on the capital structure of institutions and to miss the significance of important changes in their competitive position. Specifically, changes in technology have favored the growth of new financial institutions that perform the traditional functions of thrifts and banks at a much lower cost. In the thrift industry, for example, government-sponsored mortgage pools have spurred the development of a national mortgage market that to a large extent has replaced thrifts in the financing of home mortgages.

With the advent of a large-scale secondary market in mortgages, one might have expected the thrift industry to shrink and government's guarantees of deposits to shrink as well. Faced with a financial crisis in the industry, however, Congress in 1980 and 1982 extended new asset and liability powers to thrifts and eased the rules that constrained most of them to be mutually owned. Thrifts thus gained access to new funding sources, including brokered deposits, and were permitted to invest in a range of new assets that included commercial mortgages and unsecured commercial loans. At the same time, many elected to convert from mutual to stock ownership.

From the taxpayers' perspective, the new asset and liability powers and conversions to stock ownership backfired badly. Instead of shrinking, the thrift industry grew by 118% from 1980 to 1988. And with high growth came higher levels of risk. Between 1982 and 1988, thrifts' new asset powers, coupled with access to a secondary mortgage market and brokered deposits, exposed the government to unprecedented levels of deposit insurance liability. Unfortunately, the regulatory system did not contemplate a world of low transaction costs; thus, when a minority of thrifts seized the opportunities permitted in a deregulated environment, the regulatory system was not able to respond quickly enough to prevent losses to the insurance funds.

Excessive risk taking by this subset of thrifts created the second thrift crisis of 1987–1990. Those that exploited their new opportunities most aggressively were stock-owned thrifts that had an economic interest in increasing the volatility of the assets under their control. Consistent with their incentives, stock-owned thrifts grew faster, used higher leverage, and implemented riskier strategies than their mutual counterparts. (Mutuals in fact contributed very little to the excessive risk taking that characterized the crisis in the late 1980s.) Ironically, mutual-to-stock conversions—which were intended to infuse capital and promote safety and stability in the industry—set loose market forces that only made the problem worse.

Figure 2-1 maps the evolution of incentives and opportunities in the thrift industry and shows how, piece by piece, the old system changed in response to changes in the external environment. In this chapter we review the traditional thrift industry's functions and describe the origins of mortgage pools. We then describe the crisis of 1980–1982 and show how legislative response to it set the stage for a second, more severe, crisis in 1987–1990.

The Traditional Savings and Loan Industry and the Origins of Mortgage Pools

The modern savings and loan industry was born during the Great Depression. From 1929 to 1939, almost 1,700 savings and loan associations and 10,000 banks failed (Brumbaugh, 1988). In an attempt to prop up the U.S. financial system, Congress passed a series of laws between 1932 and 1934 that established a comprehensive regulatory framework for the banking and thrift industries. The most important aspects of this legislation for thrift institutions were the establishment of the Federal Home Loan Bank (FHLB) system to provide regulatory oversight and to serve as a source of liquidity, and the creation of the Federal Savings and Loan Insurance Corporation (FSLIC) to insure deposits at thrifts (see Figure 2-1).[1] These laws (and subsequent regulations) were designed to promote personal savings while providing funds for residential housing.

---

1. The Federal Home Loan Bank system was established through the initiative of President Herbert Hoover and was designed to function along the same lines as the Federal Reserve system. Deposit insurance for both thrifts and commercial banks was pushed by the Roosevelt administration (FHLB Board, 1983).

Figure 2–1
The Evolution of Incentives and Opportunities in the Thrift Industry, 1933–1989

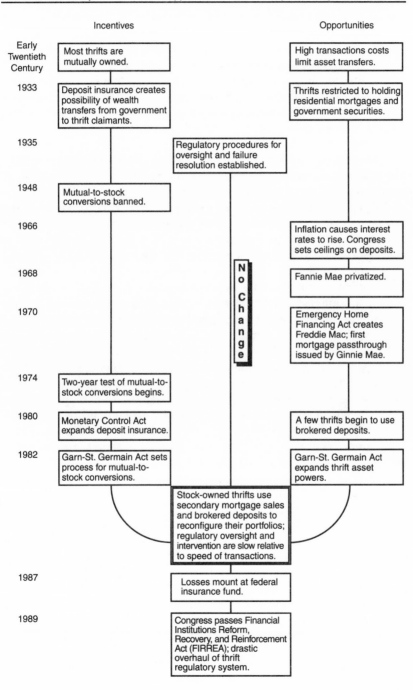

Although the system worked quite well for several decades—as evidenced by the growth of the housing industry, profits at thrift institutions, and the lack of failures—it contained several structural flaws. The first was a maturity mismatch between permitted assets (long-term fixed-rate mortgages) and liabilities (short-term savings deposits). While these asset and liability restrictions were in accordance with the goals of promoting housing and personal savings, they made thrifts vulnerable to interest rate movements. If short-term rates were to exceed long-term rates, then thrifts' borrowing costs would exceed their lending rates and they would lose money. But such an interest rate environment was virtually unheard of in the 1930s.

The second flaw in the system was a set of overly restrictive branching and acquisition regulations, which limited thrifts' ability to achieve economies of scale or scope. Fragmentation had been a hallmark of the states' regulation of financial enterprise in the nineteenth century; the federal regulatory policy of the 1930s carried this bias into the twentieth century. Thus, although the number of thrifts fell substantially in the post–World War II period, there were still five thousand in business in 1975, most of which were small local institutions.

Inefficient scale became an even greater problem after Congress passed the Interest Rate Adjustment Act in 1966, establishing interest rate ceilings for deposits at thrifts and banks. The ceilings caused industry competition to shift from price to service. Thrifts added branches and staff: by 1980, there were over 20,000 thrift offices and the industry employed 260,000 people (one for every 872 in the general population). The new offices and personnel raised thrifts' operating costs: operating expenses as a percentage of assets rose by almost 25 basis points from 1965 to 1980—a large increase given that the average thrift earned only 70 basis points on assets at the time (Carron, 1982). The combination of high operating cost and interest rate exposure left the industry highly susceptible to interest rate movements.

In 1966, and again in 1969, the country experienced brief bouts of inflation and high interest rates. Because thrifts were restricted from raising their deposit rates, depositors began withdrawing their money in search of higher returns from Treasury bills and commercial paper. Such disintermediation drew attention to the industry's structural vulnerability, but at this point Congress's primary concern was with the availability of funds to finance housing, not with the government's deposit insurance liability. Accordingly, in 1968, Congress privatized part of the existing Federal National Mortgage Association ("Fannie Mae"). In 1970, it established the Federal Home Loan Mortgage Corporation ("Freddie Mac"). The title of the law creating Freddie Mac was the Emergency Home Financing Act of 1970—an indication of how dire Congress viewed the housing problem to be. Both institutions were charged with establishing a secondary market for mortgages to ensure the availability of funds for residential housing.

Also in 1970, the Government National Mortgage Association ("Ginnie Mae"), which remained government controlled when Fannie Mae was privatized, created the first publicly traded, mortgage-backed passthrough security. This new type of security gave investors a proportionate claim to the income and principal payments from a pool of underlying mortgages. Today the primary instruments of the secondary mortgage market are mortgage passthroughs and collateralized mortgage obligations, which divide mortgage pools into interest and principal segments of different maturities.

The role of the mortgage companies is to facilitate transfers of mortgage cash flows (and attendant risks) to a broad cross-section of investing institutions, including mutual funds, pension funds, life insurance companies, commercial banks, and thrifts themselves. Because they deal with large pools of money, mortgage companies can operate at a very low cost, typically charging a spread of 50 basis points or less on a passthrough obligation. Because they are not exposed to interest rate or prepayment risk (both are assumed by the ultimate investor when the securities are sold), and because they purchase only mortgages that meet certain quality standards ("qualified" residential mortgages), they can operate with very little capital. Thus mortgage companies operate at a lower cost and with less risk than a traditional thrift.[2]

The privatization of Fannie Mae and the creation of Freddie Mac marked the beginning of a new era for thrifts in the financial system. Traditionally, thrifts had performed a wide range of functions related to mortgages: they originated, serviced, held, and financed them. Today the functions of origination and servicing are still lodged in thrifts (although real estate brokers and finance companies are competing for this business), but over 50% of all new residential mortgage originations flow into the secondary market and the market continues to grow.[3] Mortgage pools thus brought about a separation of functions that previously had been performed "under one roof." Fundamental changes in technology and transaction costs that occurred between 1960 and 1980 made such a separation possible.

---

2. The mortgage companies operate with lower risk if they sell the underlying mortgages. However, it has become more common, especially for Fannie Mae, to hold the mortgages on their own balance sheets. In 1991, FNMA held $126 billion of mortgages as assets and had $372 billion of mortgage-backed securities outstanding (FNMA Annual Report, 1991).

3. A record $189 billion of mortgage-backed securities were issued in the first quarter of 1992.

A self-amortizing mortgage with a prepayment option is a fairly complex financial contract. Even ignoring the option feature of the mortgage, the contract requires (1) substantial effort in pricing and (2) nontrivial amounts of record keeping, as interim payments must be recorded and assigned to interest and principal. In a world where all mathematical calculations had to be performed by human beings, every transfer of such a contract required costly calculations of the present value of the instrument and the impact of each cash flow (interest and principal) on the present value. Although such calculations were standardized and tabulated, they were time-consuming and could be performed only by highly skilled individuals. Total transaction volume was therefore limited by the number of people with training in this specialized field.

Given the computational cost of transferring a mortgage, it is not surprising that mortgage assets tended to stay in the institutions that originated them. This arrangement minimized total transaction costs: the mortgage could be valued once, booked once, and each receipt of interest and principal recorded once. Assets such as common stock that did not demand precise, expert valuation could trade in more liquid, national markets. Assets such as corporate bonds that demanded expert valuation but existed in naturally large units could be traded among dealers. But it would take hundreds of home mortgages to equal the size of a single corporate bond issue. Such small-scale securities did not justify the transaction costs of transfer, hence they were not traded at all. The fragmented, local thrift industry of the 1930s, 1940s, and 1950s *represented an efficient configuration of assets in a world of high transaction costs.*

The high transaction costs associated with mortgages meant that important investments in standardization that later might have encouraged trade in mortgages were not made. Each thrift evolved its own mortgage contract forms, documentation and record-keeping systems. When the cost of raw computation came down in the 1960s and 1970s with the advent of computers, lack of standardization remained a barrier to the transfer and pooling of mortgage assets. By offering to buy mortgages that conformed to certain standards, the government-sponsored mortgage companies played an important role in providing incentives for the fragmented thrift industry to standardize mortgage contracts on single-family loans.

Another barrier to trade was the existence of prepayment options. Other fixed-income securities have options attached: many corporate bonds are callable, for example. Nevertheless, as the secondary mortgage market was getting under way, investors had no previous experience with prepayments and thus no way to predict how a particular pool of mortgages might behave. Purchasers of the securities took prepayment risk, for which they demanded compensation. This meant, however, that in normal times (when short-term rates were below long-term ones), secondary market financing appeared expensive to thrifts—particularly when compared to the rates paid on *insured short-term deposits*, the industry's traditional source of funding.

Secondary market and traditional financing were not necessarily mutually exclusive, however. Institutions with broad asset powers—the ability to make a wide variety of loans and investments—might have sold mortgages and at the same time taken in insured deposits and invested the funds in other assets (within the scope of their authorization). Significantly, though, until the 1980s thrifts were largely restricted to investing in residential mortgages and government securities.[4] Thus the growth of the mortgage pools was limited by the fact that the thrifts—the primary originators—had a cheaper source of funds, *and few other permitted uses for their money.*

Although there was not much volume in the secondary mortgage markets during the 1970s, that decade served as a period of infrastructure development. By the late 1970s, technological advances with computers allowed quicker valuation of fixed-income securities, while standardized loan documentation and new security structures created the potential for a national mortgage market. Such a market had important functional advantages over the traditional thrift system. First, interest rate and prepayment risk could be borne by the ultimate investors instead of by financial institutions propped up by federal guarantees. Second, mortgage interest rates could reflect supply and demand at the national level, thereby eliminating local inequities and misallocations. Third, claims to mortgages could become more liquid, allowing investors to modify their holdings in response to short-run changes in their portfolios. Fourth, origination and servicing functions could be unbundled and opened up to competitive entry. All of these forces promised to reduce the cost of financing the purchase of a home. However, the emergence of a national mortgage market implied a radically different role for thrifts, as certain key functions would no longer be performed efficiently at the local level.

Two Thrift Crises

In 1980, the Federal Reserve attacked inflation by dramatically slowing the growth of the money supply. This caused short-term interest rates to

4. Until 1964, a federally chartered thrift could lend money for mortgages only on property within a 50-mile radius of its home office, and could invest only in U.S. Treasury securities. Between 1964 and 1982, their investment authorities were broadened to include consumer loans and nonresidential mortgages (each up to 20% of assets) and certain types of educational loans.

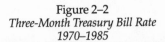

Figure 2–2
Three-Month Treasury Bill Rate
1970–1985

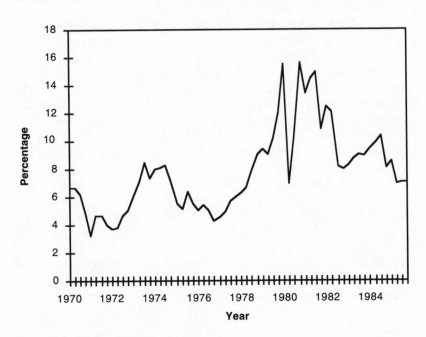

Source: Federal Reserve Bulletin (various issues).

skyrocket: three-month Treasury bills yielded over 15% in early 1980 and peaked at 16.3% in the second quarter of 1981 (see Figure 2-2). These interest rates had a disastrous effect on the thrift industry. Virtually all thrifts experienced a negative spread between their cost of funds and the yield on their long-term mortgages (see Figure 2-3). Hundreds went bankrupt as they ran out of capital to fund their losses (see Figure 2-4), and even those that survived saw their capital position (net worth) impaired significantly.

At two points in the unfolding of this crisis, Congress passed laws aimed at deregulating the industry. The Depository Institutions Deregulation and Monetary Control Act of 1980 (known as the Monetary Control Act) removed many of the liability restrictions that prevented thrifts from competing for deposits. For instance, the act planned for the removal of interest rate ceilings and raised the federal deposit insurance limit from $40,000 to $100,000. By allowing thrifts to offer competitive rates on all deposits, Congress hoped to prevent further disintermediation.

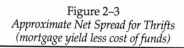

Figure 2–3
Approximate Net Spread for Thrifts
(mortgage yield less cost of funds)

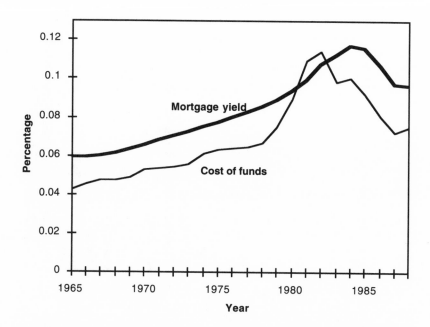

Sources: U.S. Treasury Department, Office of Thrift Supervision (1989a); U.S. League of Savings Institutions (1989).

The Garn-St. Germain Act of 1982 expanded thrifts' asset powers to allow for diversification away from long-term fixed-rate mortgages. By permitting a wider range of asset investments with shorter maturities or variable rates, Congress hoped to solve the mismatch problem. The architects of Garn-St. Germain recognized that traditional thrift banking was not sustainable in the long term: one of the goals of the legislation was to ease the transition to a new "level playing field," where commercial banks, thrifts, and other financial institutions would compete on the basis of similar products and services.

What the architects of Garn-St. Germain did not recognize was how the new asset and liability powers would be exploited by profit-motivated institutions with access to liquid markets for mortgages and deposits. Their second misapprehension was in not seeing how stock ownership (which was encouraged by the new legislation) would affect institutions' incentives to take advantage of high leverage backed by federal deposit guarantees. Finally, the architects did not realize that the

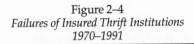

Figure 2–4
Failures of Insured Thrift Institutions
1970–1991

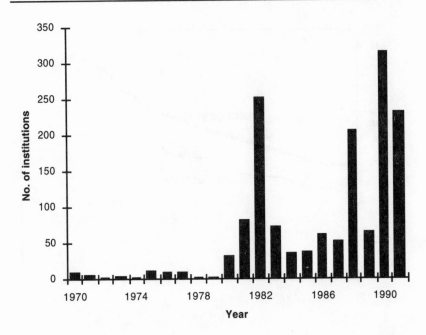

Sources: Federal Home Loan Bank Board (1983); U.S. Treasury Department, Office of Thrift
Supervision(1989).

slow process of regulatory intercession, which was tolerable in an environment of high transaction costs, was inadequate to cope with the speed and fluidity of transactions in the 1980s.

Even before the new law had time to take effect, improved macroeconomic conditions (lower interest rates and a positively sloped yield curve) returned the industry to profitability: as a whole, thrifts earned $1.9 billion in 1983, $1.0 billion in 1984, and $3.7 billion in 1985. Thus, by 1985, Congress and thrift regulators had reason to be pleased with their success in rescuing and deregulating the industry. At that time it was expected that a realignment of assets and liabilities (made possible by the Garn-St. Germain act) would gradually eliminate the structural flaws that had jeopardized the industry during the first crisis.

The honeymoon period was short-lived, however. In 1984, a regional crisis began to unfold in Texas, as crude oil prices fell from $26 per barrel to $11, causing enormous declines in real estate values. Despite the severity of the crisis in Texas and surrounding states, the bad news was by no means limited to the Southwest. Nationwide, the delinquency rate on mortgages jumped from 2.1% in 1983 to 5% in 1986, while the level of repossessed assets quadrupled. Partly as a result of losses in the Southwest, industry profits fell sharply in 1986 and turned negative in 1987. Industrywide losses of $7.8 million in 1987 grew to over $19 billion in 1989.

The pattern of the crisis of 1987–1990 was quite different from that of 1980–1982. A change in interest rates (an inverted yield curve) clearly initiated the 1980–1982 crisis; the 1987–1990 crisis occurred during a period of a normal yield curve (see Figure 2-3). In 1980–1982, the whole industry suffered a negative spread, and 85% of thrifts lost money. In 1987–1990, spreads remained positive, and less than one-third of all thrifts were unprofitable. Thus, whereas the first crisis was an industrywide phenomenon, the second exposed underlying differences in asset structure and risk taking among thrifts themselves.[5]

Stock ownership, broader asset and liability powers, access to secondary markets, and an antiquated regulatory process all interacted to give rise to the *second* thrift crisis. In the remainder of this chapter, we describe each of these effects and show how they contributed to the crisis of 1987–1990.

Mutual versus Stock Ownership

A major insight gleaned from modern financial theory is that the presence of debt changes the incentives and therefore the behavior of the residual claimants (shareholders) to an enterprise. Specifically, owners of levered equity claims hold the equivalent of a call option on risky assets (Black and Scholes, 1973). As a result, they have incentives to increase the riskiness of underlying assets and to take on additional debt (Merton, 1973; Jensen and Meckling, 1976; Green, 1984). Either action increases the value of the equity claim at the expense of debtholders. This means that debtholders must somehow constrain risk taking and leverage within the bounds contemplated by their initial contract. Of course, when debt is guaranteed by a third party, the responsibility for active oversight and control of risk taking shifts to the guarantor, which

---

5. Several authors (Barth, 1991; Brumbaugh, 1988; Kane, 1989; White, 1991; and others) have noted the differences between the two crises. These authors attribute the incentives for risk taking during the second crisis to depleted capital positions, but they do not address the issue of ownership. Esty (1992a, 1992b) and Esty and Baldwin (1992) relate risk taking to stock ownership.

in the case of the thrift industry was the Federal Savings and Loan Insurance Corporation.

In a stock-owned thrift institution, the residual claimants (shareholders) are a distinct class, and their claims can be transferred via a sale of stock. *Thus shareholders can capture the full value of the residual claim* and have strong incentives to maximize its value at the expense of debtholders or a guarantor. In contrast, in a mutually owned institution the residual claimants (depositors) are not a distinct class; there is no legal mechanism for transfer of shares, and only the face value of the deposit can be redeemed when one closes an account. Depositors in a mutual have very few ways to capture the value of the residual claim and correspondingly weak incentives to increase its value by taking advantage of debtholders or a guarantor. (In theory, excess profits in mutuals can be used to increase interest paid on deposits. Yet throughout much of the post–World War II period, deposit rates were subject to interest rate ceilings, and excess profits—when they existed—simply accumulated in reserve accounts.)

According to modern agency theory, managers and directors of mutual institutions can capture value through higher salaries and perquisites, but generally have little to gain by increasing risk or leverage (Akella and Greenbaum, 1988; Mester, 1989). The claims of a salaried manager resemble those of a bondholder more than those of a stockholder: like a bondholder, the manager is interested in avoiding bankruptcy, which might lead to termination of employment. Avoidance of bankruptcy is best accomplished by avoiding high levels of risk and by maintaining enough capital to survive emergencies. Indeed, one common criticism of managers in mutual organizations is that they are unduly risk averse.

The history of the debate over stock versus mutual ownership in the thrift industry goes back to 1948, when Congress passed the Home Owners Loan Act banning federally chartered thrifts from converting to stock ownership. Conversion opponents objected to the transfer of value from depositors to new stockholders that took place when a thrift converted. In most cases, this "windfall" of profits went to thrift insiders, who tended to buy the conversion stock.

The debate resumed in the mid-1970s, after Congress approved a number of trial conversions. Following a two-year test period ending in 1976, Congress held hearings to determine whether conversions were in the public interest. Conversion advocates described a number of advantages to the stock form of ownership: it represented a chance to bolster the industry's capital position (which had been weakened by inflation in the late 1960s and early 1970s), and it promised increased efficiency through better monitoring of managers by stockholders. Thomas Bomar and Garth Marston, respectively the former and the acting head of the Federal Home Loan Bank Board, were two of the most outspoken advocates of stock ownership at the Senate hearings in 1976:

> The objective (of conversion) [is] to strengthen the net worth positions of savings and loan associations . . . and we do believe they are good for savings and loan associations. (Bomar)[6]

> [It is] clear that conversions pose no threat to the stability of financial institutions, to the managements of institutions, and that there are no potential ill effects of depositors or any other persons, or the institution itself. (Marston)[7]

Notwithstanding the overwhelming regulatory support for conversions, the Senate Subcommittee on Financial Institutions was not convinced that conversions were equitable. As a result, it decided not to rescind the prohibition on conversions.[8]

The issue of inside ownership of stock was also a controversial topic in the mid-1970s. Proponents argued that inside ownership provided better incentives for managers to maximize firm value. A statement from a 1983 study by the Federal Home Loan Bank Board encapsulates the views of many academics, regulators, and legislators at the time of the passage of Garn-St. Germain:

> Investors who hold stock in a business firm have motivations and reactions *similar to those of debtholders* . . . Thus, stock associations provide a wider array of incentives for effective management and the avoidance of risk . . . *managers discipline themselves against excessive risk-taking* because of their vested interest in preserving their jobs and the value of any stock options they may own. (Emphasis added.)[9]

This statement runs counter to the predictions of financial theory, which states that with respect to risk taking, holders of levered equity have interests diametrically opposed to those of debtholders. Stockholders have reason to embrace—not avoid—risk and cannot be expected to discipline themselves against excessive risk taking. Discipline against excessive risk taking is usually provided by debtholders, who impose restrictive covenants as a condition of their initial investment. However, federal deposit insurance absolved most thrift debtholders of any responsibility for limiting risk.

6. U.S. Congress, 1976a, pp. 2–3.
7. Ibid., p. 87.
8. U.S. Congress, 1976b.
9. Federal Home Loan Bank Board, 1983, pp. 55–56.

Nevertheless, by 1982, support of mutual-to-stock conversions from academics, regulators, and the industry itself was widespread. In fact, the Federal Home Loan Bank Board was accepting and approving conversion applications even though it was technically illegal for a federally chartered thrift to be stock owned: from 1976 to 1981, 81 thrifts converted to stock ownership.[10] The FHLBB justified its actions by citing the urgent need to rebuild the converting institutions' capital position. Because permitting stock ownership was the only way to allow substantial numbers of thrifts to tap the public capital markets for new equity, Congress included a section in the Garn-St. Germain Act of 1982 that legalized and set forth a process to allow federally chartered institutions to convert voluntarily to stock ownership.

Asset Growth, Mortgage Sales, and Brokered Deposits

Following the passage of the Monetary Control Act and the Garn-St. Germain Act, thrifts had opportunities to raise funds by selling residential mortgages to Fannie Mae and Freddie Mac and to solicit insured brokered deposits. In addition, they could convert from mutual to stock ownership: stock-owned thrifts could issue new equity and lever the proceeds with government insured deposits. The funds generated by these actions could then be used to purchase a wide range of assets, which would change the fundamental risk profile of an institution and hence the cost of providing deposit insurance.

Stock-owned institutions did all of the above to a much greater degree than mutuals. In this section, we compare the behavior of stock-owned and mutual institutions with respect to asset growth, secondary market sales, and the use of brokered deposits. In the next section, we compare overall risk taking, and the federal government's implicit deposit insurance liability (as of 1988) for mutual and stock-owned institutions.

Growth in Assets and Share of the Industry

In 1982, after the passage of Garn-St. Germain, thrift industry assets totalled $686 billion. There were over 3,000 insured thrift institutions: 77% were mutuals, and 23% were stock owned. Stock-owned institu-

---

10. For a description of this legal controversy among the FHLBB, General Accounting Office (GAO), and Congress, see the 1979 GAO study calling for a new national policy on conversions: "The Congress should establish a national policy on the conversion issue and clarify the legal status of associations which have converted after June 30, 1976 [the date the moratorium went back into effect], and retained their federal charters." GAO, 1979, p. iv.

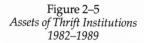

Figure 2–5
Assets of Thrift Institutions
1982–1989

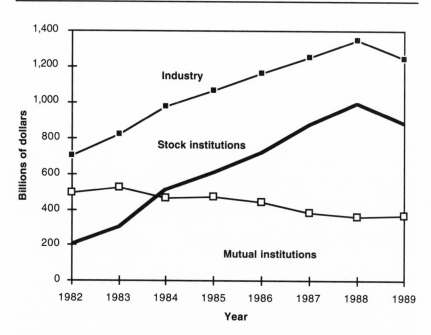

Sources: U.S. Treasury Department, Office of Thrift Supervision (1989a).

tions at that time controlled about 30% of the industry's assets; thus the average stock institution was slightly larger than the average mutual.

One of the most noticeable changes in the structure of the thrift industry in the period just after Garn-St. Germain was the transition from mutual to stock ownership. Between 1982 and 1986, close to 500 thrifts took the opportunity offered by the new legislation to convert to stock ownership, raising over $5.4 billion of equity capital in the process.[11] In addition, of the 459 savings and loan associations formed between 1980 and 1986, 75% were stock owned. The existing, converting, and de novo stock institutions then proceeded to grow at much higher rates than the institutions that remained mutually owned.

Figure 2-5 shows the growth of thrift assets and the dramatic change in ownership structure that occurred in the thrift industry in the mid-1980s. By 1988, thrift assets topped $1.3 trillion, over 70% of which

11. Federal Home Loan Bank Board, 1986.

were held in stock-owned institutions. The average stock-owned institution was now almost twice as large as the average mutual. Put another way, the average mutual that survived to the end of 1988 grew at an annual rate of 6.9%; the average stock-owned institution grew at a rate of 22.6%; and the average converting institution grew at a rate of 13.8%. Much of the growth came right after the passage of Garn-St. Germain, between 1983 and 1984. For example, in 1983, the median stock thrift in California grew by 70%, compared to 19% for the median mutual thrift.

Consistent with their equity holders' incentives, stock-owned institutions not only grew faster, but also adopted more aggressive funding strategies than did mutuals. They levered their equity, going out of their local market to obtain brokered deposits if necessary. They sold more of their qualified residential mortgages to the government sponsored agencies than did mutuals. (Funds obtained by selling mortgages were an off-balance-sheet source of funds not included in the asset figures. Therefore Figure 2-5 *understates* the stock-owned thrifts' true growth rates, as well as their share of market in 1988.)

Finally, stock-owned thrifts used the money raised from equity issues, mortgage sales, and brokered deposits to fund riskier portfolios than those sought by mutuals. Indeed, a portion of the spectacular growth achieved by some stock institutions was made possible by the fact that risky investments often initially generated high interest and fee income, which could be added to the institution's capital base and then used to support further asset growth. (Esty, 1992b)

Secondary Mortgage Markets

As indicated, secondary market funding was more expensive than short-term deposit funding throughout the 1970s, thus most thrifts chose to hold mortgages in their own asset base. Thrifts in fact were net purchasers of mortgage-backed securities between 1970 and 1981. Both in absolute dollars and as a percentage of total mortgage lending, the pools were a marginal source of funds until 1982.

In 1982, the new asset powers conveyed by Garn-St. Germain suddenly gave thrifts new uses for money. Sales of mortgages jumped from under $20 billion to over $50 billion and then held steady at that level for two years. They shot up again in 1985 and 1986, peaking at over $160 billion before dropping back to about $100 billion in 1988. Figure 2-6 depicts total mortgage sales by thrift institutions over the period from 1970 to 1989. Figure 2-7 shows the growth of government sponsored mortgage pools: by mid-1991, they topped $1.2 trillion and accounted for fully one-third of total mortgage debt outstanding.

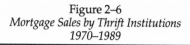

Figure 2–6
Mortgage Sales by Thrift Institutions
1970–1989

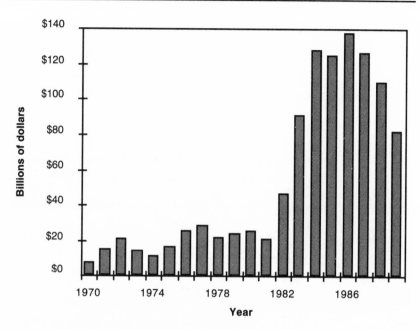

Source: U.S. League of Savings Institutions (1989).

Different types of institutions took advantage of the secondary market to varying degrees. Stock institutions were the most active: between 1985 and 1988, stock-owned institutions as a group sold 2.27 times as many mortgage-backed securities as they purchased. Mutual institutions sold 1.41 times as many securities as they purchased, while the corresponding figure for converting institutions was 1.69.

In total, more than $1.2 trillion of residential mortgages now are held in the form of mortgage-backed securities. In the traditional thrift industry, these would have been assets of insured institutions. Instead, although a certain percentage of mortgage-backed securities does find its way back to the portfolios of thrift institutions, the bulk of these assets is held by other financial institutions or by individuals. From a functional perspective this is a healthy development made possible by lower transaction costs. Risks are distributed more widely, and individuals and institutions have the opportunity to use mortgage securities to achieve specific investment goals. However, the withdrawal of these

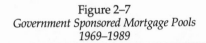

Figure 2–7
Government Sponsored Mortgage Pools
1969–1989

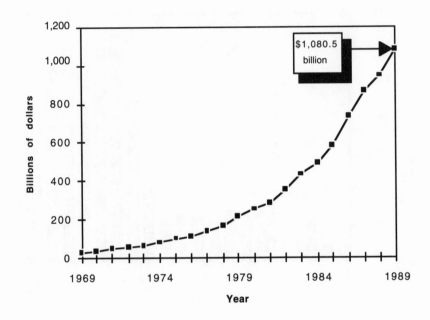

Source: U.S. Council of Economic Advisers (1991).

assets from thrift institutions necessarily changes the cost of insuring deposits in such institutions.

When assets are withdrawn from an insured institution, three outcomes are possible for the insurer. First, the original assets may not be replaced, in which case the deposit base and the insurer's liability will shrink. Alternatively, the original assets may be replaced by others of lower risk: this also reduces the deposit insurer's liability. Finally, the assets may be replaced by others of *higher* risk, thereby *increasing* the deposit insurer's liability.

The fact that the total assets of the thrift industry grew by $666 billion between 1982 and 1988 is prima facie evidence that thrift institutions did not use mortgage sales to shrink their assets and deposits. Indeed, correlating growth with mortgage sales by institution reveals that those with high levels of mortgage sales also had high growth rates both in assets and deposits. Thus opportunities to sell mortgages into the secondary market did not generally lead to shrinkage of insured deposits: instead, thrifts reallocated the funds obtained from mortgage sales to other uses permitted under the new regulatory structure of

Figure 2–8
Brokered Deposits
1978–1989

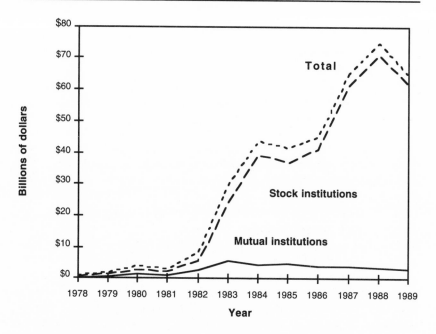

Source: U.S. Treasury Department, Office of Thrift Supervision (1989b).

Garn-St. Germain. For stock-owned thrifts, economic incentives favored selling the least risky mortgages and reallocating the funds to more risky endeavors. Fannie Mae's and Freddie Mac's requirements in terms of documentation and credit quality also made it likely that less risky mortgages would be sold and more risky ones retained in a thrift's portfolio.

Brokered Deposits

Brokered deposits are funds packaged by brokerage houses in units of $100,000, to be eligible for federal deposit insurance. They are then placed in thrifts and commercial banks on a rate-competitive basis. This funding channel first appeared in 1980, after the Monetary Control Act removed interest rate ceilings and lifted the deposit insurance maximum from $40,000 to $100,000. Brokered deposits are highly organized, low-transaction-cost flows of funds that (because of government deposit insurance) are virtually immune to risk.

Figure 2-8 shows the growth of brokered deposits at thrifts in total and by ownership class. Again, consistent with their incentives to take maximum advantage of federal deposit insurance, stock-owned institutions used brokered deposits much more intensively than did mutuals: over 95% of all brokered deposits were placed in stock thrifts.

Portfolio Risk and the Cost of Deposit Insurance

In the years just following the passage of Garn-St. Germain, stock-owned institutions used their access to equity markets, secondary mortgage markets, and brokered deposits to grow rapidly and to change radically the composition of their portfolios. Financial theory suggests that stock-owned institutions had especially strong incentives to use the new, low-transaction-cost markets to reconfigure their portfolios to take more risk. In this section, we report measures of portfolio risk for stock-owned, mutual, and converting institutions over the period 1982 to 1988, and compare risk taking across these groups. We then use our estimates of portfolio risk to make a rough calculation of the cost of federal deposit insurance for each group as of 1988.

According to the contingent claims theory, the cost of deposit insurance is an increasing function of the riskiness of returns on the underlying portfolio (Merton, 1977; Merton and Bodie, 1992). This so-called asset or portfolio risk is often defined as the standard deviation of the change in asset value, divided by initial assets (cf. Merton, 1977). However, in thrifts and other financial intermediaries, *total portfolio risk is affected by the choice of liabilities in relation to assets.* For example, an institution that matches assets and liabilities will have very low risk from an insurer's standpoint, even though its assets viewed in isolation may be very risky. The interdependence of assets and liabilities in determining total risk means that it is necessary to take account of both sides of the balance sheet when computing portfolio risk. The appropriate measure is then the standard deviation of the change in net worth, divided by initial assets. (Net worth in this definition is simply the difference between assets and contractual liabilities, ignoring the possibility of default at a fixed point in time.)

Under the assumption of independent, identically distributed observations, a cross-sectional sample will reveal the true underlying distribution as the number of observations becomes large. Thus the standard deviation of changes in net worth for each ownership class serves as an estimate of the portfolio risk of that class.[12]

12. The standard deviations calculated from cross-sectional data may under- or overestimate the true portfolio risk of a particular class. On the one hand, *common factors* (such as interest rates) that affect all thrifts in a given class lead to *correlated outcomes*, which cause the observed distribution to have a lower standard deviation than the true ex ante distribution. On the other hand, if thrifts within each class are not entirely homogeneous, the observed distribution will have a higher standard deviation than the true distribution. The most obvious source of cross-sectional heterogeneity is size differences among thrifts. The portfolio risk measure adjusts for size by dividing each net worth change by the institution's initial asset value.

Figure 2–9
*Distribution of Change in Net Worth
Nonconverting Mutual Thrifts, 1982–1988*

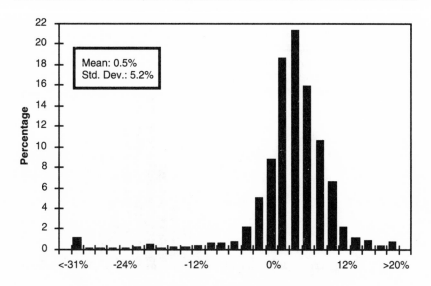

Mean: 0.5%
Std. Dev.: 5.2%

Cumulative Net Income as a % of Assets

Source: Authors' calculations based on data from the Federal Home Loan Bank Board.

We computed the change in net worth (measured as cumulative net income divided by initial assets) for approximately 2,500 thrifts in three groups: mutual institutions (1,575); stock-owned institutions (451) and institutions that converted from mutual to stock ownership (491).[13] The distributions are shown in Figures 2-9, 2-10, and 2-11. The results strongly suggest that stock-owned and converting institutions did take more portfolio risk than mutual institutions: the annualized standard deviation of the change in net worth is 27.2% for stock companies, 22.3% for converting institutions, and only 5.2% for mutual institutions. These differences in portfolio risk indicate that, as a class, stock and converting

13. Initial net worth and assets were observed at year-end 1982; final net worth as of year-end 1988. The change in net worth can be measured before or after dividends. We calculated both and found that the results were not greatly affected by the change. (The before-dividend results are displayed.) Finally, for stock-owned and converting mutuals in our sample, a portion of their ending net worth—and thus technically, some of the dispersion—was attributable to new common stock issues. To adjust for this effect, we calculated the ratio of 1982 to 1988 capital stock and allocated that fraction of ending net worth to the initial claimants.

Figure 2–10
*Distribution of Change in Net Worth
Converting Mutual Thrifts, 1982–1988*

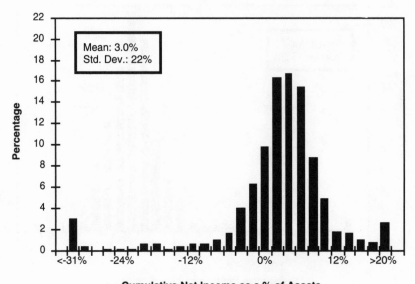

Cumulative Net Income as a % of Assets

Source: Authors' calculations based on data from the Federal Home Loan Bank Board.

institutions tended to adopt portfolio strategies that were *four to five times as risky* as those of nonconverting mutual institutions.

However, during our observation period, Texas thrifts in particular experienced severe stress due to a collapse first in the regional oil and then in the real estate markets. In addition, Texas state-chartered thrifts had very broad asset powers, which might have allowed them to adopt more risky portfolio strategies than thrifts in other parts of the country. Finally, Texas had a disproportionate number of stock-owned institutions at the start of the observation period.

Table 2-1 shows standard deviations for Texas and non-Texas thrifts, broken down by ownership class. Regional differences did indeed influence risk-taking behavior within each class. Nevertheless, the fundamental pattern—stock-owned and converting institutions exhibiting higher levels of risk than mutual institutions—is present in both the Texas and non-Texas groups. Significantly, the Texas mutual organizations—with opportunities similar to those of the stock-owned institutions—exhibited an annualized standard deviation of only 4.0%.

Figure 2–11
*Distribution of Change in Net Worth
Stock-Owned Thrifts, 1982–1988*

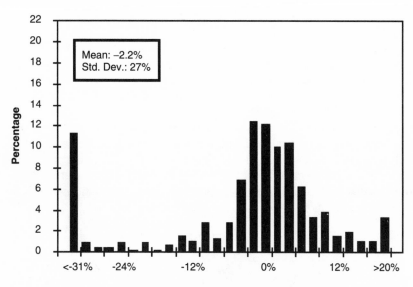

Cumulative Net Income as a % of Assets

Source: Authors' calculations based on data from the Federal Home Loan Bank Board.

Texas stock-owned institutions in contrast displayed a staggering 49.4% annualized standard deviation over the same period.

Table 2-1
Portfolio Risk

	Texas	All Others
Mutuals	4.0%	5.2%
Stock-owned	49.4%	13.4%
Converting	28.9%	22.0%

In the rest of the country, an interesting pattern emerged. Mutual institutions had the lowest risk level (5.2% annualized standard deviation), followed by stock institutions (13.4%), followed by converting institutions (22.0%). It appears that outside of Texas, existing stock-owned institutions as a group did not adopt portfolio strategies that were as risky as newly converted institutions. Converting institutions may have experienced changes in control in connection with their conversion, and as a result may have been under more pressure to increase portfolio risk to exploit the value implicit in the government guarantee. But this apparent difference in risk taking between the two types of stock-owned institutions clearly merits further investigation.

We can use the portfolio risk measures to make a rough estimate of the cost of deposit insurance for different classes of institutions. Inputs to the pricing formula are the following: the portfolio risk measure, the net worth ratio of an institution, and the surveillance period (roughly the period over which regulators can discover and act on problems in an insured institution). With these parameters we can calculate an approximate value for FSLIC's liability in 1988 for each class of thrift. The results are shown in Table 2-2. Briefly, the total cost of insuring the then-surviving population of mutual thrifts (assuming a one-year surveillance interval) was .45% of assets or $1.45 billion; the cost of insuring the then-surviving population of thrifts that converted was 5.2% of assets or $23.0 billion; the cost of insuring the then-surviving population of stock-owned thrifts was 13.1% of assets or $53.7 billion.

Table 2-2
Illustrative Calculation of the Cost of Deposit Insurance by Ownership Class, 1988

	1988 Assets ($ bill.)	Average Net Worth Ratio	Portfolio Risk	Cost as a % of Assets	Total Cost ($ bill.)
Mutuals	$322	4.6%	5%	.45%	$1.45
Converted	$442	5.0%	22%	5.2%	$23.0
Stock-owned	$402	-5.0%	27%	13.1%	$53.7

These figures represent the estimated cost of supplying one year of insurance against loss on deposits to each class of thrifts. They reflect the risk-taking behavior of each class, calibrated over the previous six years, as well as the average net worth of each class as of year-end 1988. The figures are only illustrative, but they do indicate the impact of both portfolio risk and capital (the net worth ratio) on the government's exposure to loss.

Regulation

The advent of low transaction costs in the 1970s greatly expanded the potential range and speed of transactions for all financial institutions. In the early 1980s, new asset and liability powers made these opportunities legally available to thrifts, while mutual-to-stock conversions increased their incentives to exploit such opportunities. However, the regulatory system continued to function in old ways. The types of information sought by regulators, the capital requirements placed on healthy institutions, and the speed of regulatory response to distress were adequate in a high-transaction-cost environment such as the one that existed between 1930 and 1970. These same regulatory devices were totally inadequate to cope with profit-maximizing behavior in the high-speed, low-transaction-cost environment of the 1980s.

The primary assumption underlying the regulatory system created in 1933 and 1934 was that each thrift would contain a core of high-quality immobile assets. In fact, because high transaction costs made it impractical to transfer or trade mortgages, these assets invariably stayed in the thrift that booked them. As a result, the vast majority of thrifts did indeed have a base of high-quality, illiquid assets.

The existence of these assets made both insuring deposits and supplying liquidity (through the Federal Home Loan Banks) relatively cheap. The nature of the assets could be determined by periodic examinations, and because the assets were illiquid, regulators could be assured that the portfolio would not change much between one examination and the next. Therefore regulators did not have to update their information very frequently and could move with deliberation in response to distress or failure. The core residential mortgages were also of basically high quality, thus regulators could be comfortable with relatively thin capital requirements. When they did have to move quickly to stem a run, the Federal Home Loan Bank could take the highest quality assets as collateral and not be exposed to great risk of loss.

In the 1980s, active secondary markets for mortgages combined with much broader asset powers removed the assurance that each thrift would retain a core of high-quality residential mortgages. Such mortgages could be sold to Fannie Mae or Freddie Mac, while more risky mortgages on rental housing or commercial properties remained on the books.

Low-transaction-cost secondary markets also accelerated the rate at which a thrift's portfolio could deteriorate. Faced with any type of cash shortfall, thrifts had the ability to sell or pledge their least risky assets to third parties. Alternatively, they could bid for brokered deposits. Either way, the institution would get money to fund its immediate cash deficit; its shareholders would gain one more chance at recovery; and the ultimate loser would be the government deposit insurance fund.

Lessons of the Thrift Crisis

The enormous losses in the thrift industry during the 1980s were attributable to the confluence of two important trends. Thrifts had heightened incentives to take risk at a time when they also had increased opportunities to take risk. The incentive for risk taking stemmed from the transition to stock ownership and the high levels of leverage common in the industry. The opportunities for risk taking were the result of expanded asset powers interacting with low transaction costs.

Given value-maximizing behavior on the part of equity holders, there are basically only two systems that can control a guarantor's risk in an environment of low transaction costs. The first is a system that collateralizes insured deposits; the second is a system that requires mandatory equity infusions. Both of these systems rely on high quality information and prompt regulatory intervention.

The rationale for collateralizing insured deposits is that in a world of low transaction costs, equity holders have wide-ranging opportunities (and incentives) to strip the least risky assets out of a portfolio and put riskier assets in their place.[14] High transaction costs formerly protected unsecured debtholders and guarantors from the worst effects of asset stripping and asset substitution. Today, however, low transaction costs and broad asset powers have made asset stripping and substitution more feasible, while stock-ownership incentives make risk taking more attractive to many institutions.

In the past, collateralization of liabilities was expensive because of the record keeping and the valuation requirements it imposed. However, this simply represents another type of transaction cost, which, like all transaction costs, has dropped dramatically in the past two decades. Thus it is not surprising that asset-secured borrowing and secondary asset sales have both escalated dramatically.

However, the ease with which assets may be sold or pledged in a world of low transaction costs poses a grave danger to those whose claims remain unsecured. The striking difference in portfolio risk between stock-owned and mutual institutions (discussed in the preceding section) shows how quickly and drastically institutions with the ability to restructure their portfolios can increase the government's deposit insurance liability.

Yet for both thrifts and commercial banks, the regulatory system has not completely adjusted to an environment of low transaction costs. In past eras of high transaction costs, guarantors were protected from the effects of asset stripping by the stickiness of markets. Today, markets are much more liquid than in the past, and as a result, guarantors—and unsecured creditors in general—can no longer count on the immobility of assets to protect them from risk.

---

14. For a discussion of the effect of asset stripping on the cost of providing deposit insurance, see Baldwin (1991).

If the government deposit insurance funds do not lay claim to specific assets, others will do so before them. The assets that are easiest to value and least risky will then flow out of insured institutions—as the least risky mortgages have already flowed out of the thrift industry. The end result of these developments is that the insured deposits will be used to finance risky, speculative undertakings that cannot obtain credit by other means. The federal government will then find itself in the anomalous position of watching the economic importance of insured depository institutions decline, while the cost of providing deposit insurance steadily rises.

A second way to limit a guarantor's risk is to impose strict capital requirements on insured institutions. As the analysis of the previous sections showed, the value of guarantees is sensitive not only to portfolio risk, but also to an institution's net worth position. Thus an effective way to limit the government's liability is to impose strict capital adequacy standards (based on market values) accompanied by provisions for mandatory equity infusions.

To implement these kinds of policies, regulators must have high quality information and must be willing and able to move quickly in the event something goes wrong. In an environment with low transaction costs, where an institution's portfolio can change quickly, it is critical to have accounting standards that reflect the institution's true condition. Current proposals to eliminate Regulatory Accounting Principles (RAP) and implement market-to-market evaluations move in this direction. However, in the absence of perfect information, regulatory standards should be a function of the precision with which values can be determined. For example, the enforcement of capital standards and mandatory equity infusions requires a statement of capital position. The greater the uncertainty about equity value, the more equity should be required. Thus institutions wishing to operate with thin equity cushions will quickly find it to their benefit to mark assets and liabilities to market. By doing so, other things equal, they reduce their need for capital and reduce the cost of bringing in new equity when and if it is needed.

In conclusion, the improvements in financial and information processing that gave rise to lower transaction costs have made the economy and the financial system vastly more efficient. Nevertheless, changes in technology and ownership structure have unleashed powerful new threats to the deposit insurance funds. The regulatory system that worked so well for 40 years now needs to be fundamentally redesigned to handle modern financial markets. The thrift industry of the 1980s provides a lesson on the folly of attempting to contain modern financial institutions within a regulatory framework designed for an era of high transaction costs.

References

Akella, Srinivas R., and Stuart I. Greenbaum, 1988. "Savings and Loan Ownership Structure and Expense Preference," *Journal of Banking and Finance* 12, pp. 419–437.

Baldwin, Carliss Y., 1992. "The Impact of Asset Stripping on the Cost of Deposit Insurance." Working paper #92-953, Harvard Business School.

Barth, James R., 1991. *The Great Savings and Loan Debacle.* Washington, D.C.: AEI Press.

Black, Fischer, and Myron Scholes, 1973. "The Pricing of Options and Corporate Liabilities," *Journal of Political Economy* 81:3, pp. 637–654.

Brumbaugh, R. Dan, Jr., 1988. *Thrifts Under Siege.* New York: Harper & Row.

Carron, Andrew S., 1982. *The Plight of the Thrift Institutions.* Washington, D.C.: The Brookings Institution.

Esty, Benjamin C., 1992a. "Ownership, Leverage, and Incentives: A Study of Risk Taking in the S&L Industry." Mimeo.

————, 1992b. "A Tale of Two Thrifts." Mimeo.

Federal Home Loan Bank (FHLB) Board, 1982. *Semi-Annual Financial Report,* December 31.

————, 1983. *Agenda for Reform: A Report to the United States Congress,* March.

————, 1986. *An Analysis of the Proposed Capital Requirements for Thrift Institutions: A Staff Economic Study,* August 15.

————, 1988a. *Thrift Financial Report,* Annual Reports, 1982–1988.

————, 1988b. *Quarterly Thrift Financial Report,* December 31.

————, 1989. *Thrift Financial Report: List of Mergers and Deletions, 1960-1989.*

Federal Home Loan Mortgage Corporation, 1991. Annual Report.

Federal National Mortgage Association (FNMA), 1991. Annual Report.

Federal Reserve Board, *Federal Reserve Bulletin*, various issues.

Green, Richard C., 1984. "Investment Incentives, Debt and Warrants," *Journal of Financial Economics* 12, pp. 115–136.

Jensen, Michael, and William H. Meckling, 1976. "Theory of the Firm: Managerial Behavior, Agency Costs and Ownership Structure," *Journal of Financial Economics* 3, pp. 305–360.

Kane, Edward J., 1989. *The S&L Insurance Mess: How Did It Happen?* Washington, D.C.: The Urban Institute Press.

Merton, Robert C., 1977. "An Analytic Derivation of the Cost of Deposit Insurance and Loan Guarantees: An Application of Modern Option Pricing Theory," *Journal of Banking and Finance* 1:3–11. Reproduced in *Continuous-Time Finance*. Cambridge, Mass.: Basil Blackwell, 1990.

———, 1973. "The Theory of Rational Option Pricing," *Bell Journal of Economics and Management Science* 4:1, pp. 141–183.

Merton, Robert C., and Zvi Bodie, 1992a. "On the Management of Deposit Insurance and Other Guarantees." Working paper #92-081, Harvard Business School.

———, 1992b. "Deposit Insurance Reform: A Functional Approach." Working paper #92-086, Harvard Business School.

Mester, Loretta J., 1989. "Testing for Expense Preference Behavior: Mutual versus Stock Savings and Loans," *Rand Journal of Economics* 20:4, pp. 483–498.

Resolution Trust Corporation, 1992. *Resolution Report.* Washington, D.C., March 31, 1992.

U.S. Congress, 1976a. Senate hearing, Committee on Banking, Housing and Urban Affairs, Moratorium on Conversions of Savings and Loan Associations and Mutual Savings Banks, May 13.

————, 1976b. Senate report, Committee on Banking, Housing and Urban Affairs, Moratorium on Conversions of Savings and Loan Associations and Mutual Savings Banks, September 10.

————, 1982. Garn-St. Germain Depository Institutions Act of 1982, Pub. L. No. 97-320 (October 15).

————, 1989. Financial Institutions Reform, Recovery, and Enforcement Act of 1989, Pub. L. No. 101-73 (August 9).

U.S. Council of Economic Advisers, 1991. *Economic Report of the President*, February.

U.S. General Accounting Office (GAO), 1979. *Converting Savings and Loan Associations from Mutual to Stock Ownership—A National Policy Needed*. Report to the Senate Committee on Banking, Housing and Urban Affairs, October 1.

U.S. League of Savings Institutions, 1989. Sourcebook.

U.S. Treasury Department, 1991. *Modernizing the Financial System*, February.

U.S. Treasury Department, Office of Thrift Supervision, 1989a. *Savings and Home Financing Sourcebook*.

————, 1989b. *Combined Financial Statements: SAIF Insured Institutions*.

White, Lawrence J., 1991. *The S&L Debacle: Public Policy Lessons for Bank and Thrift Regulation*. New York: Oxford University Press.

CHAPTER 3

BANKS IN THE BOARDROOM: GERMANY, JAPAN, AND THE UNITED STATES

W. Carl Kester

As global capital and product markets have become more integrated, national differences in corporate governance have been drawn into sharp relief. One of the chief differences among corporate governance systems around the world concerns the relationships maintained by major financial institutions—commercial banks in particular—with industrial corporations. Specifically, it is commonly observed that large financial intermediaries in Japan and Germany tend to have much closer, longer-term relationships with many of their industrial clients than do their counterparts in the Anglo-American family of countries.

Furthermore, there is evidence that these relationships are associated with differences in corporate investment, financing, and performance. Hoshi, Kashyap, and Scharfstein (1990), for example, find evidence that investments by Japanese corporations with close main-bank relationships are less sensitive to variations in operating cash flow than are investments by American companies, which lack such relationships. Similarly, Prowse (1990) finds that bank ownership of equity in Japan reduces shareholder-debtor conflicts and allows Japanese companies to support more leverage, other things being equal. Gerlach (1987), Kester (1991a, 1991b), and Suzuki and Wright (1985) all document the critical role that Japanese main banks (i.e., lead lenders with close, long-term relationships to industrial borrowers) play in the monitoring and control of Japanese corporations and in their restructuring in the event of financial distress. Kester (1991b) also documents this role by so-called *Hausbanken* in Germany. Although he does not examine company-bank relationships in Japan per se, nor the mechanism by which Japanese executive directors are replaced, Kaplan (1992) provides formal empirical evidence supporting the claim that Japanese boards of directors are subject to closer monitoring and quicker replacement by outside directors in association with declining performance than are their American counterparts.

In contrast to practices in many other nations, a panoply of U.S. laws and regulations serves to reduce the roles that can be played by large American financial institutions in the governance of publicly owned U.S. corporations. These were well intended at inception as safeguards against imprudent preferential lending to particular industrial clients or abuses that might have arisen from undue concentrations of financial power. But today, many of the laws and regulations are being challenged in a wave of reformist sentiment aroused by the banking crises that began the 1990s, by the growing American economic malaise, and by the spreading suspicion that current institutions of corporate governance may have played a part in both problems.

This chapter examines the American debate about corporate governance reform in a comparative international context and links it with debate about the restructuring of the U.S. financial services industry, banking reform in particular. It is argued that the relative absence of a strong voice on the part of large institutional capital providers in the governance of industrial corporations has been detrimental to the efficiency and competitiveness of American business. Besides helping preserve the financial health of the banking industry, another important objective of banking reform should be to create conditions conducive to the restoration of a healthy governance relationship between major providers and users of capital in the U.S. economy.

Financial Institutions and Corporate Governance: An International Comparison

As indicated by the data presented in Table 3–1, financial institutions as a group are substantial owners of equity in nearly every major capitalist economy. What differs, however, is the composition of ownership by the financial sector. Specifically, pension funds are the largest single class of financial institutional equity owners in the Anglo-American nations, while banks and/or insurance companies dominate institutional ownership in other nations, Japan in particular. Other nonfinancial businesses as well are more substantial owners of stock in countries outside the Anglo-American block.

Associated with these differences in ownership are substantial differences in the roles played by financial institutions in corporate governance. I will delineate major differences among various systems by comparing the governance roles played by banks and other financial

Table 3–1
Ownership Structure of Publicly Listed Corporations in Selected Countries, 1990–1991

Country	Financial Sectors					Nonfinancial Sectors			
	Banks*	Insurance Companies	Pension Funds+	Investment Companies and Other	Total	Nonfinancial Businesses	Households	Government	Foreign
Australia	-	10.7	24.5	2.5	37.7	8.9	26.4	n.a.	27.0
United Kingdom	0.9	18.4	30.4	11.1	60.8	3.6	21.3	2.0	12.3
United States	0.3	5.2	24.8	9.5	39.8	n.a.	53.5	-	6.7
France	3.5	16.6		n.a.	20.1	26.4	37.5	1.6	14.4
Germany	8.9	10.6	-	-	19.5	39.2	16.8	6.8	17.7
Netherlands	1.0	20.0			21.0	n.a.	44.0	n.a.	35.0
Switzerland	3.0	5.0	8.0	1.0	17.0	16.0	31.0	0.0	36.0
Japan	25.2	17.3	0.9	3.6	47.0	25.1	23.1	0.6	4.2

* All types, including bank holding companies

+ Public and private

Sources: J. B. Were & Son, "Australian Equity Market Profile," February 1992; Commission des Operations de Bourse; Deutsche Bundesbank; Tokyo Stock Exchange; Amsterdams Effectenbeurs; ProShare; Federal Reserve Board "Flow of Funds."

institutions in three major industrial rivals: the United States, Japan, and Germany.[1]

The United States

Predicated on the ideal of shareholder democracy and the perceived need to prevent abuse of corporate power, the American corporate governance system is a product of constantly evolving American legislation and jurisprudence. A host of laws and regulations has been used to curtail the ability of many large American financial institutions from becoming major shareholders in industrial corporations and exercising significant influence, either individually or as a group, in the governance of those corporations. The Glass-Steagall Act of 1933, for example, prohibits banks from owning stock in other companies directly or indirectly through affiliations with investment banks. The Bank Holding Company Act of 1956 prohibits banks from owning more than 5% of the voting stock in any nonbank company or from otherwise controlling an industrial firm. In addition, the U.S. tax code encourages diversification of bank-managed trust holdings so that no more than 10% of a bank's trust funds are invested in any one corporation. Finally, lenders that exert actual or effective control over a company could (under standards that remain ambiguous) be subject to "equitable subordination" of their loans in the event of a bankruptcy proceeding.[2] For their part, American insurance companies, which are regulated primarily by state laws, must abide by the most restrictive of these state laws if they wish to operate nationwide. The strictest state laws prohibit insurance companies from putting more than 2% of their assets into a single company and from owning more than 5% of the voting stock of any one corporation.

Although pension funds control nearly two-thirds of institutionally owned equities, they have virtually no representation on corporate boards as a result of laws that limit their voting power and discourage their active involvement in corporate governance. If it wishes to receive favorable tax treatment as a diversified fund, a pension fund must hold not more than 10% of any one company's stock. Other laws discourage pension funds from becoming too involved in management issues. The Employees Retirement Income Security Act of 1974 (ERISA) established a prudent standard for fiduciaries: managers of pension funds must be "prudent experts" in the business they undertake. Hence, if pension fund managers were to become active on the boards of business corporations in which their funds invest, they could become liable to meet

1. For further discussion of the laws influencing the role played by financial institutions in corporate governance, see Lightfoot, 1991, pp. 1–5; and Edwards and Eisenbeis, 1990.
2. Dickens, 1987.

higher standards of care in their investments. Although funds might attempt to coordinate themselves by initiating shareholder resolutions and voting in blocks on issues of mutual concern, they must first obtain approval from the Securities and Exchange Commission (SEC) if they wish to influence the voting of more than ten stockholders.

Like pension funds, mutual funds tend to refrain from exercising large shareholder rights in order to receive favorable tax treatment. If a mutual fund is not diversified, its income is taxed first at the corporate tax rate and then again when it is distributed to the fund's shareholders. To be considered diversified under the tax code and the Investment Company Act of 1940, a fund must have at least half its investments in companies that constitute 5% or less of its portfolio and cannot own more than 10% of any one company's stock. Even if a fund owned 5% of a company's stock, the portfolio company would become a statutory affiliate of the mutual fund and its principal underwriter. If the fund wished to exercise control with another affiliate, it would need SEC approval.

Japan

Common practices in Japan are virtually polar opposites to the U.S. experience. Admittedly, Japanese commercial banks and insurance companies are limited in the extent to which they can own equity in industrial corporations (to 5% and 10%, respectively, of any single company's stock), but historically their influence has exceeded that which would be anticipated on the basis of percentage ownership alone.

Most large publicly listed Japanese corporations maintain main-bank relationships—close, long-term relationships with one or a couple of banks characterized by (often reciprocal) equity ownership as well as the provision of debt capital. Sheard (1989) reports that a Japanese company's main bank ranked among its five largest shareholders in 72% of his sample (first or second in 39% of his sample). Prowse (1990) finds that a Japanese company's largest lender was also its largest shareholder in 57% of his sample. Commensurate with their position as lead lenders and major shareholders, main banks enjoy preferred status in the provision of a wide range of financial services to client companies and in the yields received on their loans: main-bank loans are typically priced 25 basis points above those of other banks lending to the company in question.

Historically, Japanese main banks have involved themselves deeply in the affairs of their client companies, requiring detailed disclosures of corporate strategies and investment plans on a frequent (often quarterly) basis. It was not uncommon for bank executives to require modification of these plans as a condition for the continued provision of scarce capital. Although the securitization of Japanese corporate finance in the 1980s has considerably weakened the influence of main banks over large, well-managed, and highly liquid corporations (see Kester, 1991b), they remain important suppliers of capital to smaller affiliates of these larger clients.

Main banks also have been and remain important providers of auditors and directors to many Japanese industrial corporations (see Table 3–2). Technically, most Japanese boards of directors are entirely "inside" boards—that is, all members are salaried executives of the corporation. Whereas virtually all American corporations have at least one outside director, a 1985 study by the Ministry of International Trade and Industry found that 43.5% of Japanese corporations listed on the First Section of the Tokyo Stock Exchange had no outside directors.[3] In a more recent survey, Kaplan (1991) found that 65.5% of 119 Japanese companies making up his sample had no outside directors.

Table 3–2
*Japanese Bank Representatives on Listed Companies' Boards of
Directors, by Rank, 1989*

		From Banks	
	Number	Number	%
Total Directors	36,211	1,912	5.3
Chairman	916	58	6.3
Vice chairman	68	7	10.2
President	1,982	125	6.3
Executive vice president	1,284	106	8.3
Other	31,961	1,616	5.1

Source: Toyo Keizai Shinposha, *Kigyo Keiretsu Soran,* 1989.

In point of fact, however, one or more members of a typical (21-member) Japanese board frequently are former executives of the company's main bank(s). These appointments arise from the common practice among major Japanese corporations, commercial banks in particular, of retiring those senior managers not being nominated to their own companies' boards of directors and placing them in so-called second careers as directors or senior managers of partner companies.[4]

3. See Ballon and Tomita, 1988, p. 185.
4. Placing executives evidently receives a high priority. A senior managing director of one of Japan's largest and oldest banks informed the author that this activity absorbs more than half of his bank's president's time each year.

Finally, a Japanese main bank will often take a leadership role in corporate restructurings, dispute resolution, or simply the promotion of new business for client companies. For example, the Sumitomo Bank's financing of non-Sumitomo group companies such as Nissan, Mazda, and Matsushita Electric has provided it with the opportunity to act as a go-between in arranging sheet metal supply contracts for Sumitomo Metal Industries, one of its group clients.[5] The Tokai bank stepped in to resolve a bitter dispute between labor and top management of one of its client companies, Okuma Machinery Works, over the appointment of the founder's son as the new company president. An executive vice president of the bank assumed the position of president in place of the son.

Main-bank involvement in the affairs of client companies is most dramatic when resolving financial distress. The Industrial Bank of Japan (IBJ) has been particularly prominent throughout Japan's contemporary business history in engineering the turnaround of such well-known companies as Nissan Motors, Yamaichi Securities, Chisso Chemicals, and Japan Lines, Ltd.[6] These corporate rescue operations can be as modest as helping the troubled company find new business or as dramatic as injecting new capital, restructuring assets, and replacing top management. The Mitsubishi Bank, for instance, rescued one of its client companies and a member of the Mitsubishi group, Akai Electric, a producer of audio equipment and videocassette recorders, by taking all these steps.[7] The bank quadrupled its loans to Akai, helped arrange new equity investments by other members of the Mitsubishi Group (chiefly Mitsubishi Electric), entered into a joint venture with Mitsubishi Electric to purchase and operate some of Akai's businesses, and created three new top management positions in which bank officers were placed: one as chief secretary to the president (in effect, the temporary de facto president), another as head of international business operations, and a third as head of international finance.

Throughout this entire operation, none of Akai's 11 other Japanese lenders withdrew from the credit. Such stalwartness in the face of risk may have reflected both confidence in the viability of Mitsubishi Bank's plan and an expectation among other Japanese banks that the borrower's main bank will take out the others in the event of a prolonged restructuring of limited effectiveness. This is precisely what Dai-Ichi Kangyo Bank (DKB), main bank for the Kojin Corporation, did when the

5. Gerlach, 1987, p. 129.

6. IBJ has been less successful lately, however, in the rescue of Fuji Heavy Industries, the producer of Subaru automobiles. Leadership in this restructuring has recently been passed to Nissan Motors.

7. See Kester, 1991b, pp. 69–75.

latter failed. In effect, DKB unilaterally subordinated its senior loans to all other claims against Kojin by voluntarily repaying all Kojin debts to other banks and assuming sole responsibility for recovering the loans.

Germany

As a single class of equity owners, German banks rank a distant fourth behind nonfinancial corporations, individual households, and insurance companies.[8] Nevertheless, like their Japanese counterparts, their influence on the governance of German corporations is disproportionate to their ownership. In part this is because of the concentration of their ownership among Germany's biggest and most prominent firms. As a group, they may own only 9% of domestically listed shares of *all* German companies, but they also own more than 25% of at least 33 major industrial corporations.[9]

In addition to direct share ownership, German banks act as depositories for stock owned by other classes of shareholders. At the end of 1988, DM411.5 billion of shares, or approximately 40% of the total market value of outstanding domestic shares, were deposited in German banks (see Table 3–3). When this is added to their own share ownership, nearly 50% of listed German corporate shares are directly or indirectly under bank stewardship.

Table 3–3
Securities Deposits in German Banks by Group of Investors (1988)

	Amount (DM billions)		%
Government	23.5		5.7
Financial institutions	50.2		12.2
Insurance companies	21.9	5.3	
Investment companies	28.3	6.9	
Nonfinancial business corporations	125.5		30.5
Private households and others	121.4		29.5
Foreigners	90.9		22.1
Total	411.5		100.0

Source: Deutsche Bundesbank, *Monthly Report,* May 1989.

8. Kester, 1991a, pp. 32–40.
9. Shirreff, 1987, p. 71.

This role as a share depository has been quite important to German corporate governance because of what is known as the *Vollmachtstimmrecht*—the ability of banks to vote shares held in deposit on behalf of the depositor. For many years this right of proxy was virtually automatic, indefinite in duration, and did not require instructions from the true shareholders. It was a condition of the deposit itself known as the *Depotstimmrecht*. Today it is restricted insofar as the right of proxy must be renewed every 15 months and banks must solicit voting instructions from shareholders. Nevertheless, as a practical matter, banks continue to obtain wide latitude in the voting of shares held on deposit, giving them considerable effective voting power.

As with Japanese company-bank relationships, German banks trade holdings of stock infrequently, if at all. In most cases, the equity-owning bank of a large industrial corporation will be one of its *Hausbanken* (comparable to Japanese main banks) with which it has a long history of banking business. Deutsche Bank is considered Daimler-Benz's Hausbank and has been so since it engineered the merger of the Mercedes and Benz automobile companies when they encountered financial distress following the deaths of their founders. Since then, Deutsche Bank has maintained a substantial equity ownership in Daimler-Benz, and the chairman of the latter's supervisory board has traditionally come from Deutsche Bank. Other traditional Hausbank relationships in the German automotive industry are shown in Table 3–4.

Table 3–4
Traditional German Hausbank Relationships

Company	Hausbank
BMW	Dresdner Bank
Daimler-Benz	Deutsche Bank
Porsche	Landesgirokasse öffentliche Bank und Landessparkasse
Volkswagen	Deutsche Bank Dresdner Bank

Sources: Company interviews.

The influence of German banks and other large German shareholders is exercised largely through a governing body known as the *Aufsichtsrat*, or supervisory board. This body is one of the more important safeguards embodied in the German system of governance, and one common to the systems of neighboring countries such as Austria and

Switzerland.[10] It is typically composed of 9 to 22 members, half of whom are (by law) elected worker representatives (at least one of whom, however, must be a member of the company's management). The other half of the Aufsichtsrat is elected by shareholders and consists entirely of members who are *not* full-time employees of the company. The chairman of the Aufsichtsrat must be a shareholder representative and is endowed with a (rarely used) tie-breaking vote on any matters that evenly split the board.

In effect, the shareholder-elected half of the German Aufsichtsrat is equivalent to the outside directors of an American corporation, or the nonexecutive directors of a British corporation. An important difference, however, is that these German outside directors are more commonly drawn from the executive ranks of large banks, insurance companies, or other corporations that have a major stake of some sort in the company in question. That stake may be a substantial equity investment, a long-standing lending relationship, a vertical purchase or supply arrangement, or, as in Japan, some combination of these various types of claims. Alternatively, they may be representatives of wealthy families or family foundations that own large blocks of stock. The representation of major German financial institutions on the boards of German automotive companies, and industry representation on the boards of the three largest German banks, are provided in Table 3–5. For the automotive companies, 11 of their 37 shareholder-elected representatives are themselves board members of their respective institutions; all but one are Aufsichtsrat chairmen or Vorstand speakers.

What German directors typically are *not* are strictly disinterested experts in some field appointed to give their presumably objective points of view, nor are they the sheer status lenders sometimes seen on British and American boards.[11] Instead, as a group, these directors tend

10. Briefly, by law, German *Aktiengesellschafts* (AGs—a form of limited liability of stock company) must have two boards. The *Vorstand*, or management board, typically has 5 to 15 members, all of whom are full-time salaried employees of the company, and each of whom is responsible for a "portfolio" of businesses or administrative functions. It has day-to-day executive authority over the company and is the real decision-making authority on most matters. However, it must report to the Aufsichtsrat (which usually meets quarterly) and gain the latter's consent for major investment and financial decisions. The Aufsichtsrat, in contrast, is a true supervisory board, not an executive one. The other form of limited liability company, the *Gesellschaft mit beschänkten* or GmbH, must also have a two-tiered board if it employs more than 500 people. Instead of a Vorstand, however, GmbHs have a much smaller *Geschäftsführung* (executive committee) made up of a chairman, a sales director, and a third director responsible for nearly everything else.

11. See Lawrence, 1980, p. 36.

Table 3–5
Board Relationships Among Major German Financial Institutions and Automotive Companies

Company	Number of Shareholder Reps	Institutions with Board Representations
BMW	11	Dresdner Bank*
Daimler-Benz	11	Deutsche Bank (3 reps)*^ Dresdner Bank+^ Commerzbank+^ Bayerische Landesbank Girozentrabe+
Porsche	6	Landesgirokasse öffentliche Bank und Landessparkasse+^
Volkswagen	10	Deutsche Bank+ Dresdner Bank*^ Allianz A.G. Holding+^ (insurance)

Bank		Industrial Companies with Board Representations
Commerzbank	11	Bayer A.G.*^ Hoechst AG* MBB Messerschmitt Bölkow-Blohm GmbH RWE AG+ SMS Schloemann-Siemag AG+^ Volkswagen AG+^
Deutsche Bank	12	Beiersdorf A. G.* Robert Bosch GmbH+^ Siemens A.G.*^
Dresdner Bank	11	Alt ana Industrie-Aktien und Anlagen A. G.*^ Hoechst A. G.^ Mashinenfabrik Goebel GmbH+^ Thyssen A. G.+^

* = Member of own company's supervisory board
+ = Member of own company's management board
^ = Chairman or speaker of one of own company's boards

Sources: Company annual reports.

to mirror the company's most important investor and business relationships. They also can, and from time to time will, exercise considerable influence in the shaping of corporate strategy through the appointments they make on the Vorstand.[12]

Although legally responsible for representing shareholder interests at large, German Aufsichtsrat members are also able to act as de facto representatives of, and monitors for, other stakeholder interests.[13] This appears to be particularly true for bank executives serving as directors. To the extent their banks lend to the corporation in question, the interests of creditors as well as shareholders are directly represented. Furthermore, by virtue of banks' extensive lending business and large equity stakes in the German *Mittlestand* (middle market), bank executives may also reflect indirectly the interests of smaller suppliers, customers, subcontractors, and so forth that service the needs of the large industrial corporations.

In a detailed study of board-level linkages among German industrial and financial corporations, Ziegler, Bender, and Biehler (1985) identified 453 primary interlocks and 1,175 secondary interlocks (i.e., directors of two companies associating with each other on the board of a third) among directors sitting on supervisory boards of Germany's 325 largest corporations. In general, German banks displayed the greater number of linkages. Deutsche Bank had by far the largest network of interlocks, reaching 239 other companies through primary and secondary linkages. Overall, however, they conclude that German board linkages represent "a coalescence of major interests from both the financial and non-financial sectors. Banks act more like integrators cross-connecting industrials from various economic sectors and other fractional interests."[14]

12. Alfred Herrhausen, past co-chairman of Deutsche Bank and past chairman of Daimler-Benz's Aufsichtsrat, was instrumental in collaborating with Edzard Reuter, former deputy chairman of Daimler-Benz's Vorstand, to shape and implement Daimler-Benz's ambitious diversification into high-technology businesses in 1985 and 1986. It reportedly was also Herrhausen's influence that helped push through a major restructuring of Daimler-Benz's Vorstand in 1986 that created five separate divisions and added three new members favoring diversification. In 1987, his support was said to have been critical in elevating Reuter to chairmanship of the Vorstand when the incumbent, Werner Breitschwerdt, resigned allegedly because of his opposition to the far-reaching new diversification strategy. See Ingersoll and Brady, 1987, pp. 36–37.
13. At one major German bank, for example, management's proposal to award a construction contract for a new building to a particular bidder met with vigorous opposition by a member of the bank's Aufsichtsrat who also sat on the supervisory board of a construction company that was 30% owned by his employer. He argued that better terms could have been obtained from this related construction company (Shirreff, 1987, p. 71).
14. Ziegler, Bender, and Biehler, 1985, p. 110.

In summary, the role of financial institutions in Germany and Japan, banks in particular, is more than that of efficient providers of capital, and their equity ownership in industrial clients represents far more than a mere portfolio investment. Through their activities as main banks or Hausbanks, they play a vital, multifaceted role in the governance of industrial enterprise in their respective countries. Their close and often unique relationship with borrowers affords them greater access to privileged information and establishes them in the eyes of other lenders as "delegated monitors" of their major industrial clients. They function effectively as centers of information gathering about client companies, and their responses to virtually any aspect of their client companies' activities represent important signals to other corporate stakeholders. As significant equity owners, they enjoy direct or de facto board representation through which they may exercise an active voice in the governing of corporations in which they invest.

More than just voice, however, they have the capability and willingness to suspend managerial autonomy and exert more direct, temporary control over client companies experiencing a financial crisis or undertaking a difficult transition in strategy. In effect, as selective interventionists in the management of their preferred borrowers, share-owning Japanese main banks and German Hausbanks help internalize the process of restructuring assets, financial claims, and/or top management itself, thereby reducing the use of legal bankruptcy or externally forced changes in ownership in the market for corporate control so frequently relied on in Anglo-American economies.

In this final respect, German and Japanese banks have an indirect but critically important role in the preservation of valuable, long-term contractual exchange relationships among industrial corporations. By insulating sound corporate investment programs from short-term operating cycles, by judiciously sheltering management from pressures to breach commitments to one or another stakeholder in order to improve near-term performance, yet also by acting swiftly enough to reverse performance declines before corrections become extremely costly if not impossible, major share-owning banks in Germany and Japan help ensure the independence and longevity of industrial enterprises. To the extent this is achieved across a network of companies engaged in vertical trading relationships and relying on a common main bank or Hausbank (e.g., an industrial group), the integrity of long-term commercial relationships is maintained.

As argued in the next section of this chapter, such relationships are valuable for the operating and transactional efficiencies they foster. Thus, in effect, the *corporate* governance activities of major banks and other financial institutions outside the Anglo-American economic bloc are ultimately part of a larger *contractual* governance system, the main concern of which is the support of efficient productions and exchange.

Corporate versus Contractual Governance

Prior to the Industrial Revolution, the management of business enterprises the world over was largely—if not, indeed, literally—a family affair. Product markets were mostly small and regional, labor was generally unskilled and itinerant, and sufficient capital to support production and trade was usually provided by wealthy landowners seeking to exploit agricultural surpluses and seasonal cycles of activity. Ownership and managerial control of business enterprises resided in the hands of a single family. Growth tended to take place by family branching at a rate commensurate with the accumulation of family wealth. Problems of coordination and control seldom extended much beyond the delegation of physical production activity to trusted foremen and the engagement of agents to distribute output in urban markets.

The Industrial Revolution and the subsequent evolution of large-scale enterprises fundamentally changed all this. Today's modern industrial enterprise faces vastly more complex problems of coordination and control. The larger scale of operations today has in and of itself heightened the complexity of problems originally faced by family entrepreneurs. In addition, new stakeholders such as major customers, suppliers, lenders, public shareholders, employees, and management itself have emerged as groups whose economic welfare depends (often crucially) on the activities of the enterprise in question, but whose priorities with respect to the proper focus of those activities can differ sharply one from another. Thus a major challenge facing modern capitalist economies is controlling and coordinating the actions of corporate stakeholders that are fundamentally self-interested and able to undertake some actions or to exploit some information hidden from the view of one another.

Broadly speaking, these problems of coordination and control can be classified into two categories: those associated with the separation of ownership and control in the modern corporation, and those associated with the establishment and maintenance of contractual exchange among separate enterprises.[15] Problems of the first type were initially identified by Adolph Berle and Gardiner Means (1932), and substantially extended by Michael Jensen and William Meckling (1976). The central problem treated by these writers is that because agents (managers) hired to do a job are likely to be self-interested and opportunistic, they cannot always be counted on to act in the best interests of the principals (shareholders)

15. Kester, 1991b, pp. xvi–xvii.

that engaged them. This fundamental reality induces principals to expand resources in the development of incentives and safeguards designed to reduce self-interested opportunistic behavior by agents. The cost of designing and running these systems, and the value lost because of the residual self-interested opportunism that cannot be eradicated, are the "agency costs" that rational investors must take into account when pricing the company's securities. From this perspective, the primary purpose of corporate governance is to create cost-effective monitoring, bonding, and incentive systems that will reduce the amount of foregone value associated with the separation of ownership from control.

The problems associated with contractual exchange were first identified in the economics literature by Ronald Coase (1937) and further analyzed by Oliver Williamson (1985), among others. The central problem addressed by these economists is the optimal means of organizing exchange. When should a company procure its needs in the market, and when should it internalize the market by integrating operations so as to be self-sufficient in one or more capacities? In other words, what is the optimal boundary between the administrative hierarchy of a corporation and the competitive marketplace? Reliance on arm's-length transactions in markets allows for greater specialization in production activities and the realization of scale economies, but also poses risks associated with self-interested opportunism. After a company invests in some expensive and highly specialized assets to support transactions with a particular customer or supplier, for example, that counterparty could threaten to abandon its relationship with the company if terms of trade are not shifted in its favor. The courts might be relied on to enforce the original agreement, but legal adjudication of such disputes is often too slow, costly, and cumbersome to be relied on routinely as a means of handling opportunism of this nature. Absorbing important upstream suppliers or downstream customers provides greater control over the transaction stream and relieves some of the hazards of self-opportunism, but often at the expense of efficiency. The high-powered incentives provided by competitive markets can be difficult to replicate and manage inside an organization. Moreover, there may emerge the types of conditions that Oliver Williamson (1985) labels "bureaucratic disabilities" (e.g., overextension of managerial capabilities or internal politicization of decision making).

From the perspective of literature pertaining to contractual exchange (or transaction cost economics), the central problem is to devise methods for governing agreements or relationships among companies that optimally balance the economies and hazards of transacting in the market with those of administratively controlling the same activities within an administrative hierarchy. Such a system will be referred to here as a "contractual" governance system, and will imply the entire set of incentives, safeguards, and dispute-resolution processes used to control and coordinate the actions of various self-interested enterprises interacting in bilateral exchange relationships. Following Gilson and Roe (1992), it should be differentiated from the more common term, "corporate" governance, which will imply the system used to align the priorities of managers with those of shareholders. Contractual governance may span a continuum bounded at one end by the writing of explicit, detailed contracts enforceable by court order in the event of attempted breach by one of the parties, and at the other end by implicit contracting founded on trust relationships and possibly reinforced by largely nonlegalistic mechanisms structured to encourage voluntary compliance with informal agreements.[16]

Equity's Role in Alternative Systems of Governance

An antitrust "culture" and a highly legalistic approach to contracting in the United States has driven many American corporations (particularly those competing in mature industries) to the extremities of the contractual governance continuum. That is, they tend to achieve comparatively high levels of integration; they rely on arm's-length, price-oriented transactions established through actual or de facto bidding among a large number of competitive suppliers, customers, subcontractors, and so forth; and they depend heavily on formal contracts enforced by courts. Japanese and German rivals, in contrast, have tended to stake out a middle ground.[17] They rely more extensively on implicit contracting among fewer parties that have stable, long-term trading relationships with one another. The latter are often so pronounced as to permit the clear identification of industrial groups (e.g., the Mitsubishi or Sumitomo keiretsu in Japan, and the Deutsche Bank, Daimler, and Thyssen spheres in Germany). The data presented in Table 3–6 for the automotive industry are consistent with this characterization. The American producers are all at once more vertically integrated *and* dependent on many more suppliers than are their German and Japanese rivals.

As pointed out by Gilson and Roe (1992), the disposition of equity ownership among the three rival nations further reflects the differences in their approaches to governance. In the United States, a higher degree of specialization in risk bearing has resulted in fairly clear, bright lines delineating one stakeholder group from another, making equity investors a distinct and largely separate class of claimants against the firm. The advantage of such specialization is that it tends to enhance capital

16. See Kester, 1991a, pp. 9–12.
17. Ibid., pp. 13, 41.

availability and lower capital costs by providing investors with a richer set of risk-return alternatives across which they can diversify. It also yields a clear-cut residual claimant (equity) with unambiguous incentives to monitor corporate management, for it is the residual claimant who will benefit most from efficient production and the reduction of agency costs.[18] Thus, for the contemporary Anglo-American corporation with its largely specialized stakeholders and its distinctly separate residual claimants, the problems associated with the separation of ownership

Table 3–6
Dependence of Automotive Assemblers on Outside Suppliers

Auto Assemblers	Percentage of Manufacturing Cost from Outside Purchases	No. of Primary Parts Suppliers
American		
Chrysler	75	2,300
Ford	50	n.a.
General Motors	30	5,000
German		
BMW	54	950
Daimler-Benz	65	n.a.
Porsche	65	600
Volkswagen	52	1,300
Japanese		
Honda Motor	78	300
Mitsubishi Motors	70	358
Nissan Motor	70	162
Toyota Motor	70	175

Sources: Company estimates; Dodwell Marketing Consultants, *The Structure of the Japanese Auto Parts Industry,* 4th ed. (Tokyo: Dodwell Marketing Consultants, 1990b); and the U.S. General Accounting Office, National Security and International Affairs Division, *Foreign Investment: Growing Japanese Presence in the U.S. Auto Industry* (Washington, D.C.: General Accounting Office, GAO/NSIA 0-88-111, March 1988), pp. 32–33.

from control become central to the governance issue, more so than the governing of intercorporate business relationships. The election of outside directors, the use of the proxy voting mechanism, and the relatively recent development of shareholder advisory committees have emerged

18. Gilson and Roe, 1992, p. 25.

as preferred techniques for solving many of the problems. And when these governance techniques fail, the market for corporate control can be depended on to concentrate ownership in the hands of new shareholders who may then change an underperforming company's patterns of investment, revoke other policies having a pernicious effect on shareholder value, and perhaps change management itself.

In Germany and Japan, residual claimants are not, for the most part, separate and distinct from other stakeholders. Rather, a majority of stock is often owned by a mere dozen or two shareholders who quite often possess other claims against the firm. Note the distribution of debt and equity ownership among Nissan Motors' top ten shareholders, shown in Table 3-7. Of those seven whose lending positions were known at the end of fiscal year 1990, six alone account for ¥192.1 billion of Nissan's then total outstanding borrowing of ¥579.5 billion (33.1%); the same six held shares in Nissan worth approximately ¥558 billion (20.8% of total market value). These financial institutions were neither pure debtholders nor pure equityholders. Their overall investment in Nissan was akin to owning a strip of Nissan's capital base.

Table 3–7
Debt and Equity Ownership in Nissan Motor Corp. Top Ten Shareholders, 1990

Shareholder	Equity Ownership (¥ billion)	%	Debt Ownership (¥ billion)	%
Dai-Ichi Mutual Life Insurance	150.2	5.6	n.a.	n.a.
Industrial Bank of Japan	123.3	4.6	57.3	9.9
Fuji Bank	123.3	4.6	56.5	9.8
Nippon Life Insurance	112.6	4.2	9.0	1.6
Sumitomo Bank	69.7	2.6	38.4	6.6
Yasuda Trust & Banking	69.7	2.6	25.9	4.5
Kyowa Bank	64.4	2.4	n.a.	n.a.
Sumitomo Life Insurance	59.0	2.2	5.0	0.9
Mitsubishi Trust & Banking	56.3	2.1	0.0	0.0
Nissan Fire & Marine Insurance	53.6	2.0	n.a.	n.a.
Total, top ten	882.1	32.9	192.1	33.3
Grand total	2,681.5	100.0	579.5	100.0

Source: Dodwell Marketing Consultants, *Industrial Groupings in Japan*, 9th ed., 1990–1991 (Tokyo: Dodwell Marketing Consultants, 1990a), p. 496.

Such commingling of claims is even more pronounced in other cases. It is not uncommon, for example, for a large *sogo shosha* (Japanese trading company) sitting at the center of a major Japanese keiretsu to have both purchase agreements and supply agreements with a particular industrial corporation within its group, to extend trade credit to that corporation, to take up a pro rata share of its publicly issued bonds (if any), and to own equity in it. While only one of these contracts may be dominant at any given time, it is nevertheless difficult to classify unambiguously the nature of the relationship between the trading company and the industrial corporation.

In these environments it is the Coase/Williamson problem—achieving efficiency of exchange—that is central to the governance process. The role of equity in Japan and Germany is less to vest ownership rights in residual claimants with strong incentives to monitor management than it is to bind otherwise diverse stakeholders to one another—a kind of financial glue that helps hold parties together in long-term trading relationships. It does so by attenuating frictions that normally arise among various stakeholders when they each hold separate and distinct claims. The incentives to breach contracts with suppliers and customers in the interests of transferring value to shareholders, or to borrow money and then take extraordinary risks that might benefit shareholders at the expense of lenders, are reduced when the injured stakeholders are also the company's principal shareholders. Helping troubled companies work out financial problems is also made easier when the principal providers of capital hold roughly comparable bundles of senior and junior, short-term and long-term claims against the company; conflicts of interest and free-riding problems are minimized.

The common assertion by Japanese managers that shareholder interests rank comparatively low on their list of priorities is partly explained by the fact that a substantial percentage of a large company's shareholders is comprised of its major creditors, customers, and suppliers. For most of these shareholders, their commercial trading/lending relationships with the company are as important, if not more so, than their equity investments per se. Not surprisingly, therefore, Japanese managers tend to view their proximate task as being the preservation and enhancement of these complex relationships rather than an immediate, direct pursuit of any one stakeholder's interests, such as that of exclusive equity owners.

The agency problem is addressed in Germany and Japan by placing representatives of significant share-owning stakeholders on the board, and by relying on main banks and Hausbanks as delegated monitors for other major lender/owners. The production process itself also serves as a kind of monitoring system for share-owning stakeholders in Japan. Intense product market rivalry in many industries; the organization of production into less vertically integrated enterprises; and the comparatively high levels of relationship-specific investment undertaken by factor providers, subcontractors, industrial customers, and so forth, all combine to yield substantial incentives for mutual monitoring among key stakeholders. Their interdependence, combined with their risky, relationship-specific investment and their joint exposure to fierce (in some industries) product market rivalry means that *all* suffer if their joint efforts are unsuccessful. As Gilson and Roe (1992) observe:

> The joint character of the [typical Japanese] production process assures the factor providers real time information concerning the quality of their co-venture's performance. A decrease in the quality of a part supplied by one factor provider is quickly discernible to the factor provider who must use it. Similarly, a just-in-time inventory system, while it may also economize on storage space and capital costs, also serves as a daily measure of factor performance; any inability to perform by either the supplier or the assembler becomes apparent quite quickly.
>
> ... product market competition and relationship specific investment transform the production process into a costless monitoring process. Information concerning factor performance and performance monitoring are a joint product of production.[19]

Such monitoring by large, share-owning stakeholders does not, of course, completely obviate the problem of the separation between ownership and control identified by Berle and Means. Indeed, from the perspective of Japanese household or nongroup institutional shareholders without a voice on the board, this sort of problem may actually be *worse* in Japan than in the United States. Among other things, overinvestment in declining core industries, excess personnel, excess product proliferation, and speculative uses of excess cash appear to be at least as problematic in Japan as in the United States.[20]

In the final analysis, however, the overarching effect of the Japanese and German focus on *contractual* rather than simply *corporate* governance—that is, their emphasis on promoting efficiency in contractual exchange among corporations transacting in a production relationship rather than solving the Berle and Means problem, narrowly construed—may have yielded better long-run corporate performance and more valuable enterprises in these nations compared to the Anglo-American nations, notwithstanding the fact that the Germans and Japanese may do no better (and may even do worse, on a relative basis) in the achievement of maximum potential value. Put differently, the systems of *corporate* governance in Japan and Germany may yield only "sat-

19. Gilson and Roe, 1992, pp. 29–30.
20. Kester, 1991a, pp. 169–235.

isficing," not maximizing, behavior with respect to shareholder value; but their *contractual* governance systems permit them to "satisfice" relative to a higher production possibility frontier for a given level of inputs.

While possibly recognizing deficiencies in the value-maximizing behavior of the corporations in which they invest, independent, noncontrolling Japanese and German shareholders may nevertheless acquiesce to such behavior as long as they perceive the advantages of sustaining long-term business relationships that support efficient, relationship-specific investment to be worth more than the foregone incremental value. In other words, they may tolerate agency costs associated with the separation of ownership from control as high or even higher than those present in Anglo-American corporations if the offsetting gain from bearing such costs is substantially reduced transaction costs (e.g., the greater use of flexible, implicit contracts; the mitigation of hazards associated with relationship investment; reliance on dispute resolution techniques instead of costly legal adjudication; and so forth) and greater efficiency in production arising from higher levels of relationship-specific investment.[21]

The Forces of Change

Deficiencies in Japanese and German corporate governance may, of course, eventually give rise to sufficiently large abuses of noncontrolling shareholder interests that it will ultimately pay those shareholders to resort to an arsenal of classically Anglo-American governance techniques, up to and including more frequent use of hostile takeovers to effect change. In fact, at least with respect to Japan, there is evidence that these costs are on the rise, placing considerable stress on traditional contractual relationships. A substantial buildup of liquidity on Japanese balance sheets and a widespread drive to diversify into new product markets often unrelated to core businesses have afforded incumbent Japanese managers far greater discretion in decision making than ever before. No longer vitally dependent on bank credit to fund investment programs, Japanese industrial corporations make more perfunctory, less substantive disclosures of information about past performance and future plans to their main banks. Some have been emboldened enough to reject bank executives dispatched to them to act as directors. For their part, Japanese banks, lately under pressure to meet BIS capital requirements, are becoming more performance-oriented about their equity investments. They are short-listing the companies that they will continue to serve as a main bank and disposing of their equity interests in others.[22] The recent decline in the

21. Gilson and Roe, 1992, pp. 37–38.
22. See Kester, 1991b, pp. 187–262 for further evidence of these trends.

Tokyo Stock Market has only exacerbated this tendency. In general, the slowing of economic activity in Japan has destabilized a number of traditional relationships and resulted in sales of shares previously held under cross-shareowning relationships.

Whether or not these trends mark the beginning of the end of the Japanese system of corporate and contractual governance remains to be seen. It is easy to overstate the significance of recent trends. Many sales of stably held shares are little more than efforts to book current period gains that can be used to boost sagging profits; they are followed by near-immediate repurchases. Other sales represent only a fraction of stably held stock, not the entire amount; still others are sales to some other stable owner of the stock in question, thereby causing little substantive change in the cross-shareholding relationships. Meanwhile, for all the pickup in the greenmailing of cash-laden companies in Japan, true hostile bids for control remain a rarity, as are successfully waged proxy battles. In short, corporate and contractual governance in Japan may be undergoing a period of stress and transformation, but it is premature to conclude that it is about to converge with Anglo-American practices.

In fact, there is evidence that the trend in industrial relations is in precisely the *opposite* direction: American business enterprises are beginning to adopt some of the long-term relationship-oriented practices of their Japanese and German rivals. Some of this has come at the hands of foreign rivals who carry with them the contractual governance practices of their home environments as they invest in the United States. Japanese-affiliated automakers in the United States, for example, have successfully entered into supply contracts with American auto-parts producers that are patterned after their relationships with suppliers at home. Typically, these involve heavier reliance on suppliers in the initial design and development of some auto parts and subassemblies, close coordination of production to take advantage of just-in-time delivery systems, rapid responses to needed product changes, and extensive monitoring and even occasional intrusion by the assembler into the operations of the supplier. Long-term relationships with a few suppliers, sometimes accompanied by minority equity stakes in them, are also used in the United States in lieu of the more common American practice of entering into one-year, bid-price contracts with many suppliers. However foreign this method of doing business may be at first, American suppliers that have successfully won the business of a Japanese-affiliated producer claim that they have been positively affected. Higher production efficiency, better quality, and lower costs are the benefits most commonly reported. Some American suppliers are even extending the same kind of practices to their own upstream suppliers. So too are

American automobile assemblers with respect to their direct supplier relationships.[23]

Implications for the American Financial and Industrial Sectors

Modern American corporate governance is the result of an evolutionary process rooted in America's Industrial Revolution and its ideological traditions. The nineteenth-century burgeoning of large-scale industrial enterprises requiring unprecedentedly large amounts of capital intersected with the cresting of American populism and federalism and created a climate of suspicion regarding the economic power held by these enterprises.[24] Out of this century-long tension emerged a corporate ownership structure and system of governance characterized by high degrees of specialization in risk bearing, a generally wide separation between ownership and control, and an intricate web of banking, insurance, securities, and tax laws and regulations that have restricted the ability of large financial institutions from exerting the prerogatives normally afforded by substantial ownership.

This American approach to ownership and governance was, in many respects, extraordinarily well adapted to its historic economic and political environment. Whereas in other industrializing nations many companies were nationalized, American private enterprise stayed *private* and was able to source sufficient efficiently priced capital to sustain its expansion. But recent experience suggests that the efficacy of the American corporate governance system was greatest when its exposure to "foreign" competition was limited primarily to companies domiciled in Great Britain and Canada—close relatives in terms of political and economic traditions. The tremendous success of many German and Japanese companies in global markets—indeed, even in domestic U.S. markets—during the past two decades, and the seemingly limited ability of so many American companies to respond with maximum effectiveness to these competitive inroads, has called this efficacy into question. Thus we observe American experimentation with new private ownership structures (see Jensen, 1989); the emergence of investment management companies dedicated to serving as long-term, active corporate shareholders (e.g., Alliance Capital Management Corporation and Corporate Partners, Inc.); calls for sweeping reforms of American corporate governance institutions (Porter, 1992); and efforts by industry to build and maintain stable, long-term vertical relationships using contracting techniques similar to those found among Japanese companies.

23. U.S. General Accounting Office, 1988, pp. 39–40.
24. See Roe, 1990 and 1991.

Predictably, these efforts are most readily discernible in those industries hardest hit by Japanese and German competition.

The distinction between corporate and contractual governance, and a comparison of American to German and Japanese systems of governance, lead to two major conclusions with respect to this ongoing process of change. The first is that close, cooperative, and even exclusionary relationships among firms transacting a vertical chain of investment and production (e.g., close vendor-manufacturer relationships or lender-borrower relationships) should not uniformly be castigated as arrangements leading to welfare-reducing restraint of trade. The antitrust culture of the United States has tended to tar vertical cooperation among businesses with the same brush used to blacken horizontal collusion, efficiency gains notwithstanding; nearly any tie-in arrangement or other form of customized, nonstandard contracting has typically been viewed as anticompetitive per se and subject to legal scrutiny. This is too narrow an interpretation of these arrangements. As practiced in Germany and Japan, close vertical relationships can give rise to efficiency in contractual exchange without substantial offsetting losses arising from an absence of rivalry. By tying themselves to one another in cooperative groups, yet eschewing outright ownership and control by any one company over another, Japanese and German corporations have been able to exploit the high-powered incentives of competitive markets that derive from independent ownership and management of assets, while simultaneously relying on close monitoring and selective intervention by key equity-owning stakeholders to ensure that customized agreements are appropriately adapted to changing circumstances. U.S. antitrust enforcement should remain steadfast in its mission to maintain vigorous horizontal competition but be more circumspect about calling into question seemingly exclusionary vertical relationships among independently owned corporations.

The second conclusion is that, when freed of artificial prohibitions against equity ownership or constraints on exercising the rights of ownership, large financial institutions can play broadly constructive and mutually beneficial roles in the systems governing industrial corporate performance. The experiences of Germany and Japan make this case. Within the context of their governance systems, financial institutions, banks in particular, are vital components of the *contractual* governance machinery used to support efficient production and exchange relationships. They are so by acting as delegated monitors of major borrowing clients, selective interventionists in the restructuring of client companies in advance of insolvency, and occasionally even as mediators of disputes among other corporate stakeholders or as agents in the promotion of new business between clients. Although there may be instances in which close relationships between industrial corporations and financial institutions have been abused, there is scant evidence to support U.S. concerns that such relationships will inevitably lead to widespread, systemic imprudence in financial dealing. The extensive commingling of claims against a given company and cross-monitoring among corporate stakeholders, including the providers of capital, mitigates this risk at relatively low cost in other major capitalist economies.

For U.S. industrial corporations to bridge the performance gaps separating many of them from their foreign rivals, substantial change in their ownership and governance appears necessary. Incremental improvements in existing institutions of corporate governance will surely help, but alone they are unlikely to be sufficient. The desirability, if not actual necessity, of a parallel *contractual* governance system that will enable American manufacturers to move away from the present system is already in evidence.

To facilitate the further evolution of such a system, the United States should gradually reduce many of the existing impediments to the establishment of closer ties between the industrial and financial sectors and the exercise of greater voice in corporate governance by large financial institutions. Several changes that might lie at the forefront of such reform would be the removal of the prohibition of equity ownership by banks for their own account, clarification of the conditions under which a creditor's loan will be subject to equitable subordination if it should involve itself in the affairs of a financially troubled debtor, and the easing of limitations in the ability of large equity owners to communicate directly among themselves on matters of corporate governance.

It must be emphasized, however, that there is no single "philosopher's stone" that by itself will remedy the current shortcoming of Anglo-American corporate governance. It took a century of securities, banking, insurance, tax, and antitrust legislation, and literally hundreds of judicial interpretations of those pieces of legislation, to produce the system we have today. Consequently, far-reaching reform will likely come about only through a comprehensive reappraisal of the entire corpus of laws and regulations impinging on corporate and contractual governance, and the adoption of a multitude of individual changes.

As the United States debates the scope and direction of banking reform, we should at least recognize its intrinsic relatedness to the reform of our corporate and contractual governance systems. Hopefully, from this recognition will spring the first of the changes required to establish preconditions for the evolution of a more efficient, more globally competitive American system of contractual governance.

References

Ballon, Robert J., and Iwao Tomita, 1988. *The Financial Behavior of Japanese Corporations*. Tokyo: Kodansha International.

Berle, Adolph A., and Gardiner C. Means, 1932. *The Modern Corporation and Private Property*. New York: MacMillan.

Coase, Ronald H., 1937. "The Nature of the Firm," *Economica N.S.* 4, pp. 386–405.

Dickens, Jeremy, 1987. "Equitable Subordination and Analogous Theories of Lender Liability: Toward a New Model of Control," *Texas Law Review* 65 (March), pp. 801–858.

Dodwell Marketing Consultants, 1990a. *Industrial Groupings in Japan*, 9th ed., 1990–1991. Tokyo: Dodwell Marketing Consultants.

————, 1990b. *The Structure of the Japanese Auto Parts Industry*, 4th ed. Tokyo: Dodwell Marketing Consultants.

Edwards, Franklin R., and Robert A. Eisenbeis, 1990. "Financial Institutions and Corporate Myopia: An International Perspective." Unpublished working paper, Columbia University and University of North Carolina, December 7.

Gerlach, Michael, 1987. "Business Alliances and the Strategy of the Japanese Firms," *California Management Review* Fall, pp. 126–142.

Gilson, Ronald J., and Mark J. Roe, 1992. "Comparative Corporate Governance: Focusing the United States-Japan Inquiry." Unpublished working paper, Columbia University Law School.

Hoshi, Takeo, Anil Kashyap, and David Scharfstein, 1990. "Bank Monitoring and Investment: Evidence from the Changing Structure of Japanese Corporate Banking Relationships," in R. Glen Hubbard, ed., *Asymmetric Information, Corporate Finance, and Investment*. Chicago, University of Chicago Press, pp. 105–126.

Ingersoll, Robert, and Rose Brady, 1987. "The Banker Behind the Shakeup at Daimler-Benz," *Business Week*, July 27, pp. 36–37.

Jensen, Michael C., 1989. "The Eclipse of the Public Corporation," *Harvard Business Review* (September–October), pp. 61–74.

Jensen, Michael C., and William Meckling, 1976. "Theory of the Firm: Managerial Behavior, Agency Costs, and Capital Structure," *Journal of Financial Economics* 3 (October), pp. 305–360.

Kaplan, Steven N., 1991. "Internal Corporate Governance in Japan and the U.S.: Differences in Activity and Horizons." Unpublished working paper, University of Chicago Graduate School of Business, November.

Kester, W. Carl, 1991a. "Governance, Contracting, and Investment Time Horizons." Working paper #92-003, Harvard Business School.

————, 1991b. *Japanese Takeovers: The Global Contest for Corporate Control.* Boston: Harvard Business School Press.

Lawrence, Peter, 1980. *Managers and Management in West Germany.* New York: St. Martin's Press.

Lightfoot, Robert W., 1991. "Note on Corporate Governance Systems: The United States, Japan, and Germany." Harvard Business School Note No. 292-012.

McCraw, Thomas K., and Patricia A. O'Brien, 1986. "Production and Distribution: Competition Policy and Distribution: Competition Policy and Industry Structure," in Thomas K. McCraw, ed., *America versus Japan.* Boston: Harvard Business School Press, pp. 77–116.

Porter, Michael E., ed., forthcoming. *Capital Choices: Changing the Way America Invests in Industry.* Boston: Harvard Business School Press.

Prowse, Stephen D., 1990. "Institutional Investment Patterns and Corporate Financial Behavior in the United States and Japan," *Journal of Financial Economics* 27:1 (September), pp. 43–66.

Roe, Mark J., 1990. "Political and Legal Restraints on Ownership and Control of Public Companies," *Journal of Financial Economics* 27:1 (September), pp. 7–41.

————, 1991. "A Political Theory of American Corporate Finance," *Columbia Law Review* 10, pp. 10–67.

Sheard, Paul, 1989. "The Main Bank Systems and Corporate Monitoring and Control in Japan," *Journal of Economic Behavior and Organization*, pp. 399–422.

Shirreff, David, 1987. "Bankers as Moral Monopolists," *Euromoney*, March, pp. 71–79.

Suzuki, Sadahiko, and Richard Wright, 1985. "Financial Structure and Bankruptcy Risk in Japanese Companies," *Journal of International Business Studies* (Spring), pp. 97–110.

Tokyo Stock Exchange Fact Book, 1990. Tokyo: Tokyo Stock Exchange.

Toyo Keizai Shinposha, 1989. *Kigyo Keiretsu Soran*, p. 92.

U.S. General Accounting Office, National Security and International Affairs Division, 1988. *Foreign Investment: Growing Japanese Presence in the U.S. Auto Industry*. Washington, D.C.: General Accounting Office, GAO/NSIA 0-88-111 (March), pp. 32–33.

J.B. Were & Son, 1992. "Australian Equity Market Profile," February.

Williamson, Oliver E., 1982. "Antitrust Enforcement: Where it has been; where it is going," in John Craven, ed., *Industrial Organization, Antitrust, and Public Policy*. Boston: Kluwer-Nijhoff, pp. 41–68.

———, 1985. *The Economic Institutions of Capitalism: Firms, Markets, Relational Contracting*. New York: The Free Press.

Ziegler, Rolf, Donald Bender, and Hermann Biehler, 1985. "Industry and Banking in the German Corporate Network," in Frans N. Stokman, Rolf Ziegler, and John Scott, eds., *Networks of Corporate Power: A Comparative Analysis of Ten Countries*. Cambridge, England: Polity Press, pp. 91–111.

CHAPTER 4

INTERNATIONAL INSURANCE: A RISKY BUSINESS?

John B. Goodman

Introduction

Financial services have long been at the forefront of the globalization process. In the last decade, in particular, the combination of rapid technological change and increased capital mobility provided firms with the opportunity to pry open national financial markets. Faced with these new opportunities, financial service vendors have increasingly emphasized the role of global markets in their competitive strategies. Setting an effective strategy, however, requires a clear understanding of both the prospects for, and the limits of, globalization. Successful vendors will be those who calibrate their strategies to the future structure of competition in their business.

Insurance provides a powerful illustration of the challenges confronting financial service vendors in this increasingly global environment. It is a mistake, however, to speak of insurance as a single industry. Insurance actually consists of a number of segments that differ significantly in terms of their international activity and configuration. Competition in reinsurance, for example, has long been global; competition in non-life insurance, by contrast, has remained primarily national in scope. Amidst all the pressure for global financial integration, it may be useful to observe Sherlock Holmes's well-known lesson that much can be learned by examining the dog that doesn't bark. Through a comparison of the reinsurance and non-life insurance markets, I develop a framework that explains why national markets have dominated non-life insurance. Then I examine whether broader economic changes will lead non-life insurance to adopt a global configuration and discuss the strategic implications for financial service vendors.

The Structure of Insurance Markets

Insurance has long been central to international economic activity. Centuries ago, when British merchants first engaged in foreign commerce, they gathered in coffee shops to arrange insurance for their cargos and fleets. Since that time, insurance has become a very big business. During the 1980s, worldwide insurance premiums came to exceed $1 trillion. The purpose of insurance, simply put, is to permit clients to transfer the risk of a financial loss resulting from the occurrence of specified (but uncertain) events in exchange for the payment of an agreed premium.

Beyond this general level, the role, size, and structure of the two segments of the insurance industry analyzed in this paper differ greatly.[1] Non-life can be thought of as a retail market where products are sold to both individuals and firms. Those sold to individuals, referred to as personal or mass risks, include both home and auto insurance; products sold to firms, referred to as either commercial or large risks, include catastrophic damage, fire, marine, aviation, and third-party liability insurance. Reinsurance can be thought of as a secondary market where insurance companies spread their risks. A reinsurance company provides cover only to insurers, not to individuals or (non-insurance) firms.

In 1988, the total volume of non-life premiums (net of reinsurance) amounted to $555.1 billion. As can be seen in Table 4–1, the United States, Europe, and Japan accounted for approximately 85% of this sum. Among these advanced industrial countries, demand for non-life insurance depends largely on a country's economic size. Premium volume in the United States alone represented more than 45% of the total.[2] As Table 4–2 shows, the largest non-life insurers tend to be located in the largest mar-

1. The third segment, which I observed but do not analyze here, is life insurance, which provides remuneration to a beneficiary in the event of a policyholder's death and frequently serves as an instrument of personal savings. Life insurance constitutes nearly one-half of all world premiums; but as of 1990, the life insurance industry was characterized by relatively little international activity.
2. The chapter focuses primarily on trade and investment in the United States, Europe, and Japan. Although international insurance transactions remain important for the developing countries, the advanced industrial countries constitute both the chief providers and the main consumers of insurance products. Thus I have used country-level data to analyze the levels and patterns of transactions (in both non-life insurance and reinsurance products) among these countries. Then, to understand the effects of regulation and firm strategy, I interviewed government officials in these markets, as well as senior managers from important non-life and reinsurance firms, including American International Group, CIGNA, Chubb, Continental Engineering Insurance Group, General Reinsurance, and Travelers in the United States; Sumitomo Marine and Fire, Taisho Marine and Fire, Tokio Marine and Fire, and Yasuda Fire and Marine in Japan; and Allianz, AXA-Midi, Lloyd's, Munich Re, Royal, Swiss Re, UAP Victoire, Winterthur, and Zurich in Europe.

Table 4–1
World Insurance: Gross Premium Volumes 1988 Non-Life and Life ($ billions)

	Non-Life	Life	Total
United States	254.6	176.8	431.4
Japan	70.5	214.1	284.6
Total EC 12 + Switzerland	144.7	137.1	281.8
West Germany	42.7	36.5	79.3
United Kingdom	28.1	40.9	69.0
France	26.6	25.5	52.2
Italy	15.2	4.8	20.0
Netherlands	7.8	7.3	15.1
Spain	7.5	7.2	14.7
Belgium	4.4	1.9	6.3
Denmark	2.8	2.0	4.8
Ireland	1.4	1.9	3.2
Portugal	1.0	0.2	1.2
Greece	0.4	0.2	0.7
Luxembourg	0.2	0.1	0.3
Switzerland	6.5	8.7	15.1
Rest of world	85.3	87.9	173.3
World total	555.1	615.9	1,171.0

Source: Sigma, Swiss Reinsurance Company, April 1990.

Table 4–2
Largest Non-Life Insurers in the World (1988 premiums in $ millions)

Rank	Company	Domicile	Premiums
1	State Farm	United States	23,254
2	Allstate	United States	13,289
3	Aetna Life & Casualty	United States	10,773
4	Allianz	Germany	10,425
5	American International Group	United States	8,529
6	Zurich Insurance	Switzerland	7,281
7	CIGNA	United States	7,061
8	Tokio Marine & Fire	Japan	6,689
9	Royal Insurance	United Kingdom	5,843
10	Yasuda Fire & Marine	Japan	4,934

Sources: Finance World, September 4, 1990; industry sources.

kets; as of 1988, four of the top ten were based in the United States. Still, non-life insurance is a highly fragmented business, and thousands of non-life insurance companies operate worldwide. The four largest firms have a global market share of only 10%. Within countries, however, non-life insurance appears more concentrated. Figure 4–1 indicates the top four firms in the United States received just 20% of all non-life premiums, while in Japan the top four firms received over 40%.

Non-life companies reinsure approximately 9% of their risks (see Table 4–3). Not surprisingly, the countries with the largest non-life

Table 4–3
Reinsurance Demand by Country, 1987 ($ millions)

	Gross Premiums	Reinsurance Demand	Reinsurance as % of GWP[a]
United States	413,267	31,408	7.60
Japan	236,978	15,641	6.60
Germany	81,354	13,749	16.90
United Kingdom	67,372	5,929	8.80
France	50,009	5,001	10.00
Italy	19,764	4,131	20.90
Netherlands	16,396	1,623	9.90
Switzerland	16,005	1,072	6.70
Spain	10,856	1,487	13.70
Austria	6,301	951	15.09
Rest of OECD	63,900	6,608	10.34
Rest of world	49,700	4,300	8.65
World total (excluding East bloc)	1,031,902	91,900	8.91

[a] Gross written premiums.

Source: Sigma, Swiss Reinsurance Company, May 1989.

markets—the United States, Germany, and Japan—place the largest amount of reinsurance. And, since non-life insurers reinsure only a small portion of their total book of business, the reinsurance market world-wide is considerably smaller than the non-life insurance market. In 1988, world reinsurance premiums amounted to $91.9 billion.[3]

Reinsurance is a more concentrated business than non-life insurance. Worldwide, reinsurance firms can be counted in the hundreds. In 1988, the top four firms possessed 15% of the world market (see Table 4–4). Apart from the United States, where the top four firms hold about 14% of the market, data on market share in different countries are generally unavailable because of the practices of national regulators and the signifi-cant role of foreign firms in this business.

3. Reinsurance firms estimate that non-life insurance represents about 85% of their busi-ness, while life insurance represents the remaining 15%.

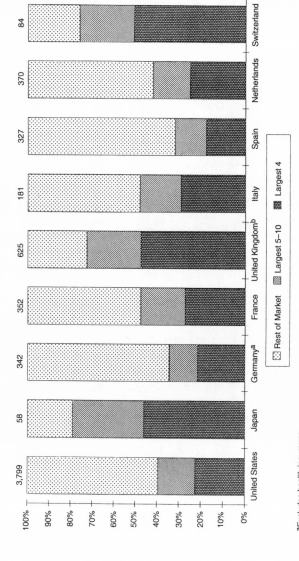

Figure 4–1

Distribution of Market Shares in Non-Life Business, 1987 (with number of firms in market noted).

aExcludes health insurance.
bRefers to worldwide business of insurance companies.

Source: Sigma, Swiss Reinsurance Company, February 1989.

Table 4–4
The Top Fifteen Reinsurers in the World by 1988 Net Premiums ($ millions)

Rank	Company	Domicile	Net Premiums
1	Munich Re	Germany	6,147.2
2	Swiss Re	Switzerland	4,186.0
3	General Re	United States	1,780.2
4	Skandia International	Sweden	1,219.3
5	Cologne Re	Germany	1,164.4
6	Hannover Re and Eisen & Stahl	Germany	1,151.3
7	Employers Re	United States	1,135.2
8	Assicurazioni Generali	Italy	1,116.9
9	Gerling Globale Re	Germany	1,040.7
10	American Re	United States	976.4
11	M&G Re	United Kingdom	976.4
12	Frankona Ruck	Germany	917.6
13	Tokio M&F	Japan	851.4
14	SCOR	France	759.9
15	Yasuda F&M	Japan	610.9

Sources: Reactions, March 1990, company data.

Even more striking are the differences in the internationalization of the two industry segments. In analyzing insurance flows, it is useful to distinguish between trade (policies sold by an insurer located, for example, in Britain to a client located in the United States) and investment (policies sold by the U.S. subsidiary of the British insurer to a client located in the United States). Of the world's reinsurance premiums, reinsurance executives estimate that some 30% to 50% is traded across borders and an additional 10% is received via investment. Non-life insurance, by contrast, is essentially a domestic business. Of all non-life premiums, only about 1%–3% is traded across borders, while an additional 6%–10% is received through investment.[4]

---

4. Data on international insurance transactions, via trade or via investment, are notoriously poor. With the exception of the United States, most countries do not collect or publish trade data, and most companies (if they list premiums obtained from abroad) do not distinguish between trade and investment. Thus the numbers presented here are the author's own estimates based on interviews with managers of leading international insurance firms and with government officials.

International Transactions in Insurance

Non-life insurance and reinsurance lie at two ends of the globalization spectrum. The different patterns of competition in these two segments are explained by differences in industry economics, in the decision-making processes of customers, and in regulation.

Industry Economics

The economics of the insurance business suggests three rationales for international expansion: to achieve scale economies, to diversify risk, and to exploit national comparative advantages. The role of these rationales differs significantly between non-life insurance and reinsurance.

Non-life insurance. Most research suggests that there are relatively few economies of scale in non-life insurance. To understand why, consider the four main activities of the insurance business: underwriting (which involves both the selection of risks and the setting of rates), sales and marketing, claims adjusting and processing (after a reported loss), and investing assets. While scale economies in investing and claims processing are sizable, they are lower in underwriting, sales, and claims adjusting.[5] Insurance executives note that an insurance company must have a large enough volume of business to attract knowledgeable and skilled underwriters and adjusters. Still, these activities are all labor intensive and constitute a large proportion of costs. Commissions paid to sales agents, for example, can represent half of a firm's expenses. The minimum efficient size (MES) of a non-life insurer is considered to be small enough that economies of scale do not constitute a significant entry barrier in larger markets like the United States and Japan. That is, MES is small relative to total industry output.[6] Even in these markets, however, there is little evidence that average costs increase with size. Thus, while major American and Japanese firms gain no advantage when they grow, they suffer no apparent disadvantage either.[7]

Of course, minimum efficient size depends on the scope of an insurer's business. An insurance company offering multiline insurance must be

---

5. For a useful description and guide to the insurance business, see Robert I. Mehr, Emerson Cammack, and Terry Rose, *Principles of Insurance*, 8th ed. (Homewood, Ill.: Irwin, 1985).

6. See Randall Geehan, "Economies of Scale in Insurance: Implications for Regulation," in Bernard Wasow and Raymond D. Hill, eds., *The Insurance Industry in Economic Development* (New York: New York University Press, 1986), p. 148. A 1974 study of the U.S. property and casualty industry concludes that MES is only about $30–$60 million in net premiums. See R.F. Allen, "Cross-Sectional Estimates of Cost Economies in Stock Property-Liability Companies," *Review of Economics and Statistics* 56 (February 1974), pp. 100–103.

7. *Sigma*, April 1991.

larger (to achieve economies of scale) than a firm exploiting a particular market niche. Many of the larger multiline firms in the United States and Japan are thought to have reached scale economies. According to one senior insurance executive in a major U.S. company: "All-state/all-line insurance companies in the United States are capitalized at about $1.5 billion; if you ask these companies if they need to double [in size], they say no."

International expansion, even for firms of this size, would allow a greater geographic diversification of risk—the second rationale for engaging in international activity—but such diversification can also be achieved through reinsurance. From the perspective of size alone, therefore, American and Japanese insurers as a whole appear to have little incentive (though perhaps no clear disincentive either) to become international.[8]

In Europe, by contrast, scale economies do not appear to have been reached by any but a few non-life insurers. The segmentation of Europe's national markets (which will be discussed) prevented most firms from becoming as large as their American and Japanese counterparts. This suggests that expansion *within* the European Community makes sense to achieve economies of scale. But a strong case for *global* expansion cannot be based on scale economies.

Exploiting a national comparative advantage is the third rationale for international expansion.[9] Such advantages do, of course, exist in non-life insurance. Firms located in the more advanced industrial countries enjoy advantages in almost every aspect of the business— from risk evaluation to asset investment. The significance of such comparative advantages shows up in the direction of insurance flows between developed and developing countries. Insurers based in the developed world have been active in the insurance markets of developing countries when not prohibited from doing so by regulation.[10] But comparative advantage tends to play a smaller role in transactions among the developed countries, where factor endowments are similar, than it does between the developed and the developing countries.

8. Although there have historically been few incentives from the perspective of scale for insurers to operate internationally, I shall argue that specific firms may—as the result of skills they have developed over time—derive significant benefit from international operations.

9. Brian Hindley and Alasdair Smith, "Comparative Advantage and Trade in Services," *The World Economy*, December 1984, pp. 369–389; Ken Tucker and Mark Sundberg, *International Trade in Services* (London: Routledge, 1988); and Ronald Kent Shelp, *Beyond Industrialization: Ascendancy of the Global Service Economy* (New York: Praeger, 1981), Chapter 4.

10. André Sapir and Ernst Lutz, "Trade in Services: Economic Determinants and Development-Related Issues," World Bank Staff Working Paper No. 480, August 1981, p. 31.

Moreover, any national advantage must overcome the existence of information asymmetries.[11]

Information asymmetries exist because insurance buyers generally know more about their own riskiness than do insurers. Asymmetries become larger when insurers venture outside their home markets, since the nature of risk (for example, the likelihood of car accidents, product liability suits, or burglaries) varies across countries.

Information asymmetries pertain not only to the nature of risk, but also to other characteristics of foreign markets, such as customer preferences and distribution channels. Japanese non-life insurers, for example, may lack the necessary expertise in the U.S. market to know how to tailor an insurance product to meet the needs of American customers. Similarly, Japanese insurers sell policies through direct agents in Japan, but in the U.S. market may operate at a disadvantage because independent insurance brokers (who shop their clients' insurance needs among various insurers for the best coverage and price) play a dominant role. The existence of information asymmetries regarding risk, distribution channels, and customer preferences often leads foreign insurers to be "selected against" on entering a new market. That is, they cannot discriminate as easily as a domestic-based firm between good and bad risks. A company trying to expand quickly into a new market (whether domestic or foreign) will therefore take on bad risks, which ultimately return in the form of higher losses. Information asymmetries thus reduce the incentive for insurers to compete abroad; and when insurers do decide to engage in international activity, such information asymmetries can be overcome only by establishing a local branch or subsidiary with underwriters who understand the market.

Reinsurance. In contrast to what we have observed for non-life insurance, there are significant economic advantages for reinsurance firms to operate internationally. First, scale economies are far more significant in reinsurance than in non-life insurance. Reinsurance is purchased in one of two ways: either directly from a reinsurer or indirectly through a broker. Economies of scale are high through both channels. Reinsurers for whom brokers serve as the principal distribution channel can provide as much cover as either regulation or prudence permits. In this segment of the market, reinsurance is primarily a capital-driven business that does not require extensive investments in marketing or loss adjustment. As a result, average costs fall per dollar of reinsurance.[12]

---

11. This is an extension of the argument presented by George A. Akerlof in "The Market for 'Lemons': Quality Uncertainty and the Market Mechanism," *Quarterly Journal of Economics* 84 (August 1970), pp. 488–500.
12. Geehan, "Economies of Scale in Insurance," p. 114.

Table 4–5
American Reinsurance Market Reinsurance Results: American Reinsurers, 1989
($ figures in thousands)

Premiums Over $500,000	Premiums Written	Combined Ratio
General Re Group	1,796,611	99.6%
Employers Re	1,113,867	104.4%
American Re	871,220	103.8%
North American/Swiss Re	630,071	116.9%
Munich Re Group	570,907	109.8%
Prudential Re Group	503,362	106.7%
Weighted Average		104.9%

Premiums Between $100,000 and $500,000		
Kemper Re	326,439	106.5%
Transatlantic Re	319,110	108.7%
Transamerica Re	280,178	104.9%
CIGNA Re	272,945	110.9%
Skandia America Group	262,162	114.4%
National Re	243,145	107.6%
Constitution Re	240,184	103.5%
NAC Re	192,323	108.5%
Continental Re Corp	184,276	104.9%
US International Re	178,920	110.5%
Putnam Re	153,280	103.0%
Underwriters Re	129,677	105.7%
SCOR Re	102,108	104.9%
Winterthur Swiss	100,096	115.7%
Weighted Average		107.8%

Premiums Under $100,000		
Reinsurance Corp of NY	98,914	125.8%
American Agr Ins Co	96,847	115.9%
Trenwick America Re	94,922	105.4%
Christiania General	93,877	104.9%
Re Capital Reins Corp	92,263	99.3%
Metropolitan Re	91,863	130.4%
PMA Re Corp	82,168	114.9%
Unity Group	77,915	112.4%
American Union of NY	72,432	116.4%
M&G America	67,073	122.6%
Executive Re	52,014	99.4%
American Royal Reinsurance Co	50,013	109.9%

Table 4–5 (cont.)

Premiums Under $100,000 continued	Premiums Written	Combined Ratio
Frankona Re	47,445	106.2%
AXA (Gamma Re)	44,201	112.7%
Philadelphia Re	43,828	123.6%
MONY Re	43,336	136.0%
Insurance Corp of Hanover	37,563	109.3%
Generali of Trieste	35,169	108.3%
Enhance Reins Co	34,559	66.5%
Abeille Reassurances US	34,028	109.3%
Finmar Re	33,697	103.6%
Stella Re-Hansa/Zurich	33,441	114.0%
Signet Re	31,313	120.5%
Phoenix Re Co	30,414	120.1%
San Francisco Re	29,464	126.4%
Belvedere America Re	29,350	117.9%
Baltica Skandinavia Re	28,096	109.4%
Gerling Global	26,382	109.6%
Great Lakes Re	25,621	105.3%
Sirius Re Corp	23,370	104.3%
Cologne Re of America	22,004	111.7%
Nordic Union Re	21,242	104.2%
United Republic Re	20,912	108.1%
Republic Western Insurance Co	20,869	94.0%
Folksamerica Re	20,462	107.3%
Vesta American Ins Co	20,186	103.9%
TOA-Re of America	17,996	124.5%
New Zealand Re	14,692	111.9%
United Re Corp of NY	11,755	112.5%
US Capital (Multiplus)	10,991	125.6%
Chartwell Re (NWNL Re)	10,105	162.7%
Unione Italiana Re	9,610	146.5%
Sorema Re (Copenhagen)	7,974	129.1%
First American Insurance	7,802	108.7%
Asset Guaranty Reins. Co	7,742	56.6%
SIRCO (Southwest)	3,690	119.8%
American Fuji Fire & Marine	3,580	191.6%
AGF Re	3,353	127.0%
Weighted Average		112.9%
Reinsurance Companies Total	10,287,424	107.2%

The largest reinsurance firms in the world tend to provide cover directly to non-life insurers, rather than through brokers. Such direct sales are considerably more profitable because they eliminate the broker's commission. Moreover, direct reinsurers tend to charge higher rates in return for technical assistance, among other things, for the evaluation of risks and claims. Reinsurers, such as Munich Re, Swiss Re, and General Re, all have large staffs of engineers and underwriters who work closely with non-life insurers. Munich Re—the world's largest reinsurer—has, for example, a staff of over 100 engineers at its headquarters who assist clients worldwide. Providing such services requires sufficient market presence and skills, which, according to industry sources, only the largest firms can provide. Thus economies of scale are high for these kinds of reinsurers as well.

The advantages of scale are particularly evident in the U.S. market. Table 4–5 lists the reinsurance results of professional reinsurers operating in the United States. Firms with premiums exceeding $500 million-have a "combined ratio"[13] of 104.9; those with premiums between $100 million and $500 million have a combined ratio of 107.8; and those with premiums under $100 million have a combined ratio of 112.9. The combined ratio is often taken as a measure of underwriting performance. The lower the combined ratio, the better the performance. The largest firms operating in the United States have probably fully exploited available scale economies. But firms based in smaller markets have to operate internationally to achieve similar scale economies.

Risk diversification also helps explain the greater international activity in reinsurance than in non-life insurance. Reinsurers, whose liabilities are spread over a broad geographic area, can smooth out fluctuations resulting from localized losses. The increase in excess-of-loss contracts which can expose reinsurers to extremely large liabilities has made this rationale particularly important.[14] More generally, reinsurance exists because it provides a market within which direct insurers can

---

13. The combined ratio is the sum of the loss ratio and the expense ratio:

$$\text{Loss Ratio: } \frac{\text{losses due to claims + loss reserves + claims + administrative costs}}{\text{net earned premiums}}$$

$$\text{Expense Ratio: } \frac{\text{expenses}}{\text{net written premiums}}$$

where net premiums (whether written or earned) are defined as gross premiums minus reinsurance costs. Written premiums are all premiums collected during a given period. An entire premium is considered written the day a policy is issued. Earned premiums, by contrast, are the proportional share of each policy's written premium for which the term of coverage has elapsed. Earned premiums are thus divided evenly over the exposure period of the policy.

diversify their own portfolios. Thus, the international expansion of reinsurance can be seen as a substitute for the lack of geographic risk diversification on the part of direct insurers.

Among the advanced industrial countries, international reinsurance appears to be driven more by the existence of scale economies and the benefits of risk diversification than by differences in national comparative advantage. In reinsurance, national comparative advantages are offset by information asymmetries—although such asymmetries may be less extensive than in non-life insurance due to the reinsurer's smaller number of customers. Because information is likely to be the most incomplete when a reinsurer enters a new market, reinsurers have also found that they are "selected against" when they first tap foreign markets.

The Customer Decision-Making Process

The decision-making processes of customers have reinforced the way in which economic forces affect international insurance transactions. The process used by non-life insurance customers differs markedly from that adopted by reinsurance customers. Insurance for personal lines or mass risks, such as home fire insurance, is a local business. According to industry executives, individuals or small business prefer to buy non-life coverage from a local company (whether foreign or domestically owned) on the ground that they will get better advice and service. Selling insurance to them has therefore historically required a local agent network and post-sale servicing contact.

In both Europe and Japan, agents (either independent or tied to a single company) are the principal distribution channel. In the United States, non-life insurers are making greater use of direct marketing for standard products. Even in these cases, however, the sheer volume of post-sale servicing requires a local network. As a result, foreign insurers entering third markets to cover mass risks have established local branches or subsidiaries.

Compared to individuals purchasing personal lines of insurance, companies that purchase insurance for large commercial risks tend to be

---

14. Reinsurance contracts are written either on a facultative basis, where risks are reinsured individually, or on a treaty basis, where the primary insurer agrees to cede a certain amount of a pool of risks to the reinsurer. Either contract can come in two forms: (1) quota share, in which a reinsurer pays a fixed portion of any loss in exchange for an equivalent fixed portion of the direct insurer's premium (minus origination fee); and (2) excess of loss, in which a reinsurer agrees to pay all losses over an agreed sum and up to an agreed limit. Reinsurers may in turn reduce their risk exposure by retroceding their policies, in essence reinsuring their own risks.

more knowledgeable and more sophisticated. Most large companies use brokers who shop for the best insurance coverage for their risks. The largest companies employ their own risk managers, who have enough experience to look outside their home market. Thus in these commercial lines of insurance some coverage will be bought from insurers located in foreign markets.

Customers of reinsurance are insurance companies themselves. When buying reinsurance, insurers often look beyond their home borders. The propensity to purchase reinsurance abroad varies by country. In general, cross-border transactions are greater in Europe than in the United States because the small size of national European markets creates a greater demand for risk diversification.

Whether insurers purchase reinsurance from foreign-domiciled companies depends, in addition, on the two types of reinsurers. Reinsurers whose principal role is to provide financial capacity—that is, to assume risk—can provide such cover from abroad. In London, for example, brokers bring policies from insurance companies around the world to be reinsured by the various underwriting syndicates at Lloyd's. Direct reinsurers that provide technical consulting services can also provide capacity from abroad, but they need closer contact with their clients. Although a local presence might facilitate such contact, it is not necessarily required. For these reasons, the purchasing decisions of customers contribute to the global nature of the reinsurance business.

Government Regulation

Government regulation further reinforces the way in which economic forces influence the level and type of international activity in non-life insurance and reinsurance. Virtually all countries regulate non-life insurance more heavily than they regulate reinsurance. Specifically, most countries require non-life insurers to be locally licensed and established, whereas reinsurers often are not under that obligation.

There are several reasons for this difference in treatment. First, national regulators generally believe that non-life insurance customers need more protection than do reinsurance customers; underlying this belief is the notion that insurance companies are more sophisticated buyers than are individuals or firms who purchase non-life insurance. Second, many nations want to keep non-life insurance premiums within their borders to contribute to economic development. Viewed from another perspective, however, reinsurance serves as a useful mechanism to transfer national risks overseas and protect national insurers from catastrophic loss. Japan, for example, encourages the purchase of reinsurance from abroad for earthquake coverage by limiting the amount of insurance and reinsurance coverage that Japanese firms can offer. Third, countries often require more insurance capacity than their own non-life insurers can supply. Allowing domestic insurance companies to purchase reinsurance from abroad enables non-life insurers to offer more coverage and to do so at a cheaper price.[15]

Sources of Competitive Advantage in International Insurance

Not only the patterns of international competition differ between reinsurance and non-life insurance; so too do the sources of competitive advantage.

Non-Life Insurance

Surprisingly, although international activity in non-life insurance has been limited, a few firms have succeeded in establishing a position in foreign markets. Figure 4-2 provides two measures of the foreign activities of non-life insurance companies. As of 1982, firms based in the United States, the United Kingdom, France, and Switzerland operated in the greatest number of countries and maintained the greatest number of branches abroad. Figure 4-3 gives the geographic breakdown of business (as of 1988) for a number of insurance companies that operate internationally. The firms with the broadest international networks include Zurich and Winterthur (based in Switzerland), Royal (based in the United Kingdom), and AIG and CIGNA (based in the United States). Nationale Nederlanden, a Dutch firm, boasts a large network, but most of this activity is in life insurance. These figures show that the firms that in the past have been most successful operating internationally have been based in the United States, in the United Kingdom, and in Switzerland. Throughout most of the postwar period, German, French, Italian, and Japanese firms, by contrast, have concentrated most of their activities in home or regional markets. The ability of U.S., British, and Swiss firms to overcome the extensive barriers to globalization in non-life insurance can be traced to both country-based advantages and national regulatory regimes.

Country-specific advantages. The most critical determinant of a firm's success in international insurance is the internationalization of its domestic client base. Non-life insurers, like banks, follow their customers overseas. As these customers—whether merchants or manufacturers—

---

15. Howard Kunreuther and Mark V. Pauly, *International Trade in Insurance*, S.S. Huebner Foundation for Insurance Education, Wharton School, University of Pennsylvania, Huebner Foundation Monograph 16 (Homewood, Ill.: Irwin, 1991).

Financial Services

Figure 4–2
Foreign Activity of Domestic Insurance Companies, 1982ᵃ

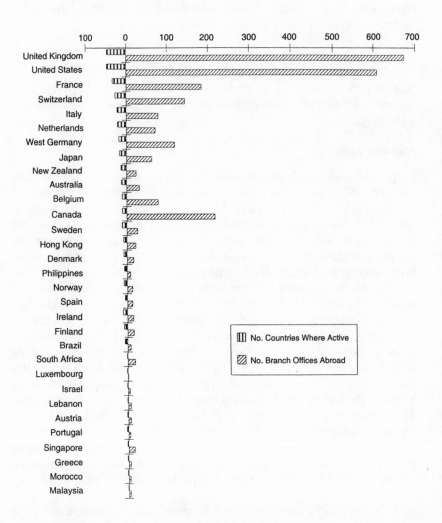

ᵃFor all countries with at least five branch offices abroad in 1982.

Source: Sigma, Swiss Reinsurance Company, February 1982.

Figure 4-3

Geographic Breakdown of Life and Non-Life Premiums of Largest International Insurers, 1988.

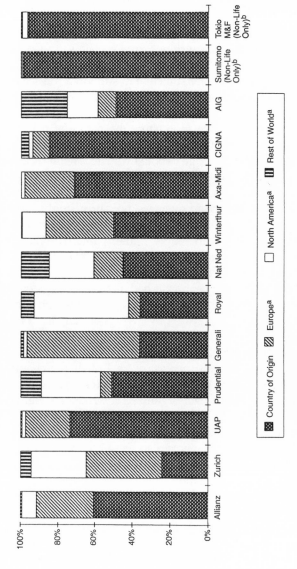

Sources: Annual reports, company data, Oppenheimer Co.

engage in foreign trade and investment, they turn to their national insurers to cover the associated risks. National ties between clients and insurers have historically been tight. To manage the overseas exposures of domestic accounts (referred to as home/foreign business), insurers often begin by establishing alliances with foreign insurers. As this business becomes more extensive, however, non-life insurers have an incentive to establish overseas facilities to provide underwriting, survey, claims, and policyholder services. But, as Henry Parker of Chubb Insurance has observed, such "home/foreign business is never sufficient to support a full-scale resident branch and affiliate operation." For this reason, "overseas facilities must compete in the indigenous market to reduce expense overhead."[16] Since most insurers lack good information about the nature of risks in foreign markets, these early efforts often lead to heavy losses. With time, however, many develop enough knowledge to both evaluate foreign risks and compete effectively against domestic insurers. This process can be seen from the earliest international activities of non-life firms.

The first insurers to expand overseas, not surprisingly, were British. The United Kingdom's development as an industrial and trading nation gave its insurers an important edge. Initially, international insurance meant marine insurance, and marine insurance meant Lloyd's. Lloyd's began as a coffee house where merchants exchanged information, but by the middle of the eighteenth century it had already established a reputation in marine insurance.[17] Other insurance companies followed Lloyd's; the Royal, for example, was created by Liverpool merchants to provide insurance for their activities.

New international lines of insurance soon developed. First came fire insurance, which became necessary as British merchants set up warehouses overseas. In the eighteenth and nineteenth centuries, marine insurance did not require a well-organized international network. Fire insurance was a different matter. To assess risks and service British clients overseas, insurers found it necessary to appoint agents to represent their interests abroad. These agents also were authorized to insure the risks of foreign nationals. But lack of knowledge about foreign markets quickly led to heavy losses. In the early 1800s, for example, a number of British insurers began to provide fire insurance in the United States only to exit that market because of mounting losses. Not until the mid-1850s did British insurers reestablish themselves in the United States.

16. Henry G. Parker III, "A Unified Europe Beckons U.S. Insurers to the Global Marketplace," *The John Liner Review* 34 (Winter 1990), p. 15.
17. On the history of Lloyd's, see D. E. W. Gibb, *Lloyd's of London: A Study in Individualism* (London: The Corporation of Lloyd's, 1972); and Harold E. Raynes, *A History of British Insurance* (London: Sir Isaac Pitman & Sons, 1950; reprinted by Garland, New York, 1983), Chapter 6.

As their business grew abroad, British insurers developed more permanent representation in the form of branches and then subsidiaries. Fire insurance provided the bulk of their U.S. business in the nineteenth century. With strong domestic bases and geographic spread, British firms offered greater financial security than did their American counterparts, and they expanded rapidly.[18] From their base in fire insurance, these firms developed greater knowledge about foreign markets, overcame information asymmetries, and branched out into casualty insurance.[19] The expansion of British non-life insurers continued within the United States, Britain's colonies, and later the Commonwealth. But penetration of continental European markets, especially Germany and Austria, was impeded by regulatory barriers.[20]

The forces driving the international expansion of British insurance operated in other countries as well. In the late nineteenth century, local manufacturers in Switzerland organized the two large Swiss insurance firms, Zurich and Winterthur; as the manufacturers expanded internationally, so did their insurers. The same pattern can be seen in the histories of large insurance companies in a range of other countries, including Japan, Germany, France, and the United States.[21] In the early twentieth century, insurers from all these industrializing nations followed manufacturers to overseas markets.

World War II disrupted this emerging intercountry pattern of insurance activity. During the war years, many insurers were forced to suspend their foreign operations and often found that their assets in hostile countries were either nationalized or liquidated.[22]

The Allied victory helped determine the postwar pattern of international insurance activity. For one thing, it abruptly ended the international operations of insurers from the Axis powers. After the war, the Allied Occupation forces barred insurers in Japan and Germany from engaging in foreign business. Even in the absence of such a prohibition, however, the war's destruction virtually ensured that Japanese and

---

18. In 1938, more than 70% of the fire premiums received by British firms reportedly came from the U.S. market. Raynes, *A History of British Insurance*, p. 270.

19. Ibid., p. 274.

20. Ibid., p. 278.

21. See, for example, William H.A. Carr, *Perils Named and Unnamed: The Dramatic Story of the Insurance Company of North America* (New York: McGraw-Hill, 1967); Michéle Ruffat, Edouard-Vincent Caloni, and Bernard Laguerre, *L'UAP et l'histoire de l'assurance* (Paris: Editions Jean-Claude Lattés, 1990); and *The Tokio Marine & Fire Insurance 1879–1979* (Tokyo: The Tokio Marine & Fire Insurance Co, 1980).

22. Prior to the war, Tokio Marine and Fire, for example, had earned more than 30% of its total premium income from foreign operations. It suspended many of these operations during the war years, although Japan's wartime imperial expansion opened access to the Chinese and Philippines markets. See *Tokio Marine & Fire 1879–1979*, pp. 114, 147.

German manufacturers would—for the immediate future—remain focused on their domestic markets, thereby depriving their national insurers of a strong overseas client base.

Moreover, the end of the war dramatically strengthened the international position of American, British, and Swiss insurance companies. Swiss insurers, because of their country's neutrality, survived the war with little loss of business, and American insurers found opportunities to expand their operations significantly. AIG, for example, sold insurance to members of the American armed forces stationed overseas; it established a position in Japan that to this day no other foreign insurer has been able to duplicate because of Japan's stringent domestic regulation.

Of course, the end of the war also had a negative effect on the business of European insurers insofar as it encouraged national self-determination throughout the European colonial system. For British, French, and Dutch insurers, decolonization brought to an end the colonial monopolies they had often enjoyed in earlier days.

National regulatory regimes.   Non-life insurance is one of the most heavily regulated industries in the world, and wide variation exists in the degree of regulation. In the postwar period, differences in national regulation have contributed to the existing pattern of international insurance activity. Broadly speaking, two types of regimes can be distinguished.

In the first, regulation is designed to protect consumers, who are thought to lack sufficient information to assess an insurer's solvency. Consumer-protection regulations apply mainly to the level and constitution of reserves held by insurers to pay future claims. In the second type of regime, regulation is intended to prevent disruptive competition. Here, regulations extend to both premium rates and policy content. The rationale for such regulation is that unbridled competition over price or policy content makes it difficult for firms to generate and maintain adequate loss reserves. In practice, however, such regulation also serves to strengthen the position of domestic insurers vis-à-vis foreign competition.[23] Because numerous differences in regulatory frameworks exist across countries, these two regimes should actually be seen as the endpoints of a continuum that runs from less to more regulation.

Regulation in the United States lies closer to the first type. The McCarren-Ferguson Act of 1945 set the framework for U.S. insurance

23. Kunreuther and Pauly, *International Trade in Insurance.* Less-developed countries have justified further regulatory barriers both to protect infant industries and to safeguard domestic capital. On regulatory barriers in the insurance industry, see also Harold D. Skipper, "Protectionism in the Provision of Insurance Services," *Journal of Risk and Insurance,* June and September 1973.

regulation. Under its terms, insurance companies are exempt from federal antitrust law as long as the individual states in which they do business oversee their rates, practices, and solvency. Allowing insurance companies to engage in collusive practices such as collective rate setting was considered necessary to prevent massive insolvencies. At the same time, state governments were charged with the task of protecting consumers and seeing to it that insurers acted prudently. The actual regulation of insurance was left to the states. Not surprisingly, wide variation developed in the extent of insurance regulation across the United States, although the National Association of Insurance Commissioners (NAIC) has brought some degree of uniformity.[24]

Yet as early as the 1950s, the price discipline that the McCarren-Ferguson Act hoped to promote began to break down. Insurance companies increasingly sought exemptions from the prices established by the various rate-setting agencies. For their part, state regulators also began to view price competition as a desirable goal. Although two-thirds of all states still regulate the price of at least some non-life lines (motor insurance being the most common), price competition has become the norm, especially in large states such as California and New York.[25] Indeed, in 1990 the Insurance Services Office, the most important rating association, stopped publishing advisory rates altogether.[26]

The ease with which firms (both U.S. and foreign) can enter the U.S. market and set prices makes the non-life business prone to boom-and-bust cycles, especially when financial market returns are high. Large profits attract new capacity. Firms then begin to cut their prices and take on poorer risks to gain premiums to invest. Eventually lower prices prove insufficient to cover rising claims, investment income declines, and insurers are forced to draw on their surpluses to pay claims. As profits fall, firms exit and industry capacity falls. Figure 4-4 traces the cycle in the United States over its last iteration, which reached its trough in 1984–1985.

Regulation of non-U.S. firms also varies by state. In general, states grant licenses to non-U.S. firms on the same terms and conditions they offer domestic insurers. Still, many states prohibit the licensing of insurance companies that are wholly or partially owned by a foreign government on the ground that government ownership provides these firms with an unfair advantage. To operate in the United States, foreign firms

24. The development of insurance regulation in the United States is discussed in Mehr, Cammack, and Rose, *Principles of Insurance*, Chapter 27.
25. See Kenneth J. Meier, *The Political Economy of Regulation: The Case of Insurance* (Albany: State University of New York Press, 1988), pp. 150, 173.
26. Merrill Stevenson, "American Insurance: Survey," *The Economist*, October 27, 1990, p. 6.

Figure 4–4
Underwriting Results and Investment Income in West Germany,
Japan, and the United States

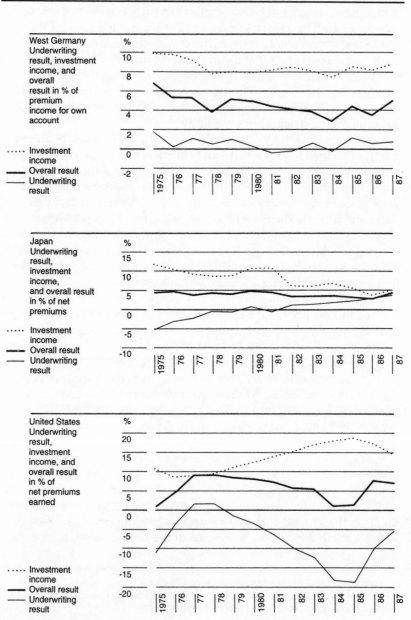

Source: Sigma, Swiss Reinsurance Company, June 1989.

must also meet different licensing procedures and solvency rules for each state (which is, of course, also true for U.S.-based insurers).[27] Apart from these direct costs, the sheer volatility of the U.S. market—a volatility that is partly the result of the relative absence of price regulation—heightens the risks and returns of entry. Foreign insurers are attracted by the potential profitability of the U.S. market on the upswing, but many have learned that operating in the United States calls for deep pockets when the market turns sour—especially in these times of skyrocketing liability awards.

Regulation in Japan, far more extensive than in the United States, is designed to prevent excessive price competition. Under the Insurance Business Law, Japan's Ministry of Finance (MOF) regulates the licensing of insurance firms, the types of investments an insurer can make, the rate of premiums, and the terms of contracts. All firms must obtain licenses from MOF before starting business. Licenses are limited in scope; that is, non-life insurers cannot sell life insurance. Furthermore, no new insurance product can be offered without MOF approval. "Premium groups" consisting of the major Japanese insurance companies generally determine rates, but endorsement by MOF still must be gained.[28] Not surprisingly, Japan's tight regulatory regime has limited the number of insurance companies operating in Japan and guaranteed higher levels of underwriting income than in the United States. It has also all but eliminated the cyclicality of underwriting income (see Figure 4-4) so prevalent in other markets.

Since insurance companies cannot compete on premium rates or policy content, the focus of competition has shifted to both distribution and service. Yet even distribution in Japan is regulated. Under the Insurance Business Law, only insurance firms and agents certified by MOF are allowed to sell insurance. Over 90% of insurance policies are sold

---

27. James Corcoran, former New York State insurance commissioner, has suggested various means to facilitate the state-by-state licensing procedure and has suggested that state-owned companies be allowed to participate in the U.S. market so long as they do not receive any injection of government funds subsequent to licensing. See James P. Corcoran, "Regulate for a Global Market," *The Journal of Commerce*, June 22, 1989.

28. Until 1980, there was only one set premium rate for each product and no room for individual company flexibility. Since 1980, there have been two types of insurance premium settings:

a) Standard premium with 10% flexibility: the rating association recommends the standard rate, which MOF must approve. Each insurance company may set its own rate within 10% of the standard rate. In practice, most firms set their premium exactly at the standard rate. These rates apply to auto, casualty, and fire insurance.

b) Individually approved rates: each insurance company determines its own rate, which must be approved individually by MOF. Hull, cargo, and various other insurance covers are determined in this manner.

through the 400,000 agents all over the country. Independent brokers, who might otherwise supply business to new entrants, are not licensed to engage in domestic Japanese business since, it is argued, they lack sufficient product knowledge to protect policyholders from losses. Thus the main source of competitive advantage is control over the distribution channel—specifically, over the number of agents. The need to build a national distribution network to compete effectively has provided significant first-mover advantages.

MOF has used its power to limit entry into the Japanese market, contributing to the high level of concentration. As of 1991, there were only 23 Japanese firms and 37 non-Japanese firms providing non-life coverage. Growth in the number of foreign firms is a relatively recent phenomenon: historically, MOF limited the number of licenses available to foreign insurers. Throughout the 1950s and 1960s, MOF granted licenses to only a few foreign firms and then strictly limited their activities. In the absence of such regulations in the early years of postwar reconstruction, foreign firms would likely have obtained a significantly larger share of the Japanese non-life market due to their advantages— risk-assessment capabilities and financial security—relative to Japanese insurers. By the time MOF did allow an increase in the number of foreign entrants in the mid-1970s, the advantages of foreign insurers relative to Japanese insurers had declined.

The ability of foreign insurers to compete in Japan was also constrained by the low levels of investment of foreign multinationals— their natural client base—in that country. Late entry into the Japanese market has further reduced the ability of foreign non-life insurers to compete for indigenous Japanese business (even though these foreign insurers are not subject to discriminatory capital or solvency requirements). As a result, their share of the Japanese market has remained at 2.8%.[29]

Regulation of premiums and, more specifically, policy content provide an additional layer of difficulty for foreign firms in Japan. Foreign insurers report that their applications to MOF to introduce new products into the Japanese market have met with long delays, often giving Japanese insurers time to develop similar products. Of course, the absence of regulation does not mean that product introduction carries a sustainable advantage: competitors can quickly introduce similar products. None-

29. Approximately 2.5% of the Japanese market—nearly the entire share of all foreign firms—is held by AIG, which, as we have noted, entered the Japanese market just after World War II. Early entry, especially at a time when the Japanese economy was weak and foreign companies enjoyed a strong reputation, enabled AIG (then AIU) to build an agency network that by the late 1980s numbered approximately 10,000. The company is now the 16th-largest non-life insurer in Japan.

theless, the extent of Japanese regulation on policy content has worked to eliminate even any short-term advantage a foreign innovator might enjoy.[30]

Japan's domestic regulatory regime has also influenced the willingness and ability of Japanese insurers to compete abroad. By enabling Japanese insurers to earn higher profits in the home market, Japan's regulatory regime reduced the attractiveness of international expansion.[31] In addition, the stability of prices and income in the Japanese market has slowed the development of the underwriting skills necessary to compete in more competitive markets. When the major Japanese insurers began to enter the U.S. market in the 1970s, for example, they were not sufficiently knowledgeable about selection, pricing, and differentiation. As a result, brokers, who occupy an important role in the American market, tended not to bring their best business to the Japanese firms. This experience proved particularly costly when the U.S. market turned sour at the end of the decade. Since that time, Japanese non-life insurers have proceeded with great caution in overseas markets and have limited their activities to serving their Japanese clients investing abroad.[32]

In the European Community (EC), substantial differences exist in national regulatory regimes. Those differences can be seen most clearly through a comparison of insurance regulation in Germany and the United Kingdom.

Germany has the strictest regulatory regime among EC members; it includes state control of premiums in many types of insurance, prior approval of the wording of contracts, and standardization of policy

30. Recently, MOF has shown some willingness to speed up the approval process and to allow foreign firms to introduce differentiated products. In October 1990, after three years of trying, Chubb & Son, a medium-sized American insurer long active in international markets, received authorization from MOF to offer director's and officer's (D&O) liability insurance on the Japanese market for the first time. The right to write these policies was granted to Chubb, AIG, and Taisho (the fourth-largest Japanese insurer), but no other insurers, for a three-month exclusive period. See Henry G. Parker III, "Globalization of the Insurance Industry—Its Consequences for Insurance Markets, Brokers, and Risk Managers," presentation at the Society of CPCU/Colorado Chapter All Industry Day, Aurora, Colorado, November 2, 1990.

31. The rapid growth of maturity-refund insurance (a non-life insurance policy with a savings component) has been especially important to the attractiveness of the home market. Maturity-refund insurance premiums rose (as a percentage of total written premiums) from 10% of the market in the late 1970s to 40% in the mid-1980s (The Marine and Fire Association of Japan, *Fact Book Fiscal 1988: Non-Life Insurance in Japan*, p. 13). Writing maturity-refund insurance has been particularly difficult for foreign insurers, given the reserve level required by MOF.

32. In 1988, direct premiums written abroad by Japanese insurers totalled 50 billion yen, less than 1% of the non-life net premiums written in Japan (The Marine and Fire Insurance Association of Japan, *Fact Book Fiscal 1988: Non-Life Insurance in Japan*, pp. 4, 18).

clauses.[33] Italy has taken a similar approach. By contrast, the United Kingdom (and to a lesser extent, the Netherlands) has focused regulatory efforts on ensuring the solvency of companies. The United Kingdom does not regulate contract terms or premium rates and requires no prior approval. Companies are largely free to write any business on any terms they like as long as they establish adequate reserves. Consumers are left to compare policy terms and prices.[34]

The patchwork of regulation in the European Community has kept national markets largely segmented, creating widely varying product prices across boundaries (see Table 4-6). Differences in national regulatory regimes have also affected the performance of companies in their markets. The more heavily regulated markets tend to exhibit lower cyclicality and better underwriting results than do the more competitive markets. These differences, of course, influence the entry calculations of foreign firms.

The stability of underwriting results has made the German market (see Figure 4-4) very attractive to foreign firms. Yet the regulation of both policy content and rates has made it virtually impossible for them to compete on the basis of either price or product innovation. A firm seeking to become a significant player in the German market has to put together a distribution network. This, too, is difficult, since captive agents and company sales people sell some 80% of all policies. Allianz, the dominant German firm, enjoys a distinct advantage here with its 43,000 agents.

Regulation in the United Kingdom is virtually the mirror image of that in Germany. The dominant role played by brokers makes entry into the British market much easier. With little regulation to stall enterprise, competition is rampant on both rates and policy conditions. As a result, many foreign firms have entered the market only to find it difficult to compete profitably. New entrants also run the risk of being selected against—that is, of being offered the worst risks. Hence the share of the British market held by foreign branches or subsidiaries has remained fairly low.

Competition has made product innovation a hallmark of the British market, and it has provided some advantage to British firms, including

---

33. Strong similarities can be seen in the German and Japanese approach to insurance regulation; this is not surprising, as the Japanese government based its regulatory regime partly on the German model.

34. See Sam Aaronovitch and Peter Samson, *The Insurance Industry in the Countries of the EEC: Structure, Conduct, and Performance* (Luxembourg: Office for Official Publications of the European Communities, 1985), pp. 28–29. For a more detailed description of insurance regulation in the European Community, see Coopers & Lybrand, *International Insurance Industry Guide*, 4th ed. (London: Lloyd's of London Press, 1988).

Table 4–6

Insurance Price Comparisons (percentage differences in prices of standard insurance products compared with the average of the four lowest national prices in 1986)

	Life insurance[a]	Home[b]	Motor[c]	Commercial fire, theft[d]	Public liability[e]
Belgium	+78%	-16%	+30%	-9%	+13%
France	+33%	+39%	+9%	+153%	+117%
Italy	+83%	+81%	+148%	+245%	+77%
Luxembourg	+66%	+57%	+77%	-15%	+9%
Netherlands	-9%	+17%	-7%	-1%	-16%
Spain	+37%	-4%	+100%	+24%	+60%
United Kingdom	-30%	+90%	-17%	+27%	-7%
West Germany	+5%	+3%	+15%	+43%	+47%

[a] Life insurance: average annual cost of term (life) insurance.

[b] Home insurance: annual cost of fire and theft coverage for a house valued at 70,000 European Currency Units (ECU); contents valued at 28,000 ECU.

[c] Motor insurance: annual cost of comprehensive insurance for a 1.6 liter car; driver had ten years of experience.

[d] Commercial fire and theft: annual coverage for premises valued at 387,000 ECU and stock valued at 232,000 ECU.

[e] Public liability: annual premium for engineering company with twenty employees and an annual turnover of 1.29 million ECU.

Note: In 1986, 1 ECU = $0.9825.
Source: EC Commission.

Lloyd's, that have developed a reputation as the leading insurers for complex risks.[35] The absence of regulation has therefore strengthened the global position of British non-life insurers built on the base of their domestic clients' overseas operations. As a result, Britain has become the leading exporter of insurance products in the European Community.[36]

Firm-specific advantages. The importance of the domestic client base and national regulation in structuring international competition has made it difficult for most firms to compete beyond their national borders. Absent access to a particular client base, the key source of competitive advantage is human capital, which is essential to careful risk evaluation, customer service, and investment. If a non-life insurer wishes to compete successfully in foreign indigenous business (that is, if

35. On the importance of domestic rivalry in explaining the international success of British firms, particularly Lloyd's, see Michael Porter, *The Competitive Advantage of Nations* (New York: The Free Press, 1990), p. 265.

36. Approximately, 44% of the United Kingdom's net non-life premium income derives from outside its borders (Robert L. Carter, "The United States and the European Community: Insurance"; paper delivered to the American Enterprise Institute's conference, "The United States and Europe in the 1990s," Washington D.C., March 5–8, 1990).

it wishes to enter foreign markets to serve foreign clients, rather than to follow its own domestic clients who have entered the foreign market), it must acquire qualified personnel who are knowledgeable about that market. To do so, foreign firms are likely to have to pay a premium—either directly in the form of salaries or indirectly in the purchase of an entire firm—which places them at a financial disadvantage relative to domestic firms.

Firm-specific advantages do exist, however, in particular segments of the non-life insurance market. These advantages are most apparent in specific niches, such as travel insurance, director's insurance, and especially global protection for multinationals. Providing global services to multinationals requires a network of offices throughout the world. The ability to cover a firm's risks worldwide can enable an insurer to attract and retain multinational business, even if its own country-based advantages decline.[37] Such firm-specific advantages, as I shall argue later in the chapter, are likely to increase in the future.

Reinsurance

The firms that dominate international reinsurance activity in the postwar period have been based in Germany, Switzerland, and the United Kingdom. Of the top three reinsurers in the world (listed in Table 4-4), only Munich Re and Swiss Re receive a large percentage of their premiums from outside their home markets. Approximately 45% of Munich Re's premium income and 94% of Swiss Re's premium income is received from foreign business.[38] By contrast, only about 7% of General Re's premium income comes from business outside the United States.

Table 4-4 does not include Lloyd's of London, which has a unique status in the international insurance community. Lloyd's is a market rather than a firm; underwriting syndicates at Lloyd's, composed of individuals referred to as "names," provide both insurance and reinsurance for risks around the world. In 1988, the total net premium income received by underwriting syndicates at Lloyd's amounted to $7.6 billion; some observers estimate the amount of reinsurance premiums at

37. The most prominent example of such a firm is AIG, which initially served as an underwriting agent for other American insurers in the Far East. With time, its network expanded, and in the 1960s it transformed itself from an underwriting agent to a direct underwriter of insurance around the world. AIG has become recognized as the leading global insurance company.

38. Both Munich Re and Swiss Re have extensive international networks. Swiss Re, for example, receives 52% of its premium income from Europe, 28% from North America, and 14% from the rest of the world.

approximately $3.8 billion, of which about two-thirds is thought to have come from foreign (i.e., non-British) business.

Why is it that American firms are active in international non-life insurance but are much less present in international reinsurance? And why are the most international of the European reinsurers based in Germany, Switzerland, and the United Kingdom rather than in other European countries? Part of the explanation lies with country-level factors—in particular, the degree of internationalization of the domestic economy and access to capital. The strategies of individual firms have also played a large role. Firm strategies exert a more important influence on patterns of international activity in reinsurance than in non-life insurance, due to the significance of first-mover advantages. Those advantages result from the importance of a firm's reputation for financial strength, for which size is often seen as a proxy.

Country-specific advantages. Country size and capital market development have created important sources of competitive advantage in reinsurance. Country size is important because of large economies of scale which result from the fact that reinsurance contracts involve a large volume of business. A reinsurer can substantially increase premium volume without a proportional increase in its costs. As I have argued, scale economies in big markets such as the United States and Japan were so large that reinsurers there gained no economic advantage in expanding overseas. These markets were also large enough to permit a sufficient geographic distribution of risk.[39] But the small size of individual national markets in Europe forced reinsurers there to become international (or at least European) to achieve similar scale economies and geographic distribution of risk.

Yet country size alone cannot explain why some countries developed successful internationally oriented reinsurance firms while others did not. In Europe the international operations of reinsurers have been strongly affected by the reputation of their domestic capital markets and their domestic currencies. The importance of domestic capital markets stems from the fact that reinsurers must have sufficient capital to back their contracts and to increase the volume of the business they accept. Therefore minimum capital standards, if not required by the government, are imposed by the market, since direct insurers evaluate the financial stability of reinsurers. Similarly, reinsurers in countries with internationally attractive currencies also enjoy an advantage, as they appear to be

---

39. The ability to achieve geographic distribution of risk is greater in the United States than in Japan. Still, the profitability of the domestic market—resulting, as we have seen, from the regulation of rates and terms—gave direct insurers fewer incentives to reinsure their risks.

better able to pay claims in the future. These two features distinguish the United Kingdom, Germany, and Switzerland. The development of a vibrant capital market in the United Kingdom contributed to the ability of Lloyd's to bring capacity to the reinsurance market, not to mention the international strength of its financial sector more generally. In Germany and Switzerland, capital availability was historically ensured by close relations with banks; moreover, both the Deutschmark and the Swiss franc have become "strong" currencies in the postwar period. These features have contributed to the financial integrity of reinsurance firms, enhancing their reputation with direct insurers. The dominance of German, Swiss, and British reinsurers over those oi ⁻rance, for example, is partly the result of France's postwar decision to nationalize the direct insurers, which in some sense turned the government into the main reinsurer.

Firm-specific advantages.   The advantages of size, capital availability, and currency stability were shared commonly by reinsurers in Germany, Switzerland, and the United Kingdom. Yet in each of these countries, only one major international reinsurer developed: Munich Re, Swiss Re, and Lloyd's. Each of these firms developed specific advantages that underlay its existing position. The development of Lloyd's as a market, rather than a firm, created a significant advantage, for it could combine extensive capacity with flexibility. At Lloyd's, brokers could place virtually any kind of risk. Much of the success of both Munich Re and Swiss Re, by contrast, lay in the development of close relationships with direct insurers. Munich Re, in fact, helped to establish a number of direct insurers in order to provide it with a steady flow of business, and it now holds a 25% stake in Allianz, which in turn owns an equal stake in Munich Re. Both reinsurers invested heavily in the development of engineering and risk analysis to assist non-life insurers with their evaluation of risks. The ability to offer such services did not create an unsurmountable advantage, but it raised considerably the costs of entry for potential competitors.

Moreover, as Munich Re and Swiss Re began to expand within Europe, they added capabilities that gave them two other sources of competitive advantage. First was simply the ability to manage activities across countries. Originally, these two firms did not need to spread their business beyond Europe to achieve economies of scale or geographic distribution of risk. But as the changing economics of the industry gave reinsurers an incentive to become even larger and more global, these firms had more experience than newer entrants or their American counterparts in managing a global network.

Second, early expansion and growth enabled the European reinsurers to develop a reputation for reliability. The importance of reputation derives from the fact that reinsurance essentially involves a *promise* to pay in the future. In purchasing reinsurance, a direct insurer is concerned not only about price, but also about dependability. In other words, will the reinsurer pay (or be sufficiently solvent to be able to pay) a claim within the span of the contract? Firm size, according to managers of both insurance companies and reinsurance firms, often serves as an indicator of dependability.

The Evolution of Competition

Three developments in recent years have led many analysts to predict that competition in non-life insurance will come to resemble the global pattern of competition we have seen in reinsurance. First, rapid change in information technologies, combined with even more rapid financial innovation, is increasing potential economies of scale in the industry and offering the prospect of greater gains through international expansion. Second, a number of manufacturing industries are themselves becoming more global, thus creating demand for global insurance services. Third, the pattern of regulation is changing.

The European Community has become a natural laboratory for observing the evolving pattern of competition in non-life insurance. The EC's 1992 program is designed to create a single market within which goods, services, capital, and people can flow freely. Already, firms in a multitude of industries have expanded across Europe to take advantage of these new opportunities. Insurance is no exception. A major thrust of the 1992 program is the creation of a common insurance market. Since 1990, non-life insurers in one member state have been able to sell policies to large companies located in another member state—a development that affects 30% of all non-life insurance in the Community. (The Appendix describes the process of insurance deregulation in the European Community.)

The EC's success in dismantling national regulatory barriers and establishing a common insurance market for large commercial risks has led many European non-life insurers to reevaluate their strategies. In Europe, non-life vendors are quickly seeking to establish positions in other markets to provide better service as their own customer bases become more European. Many insurance executives have concluded that having a "critical mass," or sufficient presence, in the major European markets will become an important source of competitive advantage. This focus on critical mass reflects the need to have a strong local distribution network.

The Second Non-Life Directive (adapted by the European Council) permits insurance for large risks to be sold—i.e., traded—across borders. International trade in insurance products for such risks will increase as large firms make greater use of brokers to shop around for better and cheaper coverage.[40] But international success will still depend upon having a strong local presence, since even pan-European clients will demand local service; moreover, many commercial risks and most personal risks will remain a local business. As a result, any company that seeks to compete across Europe will require a pan-European network.

The importance of having a pan-European network also reflects the difficulty of competing on product innovation and quality. Arthur Andersen's recent survey of insurance executives suggests that in Europe (as in Japan) product innovation is unlikely to create a sustainable advantage. Although "a short-lived competitive advantage could be gained by a foreign entrant through the introduction of a new product... this would be impossible to sustain as the product was copied by local companies with greater distribution power."[41]

Developing a European distribution network through internal growth is both slow and difficult, especially given the dominant role played by agents in many EC countries. Moreover, as we have seen, a company trying to enter a market faces high barriers to entry in the form of information asymmetries. For these reasons, most insurers have sought to grow through acquisition. In the last several years, the European Community has witnessed a vast number of acquisitions, both within and across countries (see Table 4-7). For example, Allianz's acquisitions have included French, Italian, and British companies. In 1989, Groupe Victoire, a major insurer in France, purchased the number-two German insurer, Colonia, for a reported $2.5 billion.

Given the cost of such acquisitions, a company's financial strength has turned out to be an important source of competitive advantage. Among European insurers, Germany's Allianz is in an enviable position. This major insurer enjoys the benefits of having both a stable ownership structure and a dominant position in a previously regulated market. Allianz and Munich Re each hold 25% of the other's shares, and such stable ownership has helped avoid shareholder demands for high dividend payments. Allianz pays out only 16% of net income in dividends, compared to about 50% for both American and British insurers. As a result, the company has been able to build up significant reserves that can now be used for acquisitions. Similarly, Germany's previous system of regulation made it difficult for new firms to compete in the German market.

40. United States International Trade Commission, *1992: The Effects of Greater Economic Integration within the European Community on the United States, First Follow-Up Report,* USITC Publication 2268, Investigation No. 332-267, March 1990, pp. 5–19.

41. Arthur Andersen, *Insurance in a Changing Europe 1990–1995* (London: The Economist Publications, 1990), p. 15.

Table 4–7
Insurance Industry Mergers and Acquisitions: Europe, 1986–1990

Firm	Acquisition	Year
Allianz (Germany)	Cornhill (United Kingdom)	1986
	RAS (Italy)	1987
	Hungaria Buztosito	1989
	Compagnie Mixte Insurers Ercos (Spain)	1989
	East German State Insurer	1990
	Fireman's Fund	1990
Groupe Victoire (France)	Colonia (Germany)	1989
	La Previsara Hispalense (Spain)	1989
	Prudential Italia (Italy)	1990
UAP (France)	Royale Belge	1989
	Allsecures (Italy)	1990
	GESA (Spain)	1990
UAP Re	SCOR (France)	1990
SCOR	Deutsche Continental Re (Germany)	1989
AGF (France)	Insurance Corp of Ireland	1990
	Assubel-Vie (Belgium)	1989
	Kosmos (Greece)	1989
	Canada Surety	1990
GAN (France)	General Portfolio (United Kingdom)	1990
	Alianza de Seguros	1990
Zurich	Maryland Casualty	1988
Winterthur (Switzerland)	General Casualty of Wisconsin	1990
	Intercontinentale (Italy)	1989
	Transatlantische Allgemeine (Germany)	1989
	Wand AG (Germany)	1990
Bernoise (Switzerland)	Amaya (Spain)	1990
Swiss Re	Lloyd Adratico (Italy)	1989
Royal (United Kingdom)	Lloyd Italico	1989
GRE (United Kingdom)	Polaris Vita (Italy), Sipea (Italy), Cidas (Italy)	1989
Minet (United Kingdom)	Anglo-Swiss (Switzerland)	1989
	Essar (Hong Kong)	1990
	Essar (Norway)	1990
Norwich Union (United Kingdom)	Plus Ultra (Spain)	1990
Generali (Italy)	Business Men's Assurance (United States)	1990
	Union Suisse (Switzerland)	1989
Netherlands Re (Netherlands)	Victoria Insurance (United Kingdom)	1990
NV AMEV (Netherlands)	Groupe AG (Belgium)	1990

Sources: Annual reports, newspaper reports.

Thus Allianz was able to maintain a strong hold on domestic distribution (roughly 16% of the German market), thereby strengthening its capital base and providing resources that the company can use to expand internationally.

Allianz's position in the European market has deepened a concern felt by other European insurers about achieving critical mass. Although no insurer has a well-defined understanding of optimal size or reach in the new market, all are convinced that it is vital to become larger. In this time of uncertainty when insurers grope to find optimal size, it is not surprising that they are playing follow the leader.[42] After Allianz bought the Italian insurer RAS, for example, other companies—including Winterthur, UAP, and Victoire—also made significant acquisitions in Italy. To ensure that they do not miss an opportunity, European insurers seem to be seeking to match as closely as possible the moves made by their competitors. Holding a position in the Italian non-life insurance market, for example, may in fact not be critical to a firm's success, yet no large insurer wants to run the risk of being absent from that market if in the future it turns out to be critical, especially if powerful competitors such as Allianz have already entered that market.

The evolving pattern of competition in Europe provides some indication of the potential evolution of competition in insurance globally. To be sure, national markets will remain for a vast number of non-life products. But as non-life insurance customers become more global, demand for global insurance services will increase. As a result, competition in non-life insurance will approach, but probably will not reach, the global configuration we have seen in reinsurance.

On the one hand, there is likely to be an increase in the number of global multiline insurance firms. Among the larger non-life insurers, the trend toward globalization has already sparked greater interest in establishing new global networks or enhancing old ones. In 1990, for example, Allianz acquired California-based Fireman's Fund; and French insurer AXA-Midi has recently taken a major stake in the Equitable. On the horizon are the major Japanese non-life insurers.

In the 1980s, foreign business represented a relatively small proportion of the total premium income of Japan's major non-life insurers—Tokio, Yasuda, Taisho, and Sumitomo. As we have seen, this pattern reflected both the profitability of the domestic market and the problems encountered by these firms in foreign markets in the past. Insofar as these four insurers are concerned, all insist that their interna-

---

42. The dynamics of such behavior are described in F.T. Knickerbocker, *Oligopolistic Reaction and Multinational Enterprise* (Boston: Division of Research, Harvard Business School, 1973).

tional activities are based on their desire to serve Japanese clients operating abroad. The continued expansion of Japanese manufacturers into foreign markets should lead these insurers to establish a greater overseas presence, thereby increasing their knowledge about conditions in these markets. With this greater knowledge, their willingness to begin to engage in indigenous business—or, as in Europe, to expand their presence through acquisition—will undoubtedly increase. In this regard, Japan's domestic regulatory regime, like Germany's, has provided its large non-life insurers with a particularly strong capital base. This guarantees the means for future international expansion.[43]

The emergence of strong international insurers from Germany and Japan will create an important test for the existing international insurers. Faced with this new competition, they will need to sharpen their skills to sustain growth. Such skills will involve the creation of better techniques of risk forecasting, marketing, and global management.

More common, and perhaps more successful, than the global multi-line companies, however, will be those firms that have the ability to target profitable market niches. Focused niche strategies enable non-life insurers to target those segments of the market where demand is most homogeneous and therefore where information about foreign conditions is most readily available. Consider Chubb and Hartford Steam Boiler, two U.S. insurers with excellent reputations for service in the home market. Chubb has moved aggressively to develop markets in Europe in those niches with which it was most familiar. In the mid-1980s, for example, it successfully introduced "all-risk" property insurance in the German market. (German insurers had previously provided separate policies for different kinds of risks.) More recently Hartford Steam Boiler, in a joint venture with General Re, established the Engineering Insurance Group to market its services to European engineering firms.

For both types of competitors—broad market vendors and niche players—the key to success in a world of greater international competition will be an ability to manage a global network. The tension intrinsic to this challenge is between centralizing to derive benefits from the existence of a global network and decentralizing to be responsive to the continuing differences within national markets.

In a world of greater international insurance competition, non-life vendors also have an increased stake in establishing a common set of rules. For good reason, all countries regulate their non-life insurance industries. In some countries, such as Germany and Japan, a high degree

43. On the effect of regulation on the foreign activities of Japanese service firms, see Peter Enderwick, "The International Competitiveness of Japanese Service Industries: A Cause for Concern," *California Management Review,* Summer 1990, pp. 22–37.

of regulation has provided financial advantages to the existing firms, albeit at substantial costs to consumers in terms of price and product availability. In others, regulation has been designed primarily to ensure the solvency of non-life insurance firms. The growth of international insurance transactions calls into question the existing patchwork of regulations; indeed, for this reason it is appropriate that setting rules for international insurance transactions is on the GATT agenda. By itself, a resolution of the GATT round is unlikely to have an immediate effect on international insurance transactions in the three major markets of the world. But it is surely necessary to create a framework for the changing pattern of international competition that is occurring as a result of the globalization of the world economy.

Conclusion

To observers of the contemporary banking industry, the preceding analysis of non-life insurance firms and reinsurers may have struck a familiar chord. Regulation around the banking world is also a patchwork of incentives and barriers. In America, it leans heavily toward consumer protection ("full disclosure"), the protection of small banking institutions from the encroachment of the large, and the fencing off of proprietary fiefdoms. Japan's regulators protect the profitability and stability of its banking and insurance institutions as pillars of national prosperity and discourage the encroachment of outside innovations. This is a source of both strength (financial) and weakness (inability to succeed in global markets).

Similarly, both insurance and banking are experiencing the same waves of change—the dismantling of regulatory barriers, a convergence of regulation (especially in the European Community), and a movement of prime customers across national borders. Faced with these changes, both are finding competitive advantage in similar places. Financial strength matters when striking out into unchartered terrain, as early losses can be expected; it also makes strategic acquisitions possible. The ability to create productive innovations is also an important strength. And, of course, the ability to find and exploit attractive niches is a competitive advantage to both insurers and bankers.

As the world's major corporations continue their expansion across borders, both non-life insurers and reinsurers, like bankers, will be compelled to follow them. Increasingly these moves will create pressure for national regulators to adopt common—or at least similar—rules. Firm strategy and regulation are likely to have a profound effect on the nature of competition. Thus, by the early decades of the twenty-first century, the insurance industry may indeed be very different.

Appendix

The Creation of a Single European Insurance Market

Insurance has long been seen as an essential element of the Common Market.[44] The Treaty of Rome provided for both freedom of establishment and freedom of services in insurance. (Freedom of establishment is defined as the right of a company in one state to set up branches in another state; freedom of services is defined as the right to market products throughout the European Community without having to establish a branch in every member state.) In 1961, the Council adopted an ambitious program to institute both freedoms in several rapid stages. Both freedoms would be applied first to reinsurance. Second, freedom of establishment would be instituted for both non-life and life insurance. Third would come freedom of services.

In 1964, the Council adopted the first directives relevant to reinsurance. However, since few actual barriers to either investment or trade existed, the directive served primarily to reaffirm the existing situation. Action in the area of direct insurance proved more difficult. Not until 1973 did the Council abolish restrictions on the freedom of establishment in non-life insurance and provide for common standards in setting Communitywide solvency margins. This made it easier for EC insurance companies to enter other EC national markets, but once inside they still had to meet local regulations. As a result, the EC insurance market remained fragmented.

Also in 1973, the Commission proposed a directive to provide for freedom of services for non-life insurance. No progress could be made on this issue, however, due to strong disagreement among the member states. Support for a more liberal regime came from both the British (who had just joined the Community) and the Dutch; the Germans and the French, on the other hand, resisted efforts to facilitate cross-border insurance transactions.

In the mid-1980s, two developments gave new impetus to this initiative. The first was the ruling of the European Court of Justice in a series of insurance cases.[45] The court began by affirming the right to

---

44. This discussion is drawn from Bill Pool, *The Creation of the Internal Market in Insurance* (Luxembourg: Office of Official Publications of the European Communities, 1990).

45. The lead case involved a Bavarian insurance broker named Schleicher. Herr Schleicher had arranged for the insurance on his German clients' stocks of furs to be placed through British brokers with London insurers that did not hold an authorization to operate in Germany. Since a condition for such authorization was that the insurers be established in Germany, Schleicher's act violated the German insurance supervisory law. After Schleicher lost his case at the national level, the Commission took the issue to the European Court of Justice. Case 205/84, *Commission v. Federal Republic of Germany* (1986).

provide services freely across national borders. However, it noted that insurance was a special area, in part because of the lack of harmonization of national insurance laws. Where the need for policyholder protection existed, the state in which insurance services were being provided could still require the insurer to be authorized. But the court held that the need for consumer protection was not the same in every case. And where such protection was not required, there was no need for national authorization. The court's ruling left it to the Commission and the Council to determine where consumer protection was required and where it was not. The second development was the signing of the Single European Act (SEA) in 1985, which introduced qualified majority voting for most of the measures (including those in the area of insurance) needed to bring about a single market.

These two changes gave new impetus to negotiations over freedom of services in non-life insurance, which in 1988 led to the EC Council's adoption of the Second Non-Life Insurance Coordination Directive, a compromise between the advocates and opponents of freedom of services in insurance that essentially followed the distinction outlined by the court in its earlier ruling. The Second Non-Life Directive distinguishes between purchasers of cover for large risks, believed to be able to protect their own interests and buy their own insurance, and mass risks, for whom national protection by the host state is still considered justified. Large risks are defined as those meeting two of the following three criteria:

- 250 or more employees
- minimum of ECU 12 million revenue
- minimum of ECU 6.2 million assets

The directive took effect in July 1990, except for Greece, Spain, Ireland, and Portugal, which were granted a longer transition period. Insurance executives in the Community estimated that the directive would affect approximately 30% of all non-life insurance. Negotiations are now under way to extend freedom of services to all non-life insurance. EC officials and national regulators do not expect that this agreement will be implemented until the mid-1990s at the very earliest.

CHAPTER 5

CUSTOMER RELATIONSHIPS IN THE 1990s

Dwight B. Crane and Robert G. Eccles

Relationship is a word used often by investment and commercial bankers and their customers. It is also used by many professional services firms and in a large variety of industries. Generally speaking, it refers to a situation in which the supplier has a preferred vendor status. In financial services, the word *relationship* is often contrasted with the word *transaction.* When we did a study of management in the investment banking industry in 1986, at the peak of the 1980s bull market, investment bankers often told us that customers were becoming more transaction- and less relationship-oriented.[1] "Loyalty is a basis point" was the phrase used by many to succinctly capture this situation. The investment bankers we talked to insisted they wanted and valued relationships and were working hard to build them. Ironically, customers (issuers of securities and M&A clients) professed a sincere desire for relationships but opined that it was the bankers who had become more transaction-oriented as they shopped "the product of the week" in this deal-rich decade.

The end of the bull market and the beginning of a new decade has brought about the predictable reaction to the go-go 1980s—even sustained in the current strong market—with calls for renewed financial sobriety and a return to basic values. We thought it would be interesting to reexamine the issue of relationships in this new environment. Toward that end we interviewed a number of investment and commercial bankers, with particular emphasis on roughly 20 mid- and senior-level investment bankers at two leading New York City firms. We also talked with several financial officers, focusing primarily on five large multinational firms, three in the United States and two headquartered

---

1. Robert G. Eccles and Dwight B. Crane, *Doing Deals: Investment Banks at Work* (Boston: Harvard Business School Press, 1988).

in Europe. All five companies were active users of investment banking services, sometimes provided by commercial or universal banks. (We will use the terms *banks* and *firms* to refer to all banking institutions that provide investment banking services.)

Not too surprisingly, we found a view that the pendulum is swinging away from a transaction orientation (which in the 1980s the buyer and seller accused each other of having, while asserting their own commitments to a relationship) to a greater relationship orientation (which each agrees the other wants). Abetting this swing is the possibility that equity-driven markets such as we have experienced for the last several years lead to more of a relationship orientation than did the debt-driven markets of the 1980s, as equity is a more strategic decision made at a higher level in the customer organization.[2]

The promiscuity of the 1980s is being replaced—if not with monogamy, then at least with a controlled form of polygamy. Most of an issuer's domestic business is done with a small group, perhaps two to five firms. The number of firms in the group is directly a function of how much business the customer has to spread around. When the members of the group are roughly equal, the customer is using a *core group* model for managing its investment bankers. A number of frequent issuers shifted from use of a single, *dominant* or lead investment bank to a core group during the first half of the 1980s, but the use of a core group has stabilized in more recent years (see Figure 5–1). Similarly, the growth in the number of investment banks used has slowed, and the number of commercial banking relationships has declined (see Figure 5–2). Our conversations with customers and these data suggest that even though companies have shifted away from a single dominant bank, the total number of relationships with financial service firms is declining, and the bulk of the business is being spread across a relatively stable set of banking firms.

The Problematic Nature of Relationships

This plausible but simple story masks a curious difference in perspective between issuers and investment banks about the meaning of a relationship. Issuers describe relationships in rather straightforward business terms. They consider that a relationship exists if a bank is on their list of firms who would be invited in to discuss and then bid on a deal. Indeed,

2. Petros G. Kitsos, "'High-Tech' Products and Relationship Management in Investment Banking." Student paper submitted for Management of Financial Institutions course, Harvard Business School, May 1992.

Figure 5–1
Frequent Financers Using Core Groups

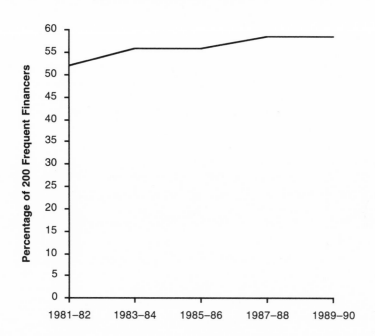

Source: Securities Data Corporation and authors' analysis.

each of the companies we talked with had a defined (if not disclosed) list of investment banks that would be included in such a discussion. For these financial officers, the strength of their company's relationship with a bank was measured directly by the share of their business that went to that bank. Investment bankers, on the other hand, talk about relationships in more personal and intimate terms using such words as "strategic advice," "confidence," and "trust." One banker said that he had a relationship with a customer if he had "access based on his credibility." Another stated she had a relationship if there was "mutual respect."

Thus like the 1980s, although in different ways and for different reasons, a lack of alignment exists between customers and investment banks in how they perceive one another. As a result, the word *relationship* means different things to different parties. The confusion this introduces is compounded by the fact that both customers and investment banks use the word *relationship* in many different ways within the broad umbrella definitions we have described.

Figure 5–2
Number of U.S. Institutions Used (per company surveyed)

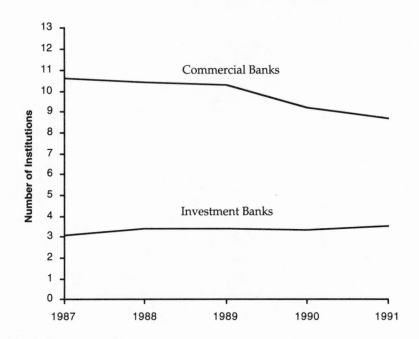

Source: Greenwich Associates, *Large Corporate Finance*, various issues.

View of Investment Banks

In one investment bank, managers had established categories of relationships based primarily on the volume of business done, not unlike the approach taken by companies that talked to us. "Excellent" relationships were those in which the firm earned a certain level of revenues and lead-managed at least half of the client's deals. (We have changed the category names to disguise the investment bank.) In effect, an excellent relationship existed when the firm got "more than its fair share of the customer's business." These relationships were attenuated versions of the monogamous relationships of yore, when a bank received all of a client's business—something rarely found today. Clearly the criteria for a relationship have been weakening over the years.

"Good" relationships were less precisely defined but referred to situations in which the bank received a reasonable amount of business but less than that in an excellent relationship, in both absolute (revenues) and relative (percentage of lead-managed deals) terms. In these relationships a firm "got its fair share" of the client's business. Both excellent and good relationships would fit the customer's definition of a relationship in terms of the economic and opportunity-to-bid criteria used to define its existence. To have an excellent or good relationship in the bank's terms, the firm had to be on an approved bidder's list in order to have sufficient opportunity to get enough business to qualify for a first- or second-tier relationship.

Stretching the definition of relationship further, this investment bank also defined transaction and calling relationships. "Transaction" relationships existed when the bank had done at least one deal for a customer within some reasonable period such as a year or two. "Calling" relationships—stretching the term to its limit—existed when no business had been done, but there was hope of doing some because the company was at least willing to talk to bankers from the firm. Clearly these are much weaker relationships than those with excellent or good customers, and given that they are defined in such different ways (a single done deal for transactional relationships and conversations about potential deals for calling relationships) one has to ask whether they qualify as relationships at all.

From the viewpoint of bankers at this firm, though, the definitions of weaker relationships were as meaningful as the definitions of excellent and good relationships. In their view, the common definition of what determined the existence of a relationship was willingness of the client to engage in dialogue that involved the sharing of information, whether or not business had been done. A relationship existed when an issuer returned phone calls and was available for meetings and presentations in order for the firm to present ideas. Those who used this definition emphasized that such a modest definition was actually quite important because clients had only so many hours (or minutes) in a day to talk to investment bankers and had to make choices about how many to spend time with. These bankers also emphasized that in the "more relationship-oriented 1990s," clients had reduced the number of banks they were willing to do "mere transactions" with. So while relationships were not what they used to be, merely to be heard by a client put the firm in a good position to eventually develop a good or even excellent relationship. One banker noted, "All I want is access. If I have it, I have an opportunity to show my ability to add value."

Others in this firm added the criterion of the client *sharing* information to its willingness to *receive* information. Here, too, clients were regarded as selective in whom they would share information with about strategy, financing needs, and so forth, which would enable the bank to develop intelligent and relevant proposals for the client. As one banker

said, "I have a relationship if I am getting confidential, strategic information about the company." Firms not receiving this information were
regarded as being in the low probability situation of making virtually
random blue-book pitches with little chance of hitting the target.

We were struck by the relatively modest criteria used to determine
whether or not a relationship existed, but we found similar ideas at another investment bank we interviewed. Bankers at this firm also
emphasized the importance of dialogue and information sharing in
determining whether or not a relationship existed. One said, "I have a
relationship if I see them a lot and they have confidence and trust in
me on important issues." While agreeing that relationships are tied to
contacts and information exchange, some of the bankers at this firm
had a more stringent definition of relationships: a relationship did not
exist for them unless they had access to the CFO and CEO and provided those individuals with strategic advice and counsel. They noted
that a relationship could exist even when no transactions had been
done for some time—although the expectation was certainly that
when the time came to do one, the firm had a good shot at getting it.
Conversely, simply doing transactions did not mean that a relationship
existed, and examples were given where this was the case. Thus transactions were neither a necessary nor a sufficient condition for the existence of a relationship.

To summarize the perspective of investment bankers, access and
information exchange—not the volume of transactions—were the key
elements in the definition of relationships. Bankers differed in the
threshold required to meet the minimum standard of when a relationship existed. Weak relationships involved regular access to someone on
the corporate financial staff and included some information exchange
and an opportunity to discuss commodity transactions such as "plain
vanilla" debt deals. Strong relationships involved regular access to the
CFO and CEO, the exchange of confidential strategic information, and
the opportunity to bid on strategic products such as equity deals and
M&A transactions.

The Customer's Perspective

Variations in the meaning of the word *relationship* existed for issuing customers as well. At one extreme, the senior financial officers at one company stated a definition consistent with the investment bankers' notion
of a calling relationship: they said they had a relationship with any bank
that called them to present an idea. (Consistent with this low threshold
for the definition of a relationship, that company did not reciprocate

much other than a willingness to listen to banks meeting the minimum threshold.) At the other extreme, some companies acknowledged the existence of senior advisory relationships, to which most investment bankers aspire.

But whereas investment bankers were generally willing to conceive of a relationship as existing even without the occurrence of transactions in the recent past, for customers relationships were almost always defined by the existence of business. One senior financial officer acknowledged frequent contact with a well-known investment banker and a high degree of respect for him, but the financial officer declined to call it a relationship because he had not done any business with that person's firm in quite a while.

Every company we talked with, even the company that accepted the phone-call definition of a relationship, had a defined set of banks that would be invited to discuss potential transactions and to bid. And, typically, the relationship or role of each bank was clearly defined in the view of the corporate financial officers. Banks included in the top tier of firms invited to bid on all transactions were there because of the stream of creative ideas they presented and their excellent execution in the past. Other banks had more of a product relationship with the company because, for example, they were good at derivative products, provided important access to the German market, or had invented a particular product of interest.

The larger the number of completed transactions and the fees involved, on both an absolute and a relative-to-other-firms basis, the stronger the relationship. These customers often kept careful track of the total amount of business going to each of the banks on its selected bidder's list. They also helped make sure that sufficient business was going to each bank to maintain its interest in the company. One company called a particular investment bank first when thinking about a transaction, not because it was the company's most important bank, but because it took longer to respond with its ideas.

The customer definition of relationships based on amount of business done is not incompatible with the investment bank definition of relationships based on information exchange. Obviously the latter is necessary in order for the former to occur. But information can be exchanged without leading to transactions. In these circumstances, it appears that the result is a one-sided relationship. The investment bank says there is one, while the customer says there is not. This raises the question of whether relationships, like the tango, require the consensual participation of two parties *who share a common definition of what it means to have a relationship.*

Prospects versus Reality

To complicate matters still further, while investment bankers have more modest criteria for the existence of a relationship than do customers, bankers describe them in more intimate and fulsome terms than financial officers do. In describing good relationships, investment bankers use such terms as "has confidence in my judgment" and "seeks my advice on strategic issues." The image conveyed is one of trusted business adviser on corporate and financial strategy with whom the CEO (ideally) and/or CFO shares his or her innermost thoughts, hopes, and fears. Transactions are almost a mere by-product of this—although competence in execution is a must—because they are simply a part of implementing a larger vision. And because of all of the useful advice that has been provided along the way, often for free or a modest retainer, the customer is not aggressive about seeking the lowest price possible on the transaction.

Of course, not all of a firm's relationships, including the best ones, fit this description. But at least some do, and they set the model for what relationships should be. Although we have only limited data on this, we believe that the model represents quite a small percentage of relationships—however defined—between typical investment banks and their customers, and so it is more a *statement of intention or objective* than a description of prevailing reality. Thus, when describing and defining relationships, investment bankers have a tendency to talk about them in terms of *what they could be at their very best*. For example, they like to make a distinction between "clients," with whom one has relationships, and "customers," for whom one does transactions. This is quite natural given that this ideal state, although a far cry from relationships in the good old days, is the best one for them in being able to provide a broad range of services and being compensated for doing so.

Customers, in contrast, speak of their relationships with investment bankers in more limited and economic terms, even though they tend to have a higher standard for what it takes to be involved in one. They regard banks as providing a useful set of services and as a source of ideas, but not as the confidantes that bankers describe themselves to be. While their ideas and transaction capabilities are valued, they are appreciated through a more distant and less intense relationship. From the customers' perspective—and they describe themselves as customers rather than as clients—they decide what they want and let their "relationship" banks bid for the opportunity to do a transaction through the presentation of ideas and pricing. Although they do not select on price alone, the all-in cost of a financing is an important variable because only banks perceived to have the ability to successfully execute the transaction are invited to bid. Relationships are not described in terms of what they could be based on future possibilities, but in terms of *what they are now* based on having won and successfully executed enough transactions in the past to stay on the bidders' list.

The lesser importance accorded the investment bank by the customer is also to be expected for several reasons. In order to maintain some degree of parity and perceived fairness in the selection process, all members of the core group need to be treated roughly the same way. One large multinational corporation is scrupulous about this. Its first-tier banks are disclosed to one another and each is given information about company plans. All are invited to bid on transactions, and all must agree to participate in each deal even if they are not chosen to lead.

Customers have two other incentives to minimize the importance of investment banks: power struggles and professional rivalry. As in any supplier/buyer relationship, the relative power balance influences the price of the exchange. A customer who limits itself to one bank or who espouses a central role for this bank makes itself vulnerable to transaction fees that reflect a premium for such an essential contribution. The obvious way to keep this from occurring is to do business with several firms and to avoid excess enthusiasm about their value-added.

This power struggle between organizations ultimately reduces to one between individuals, which introduces the problem of professional rivalry. The corporation's financial staff is the primary contact for the investment bankers—despite their desires, the total time investment bankers spend with CEOs is small. As finance professionals, the staff and the bankers share a common expertise and vocabulary, but they also need to share credit for the value they provide. Astute investment bankers know this and go out of their way to make members of the financial staff look good in front of their bosses and ultimately the CEO. Nevertheless, when describing the relationship, financial staff have an obvious incentive to downplay the contribution of their bankers lest they appear as less than competent and as deserving the often significantly lower compensation they receive—which is itself another source of irritation.

Whose Relationship Is It Anyway?

Explicit recognition of individual roles and relationships introduces yet another layer of complexity, and again the descriptions offered by investment bankers and customers differ. The investment bankers we interviewed spoke of the relationship in very personal terms, emphasizing their particular contributions and the particular individuals in the customer organization with whom they had relationships. They talked about their own competence, credibility, trustworthiness, and helpfulness as being key to establishing a good relationship. This is to be expected because they are responsible for developing relationships, and their compensation is heavily dependent on the quality of relationships they develop. The importance of building relationships is reflected in the fact that the bankers in one firm were recognized and rewarded for developing a relationship even when it had yet to produce significant revenues.

Customers, on the other hand, talked about relationships almost exclusively in institutional terms. Rarely did they mention the name of an individual banker and instead emphasized the resources a particular firm brought to bear in servicing their needs or the particular role they expected the firm to fulfill. In one instance, a company we interviewed was not aware that a major firm had assigned a senior relationship manager to oversee their worldwide relationship. Apparently, the relationship manager decided it was not worth telling the company about his global role, thinking—probably correctly—the company did not really care to have its relationship managed in this way.

Although companies did not assert that the identities of the individuals assigned by the bank to cover them were irrelevant, they felt that a number of very viable choices existed. One financial officer felt that a really good relationship manager could help an investment bank get in the door to present an idea or a bid, but that was about it. Only when problems emerged did the particular person become an issue, and then it was simple to have him or her replaced. While investment bankers recognized the need to manage this negative chemistry, they also described a positive chemistry that was hardly mentioned by financial officers.

The low importance assigned to particular relationship managers shows up clearly in customer surveys. In the Greenwich Associates surveys, when companies were asked what factors influenced the choice of an investment bank to lead a financing or M&A transaction, the quality of the relationship manager was ranked eighth or ninth. As shown in Figure 5–3, 40% to 50% of the companies mentioned factors such as "innovative ideas" and "understanding of the company's needs," while less than 15% mentioned "capable relationship manager" as an important factor in selecting an investment bank. Lest this result be interpreted as a U.S. phenomenon, we tried out a similar question with a group of about 20 European corporate financial officers. We obtained a similar result, despite the perception that closer relationships exist between European companies and their banks.

What customers seem to be saying is that they are looking for creative and useful ideas as well as execution capabilities. They are willing to spend time with bankers so that the bankers can learn about the com-

Figure 5–3
Factors Used in Selecting a Lead Manager

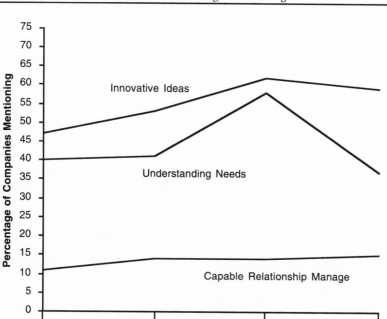

Source: Greewich Associates, *Large Corportate Finance,* various issues.

pany and its needs. But to the extent that "the relationship" needs to be managed, they feel that they can manage it themselves and are not dependent on a particular investment banker to do so.

The institutional, rather than individual, nature of the relationship from the customer's perspective also provides one explanation for why investment banks are frequently disappointed when a so-called rain-maker is hired away from a rival firm. Only in exceptional circum-stances is a customer so committed to a particular banker that it will place a higher priority on that relationship relative to the institutional one and follow the person from firm to firm. More commonly, when individuals leave or receive new assignments, they are replaced by someone else and the institutional relationship remains largely intact unless the bank drops the ball.

This is obviously the preferred situation to the senior management of an investment bank. The last thing they want is for their individual bankers to be able to hold the firm hostage by controlling customer relationships. Thus another, and rather subtle, power struggle over who owns the relationship is going on between the individual banker and his or her firm.

From the bank's perspective, a delicate balance needs to be struck. If the role of the individual banker is reduced too much, he or she will have no credibility in the eyes of the client, being perceived as unable to commit and deliver the desired resources of the firm. But if this role is too great, the relationship with the firm may be unstable. Furthermore, the banker may have an incentive to put the interests of the client over those of the firm because the costs of doing so are largely borne by others while the benefits—present and future—largely accrue to the banker. This is especially dangerous given the strategy of investment banks to incur substantial costs in delivering value—in the form of advice, special studies, and market information—as a way of creating obligations that are hopefully converted into transaction fees in the future.

Thus, relationships need to be considered at both the institutional and individual levels. Both financial staff and investment bankers described a common model of relationships matched by hierarchical level (e.g., investment bank associates with assistant treasurers and vice presidents with treasurers), as well as relationships matched by function or specialty (e.g., commercial paper traders with cash managers and M&A specialists with CFOs or CEOs). These relationships usually vary in intensity and can involve cross-organizational collaborations for purposes of intraorganizational power struggles, as when an associate and assistant treasurer band together to convince the CFO to do a particular kind of transaction.

The existence of relationships at the individual and institutional levels raises questions that we can articulate but not answer. Can multiple strong individual relationships exist without there being an institutional relationship? Can an institutional relationship exist without individual ones? Is there a life cycle involved in the building of an individual relationship with a new client into an institutional relationship? Is there a life cycle from a single product relationship to one with several products that eventually results in an overall relationship? To what extent can an overall relationship be used as leverage into a product relationship in a product area the firm is just developing? Can a failed institutional relationship be resurrected through one or more good individual ones? Which is worse, a bad institutional relationship or no relationship at all?

What Does It Matter?

The fact that buyers and suppliers describe relationships in different terms is not all that surprising. Nor is the fact that the word *relationship* has many different meanings, even within the same organization. What is at issue is whether this is of interest to anyone other than linguists. We believe that it is, and for a very simple reason. Customers and investment banks allocate resources based on their own definitions of a relationship. In the case of customers, these resources are transactions that give firms the opportunity to earn fees. The rules they establish for awarding these transactions are based on the value they perceive the banks as adding. They are unwilling to pay for things they regard as unimportant or for potential future contributions.

Investment banks, on the other hand, seek to capture the greater value they perceive themselves as providing. They are also willing to incur current costs in the hope of getting future fees. This gives the customer an opportunity to receive services that he or she may never have to pay for. In the worst case, the investment bank will give up on its efforts with a prospective customer, but there will always be another one willing to take its place. Currently there are more capable investment banks than even the most active issuer needs in its core group to obtain necessary services and the desired level of price competition.

Customers, however, should recognize that there is a price to pay for letting its investment banks pursue the ideal relationship they wish to have. The price is paid in the form of time spent providing information, listening to ideas of limited relevance, and handling indignant phone calls from bankers left out of deals or placed in an unacceptable position on the tombstone.

The implications of this are very practical. Both customers and investment banks need to determine their respective resource allocations based on a mutually agreed-on definition of a desired relationship. This may end up being more than the customer wants and less than the investment bank desires. But it is a way to avoid wasting resources in pointless conversations, blue-book preparations, calling activity, and coordination costs that exceed their benefits. While the value of these wasted resources is obviously difficult to measure, we suspect it is very high.

The point we are making is simple to understand but difficult to implement. A number of barriers inhibit the ability of investment banks and their customers to sit down and speak frankly about what each side is looking for and needs. Commercial banks and their customers do this regularly, but it is very rare for investment banks. One of the highest barriers to constructive dialogue is the power struggle between bankers and customers over their relative dependence on one another. As we have discussed, each engages in strategies designed to gain the upper hand in fee and other negotiations. The professional rivalry between corporate financial staff and investment bankers is another serious barrier to discussion of what the relationship means to each. As with all relationships, discussing the relationship is difficult. But if there is no easy and natural opportunity to talk about the relationship in the normal context of doing business together, then does the relationship exist? If it does not exist, then it need not be discussed.

While we have described what is a fairly large disparity between customers' and investment banks' perception of their relationships, we do not mean to imply that this general depiction applies in all circumstances. Obviously it does not, but when strategies for controlling relationships lead to self-delusion, the result is squandered resources for both parties. The implication of this is that for each firm, for each customer, and for each person involved in "the relationship" from both sides, an effort should be made to be aware of how the term *relationship* is being used. Doing so and clarifying differences does not require some kind of special—and ultimately sterile—exercise in vocabulary. It can occur productively in the context of account reviews or more informal conversations.

CHAPTER 6

SECURITIES UNDERWRITING AND INVESTMENT BANKING COMPETITION

Samuel L. Hayes, III, and Andrew D. Regan

Introduction

Back in the "old days," a couple of decades ago, the U.S. securities business was relatively uncomplicated and the protective walls of the Glass-Steagall Act kept out upstarts. The securities underwriting business was a lucrative engine that powered the competitive hierarchy of Wall Street. But by the early 1990s, underwriting revenues—while much larger in absolute dollar terms—were in secular decline, viewed either as a percentage of a securities firm's revenues or in terms of the spread of gross profit on the actual volumes of new capital being raised. The engine that could suddenly couldn't.*

Several trends prompted this change in circumstances. One was diversification, initially forced on securities firms by their corporate clients and institutional customers, but ultimately embraced by the firms themselves as an attractive and profitable antidote for the cyclical nature of investment banking. Another was an increased level of sophistication among clients and customers, which devalued the pricing and distribution of plain vanilla public financings. As a result, spreads on these deals steadily eroded throughout the 1970s and 1980s.

Another important influence on American securities underwriting was the appearance of increasingly attractive alternative financing opportunities abroad, particularly in the London Euromarkets. Not only was the all-in cost of money often cheaper in London, but the lack of regulatory review and negligible due diligence requirements characteristic in these off-shore markets permitted faster financings than in the United States.

* The authors gratefully acknowledge the assistance and input of Joseph Auerbach, Class of 1957 Professor of Business Administration, Emeritus; Sarah Woolverton of HBS Statistical Research Services; and Research Associate, Emeritus, Jack Case.

145

At the same time a philosophical sea change regarding *de*regulation of financial services was emerging—first in America and later abroad. In the United States both political parties, most of the academic community, and the Washington-based oversight bureaucracy embraced this conviction, which led to a series of reforms: most notably the end of fixed commissions in 1975 and the integration of disclosure in 1979. These moves substantially altered the terrain on which the securities business was conducted. The new philosophy stressed paperwork reduction and financing flexibility.

Shelf registration, one of the most important deregulatory initiatives reflecting the new philosophy, prompted the research underlying this chapter.[1] The shelf procedure allows certain companies meeting minimum size and other requirements to register large blocks of securities with the Securities and Exchange Commission (SEC) and signal the intent to sell them to investors in unspecified amounts at unspecified points within the succeeding two years. Sanctioned under Rule 415 of the Securities Act of 1933, this financing form has been called shelf registration because issuers are permitted to register predetermined amounts of securities and leave them "on the shelf" in anticipation of a window of opportunity through which they can be passed quickly to investors without the normal fuss and bother of conventional SEC registration procedure.

It was expected that shelf registration opportunities would foster broader competition for this financing business among securities underwriters and that the overall cost of funds to qualified capital seekers would be materially reduced. Reasoning held that if competition in American securities underwriting could be altered so that vendors lacking ongoing business relationships could approach corporate issuers with attractive bids on blocks of to-be-issued securities, benefits would accrue to the entire capital-raising system.

Competition in underwriting has indeed been altered in recent years by a number of developments, including the advent of shelfs, but not always in the directions originally envisioned. Our research on post–Rule 415 underwriting indicates that the introduction of shelf registration has not had a fundamental impact on the competitive structure of the securities underwriting sector; the U.S. underwriter hierarchy has

---

1. The research for this chapter is based primarily on two sources: a series of interviews with corporate debt syndicate personnel at each of the Big Six bulge-bracket firms (First Boston, Goldman Sachs, Merrill Lynch, Morgan Stanley, Salomon Brothers, and Shearson Lehman) plus a representative group of major bracket firms (Donaldson, Lufkin and Jenrette, PaineWebber, Prudential Securities, and Smith Barney); and a series of data enquiries to the Securities Data Corporation for information on issuance activity in the debt market as a whole and in the Rule 415 market in particular.

not been materially altered. And while spreads on plain vanilla financings have been eroded during the period since Rule 415 was first adopted, there is no compelling evidence that this erosion is directly linked to the introduction of shelfs. Rather, margin compression may have been spurred in part by competitiveness among the major vendors in the market amid a general perception that power has been shifting steadily away from vendors and toward issuers and investors.

As our research progressed, however, we became convinced that shelf registration could not be examined in isolation. Rule 415 had to be understood within the overall context of financial market evolution. Ultimately we concluded that the introduction and growth of shelfs, though clearly significant, was not a seminal event in and of itself. From a strictly regulatory perspective, Rule 415 is perhaps best understood as an important step in a long transition to a market-based system of regulation and disclosure. Viewed more broadly, however, Rule 415 is part of a wider series of changes impacting the marketplace that should give leading securities vendors no reason for complacency. The private and public primary capital-raising arenas appear to be converging to a point where particular financings can be difficult to categorize. A different group of competitors is gaining importance in the private markets, and if and when these two financing markets do fully converge, the consequences for the competitive vendor hierarchy could be quite significant.

The First Decade of Rule 415

Figure 6-1 and Figure 6-2 illustrate the part that shelf registered offerings played in the overall growth of both debt and equity financing during the years 1980–1991. Obviously the overwhelming impact of Rule 415 has come in debt underwriting (including medium-term notes, or MTNs). The 1980s was, of course, a period dominated by debt financing; however, as the *proportion* of shelf registered equity suggests, Rule 415 has been only nominally utilized in raising new common.[2]

Modest Equity Usage

The minimal reliance on shelf registrations in equity financings can be attributed to several factors. One is the dampening influence of the "overhang" of already registered securities on stock prices. The potential dilutive impact of these additional shares could be expected to be discounted in the current market price of the outstanding common. There is also the possibility that an equity shelf announcement could

2. An appendix containing key source data on Rule 415 activity can be found at the end of this chapter.

Figure 6–1
Shelf Debt+MTN in All Industrial, Financial, Utility Debt+MTN Issues
1980–1991

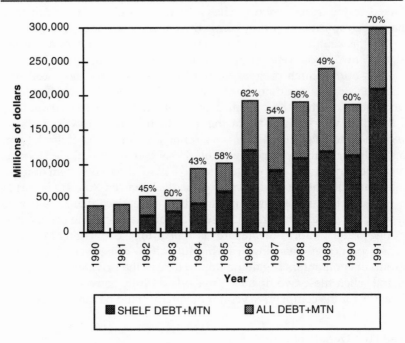

Source: Securities Data Corporation.

send a negative signal to the market that the shares were, in the view of insiders, fully priced, or that excess financial leverage (and possibly lender pressure) was forcing the sale of new equity.[3]

Broad Adoption in the Debt Markets

In contrast, by the end of 1991, the shelf registration format—from a standing start in Spring 1982—had captured upwards of 70% of all debt

3. The modest employment of Rule 415 in the equity markets prompted the SEC to propose in April 1992 further rule changes to encourage corporate issuers to utilize the shelf registration route for new equity financings. It is not clear what kinds of further regulatory concessions would overcome the drawbacks mentioned. To date only a few notable equity issues have been executed under Rule 415. Acquisitive companies in rapidly consolidating sectors such as the cellular telephone industry have filed equity shelfs to be ready for quick share-for-share merger offers that surface.

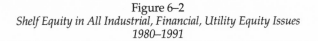

Figure 6–2
Shelf Equity in All Industrial, Financial, Utility Equity Issues
1980–1991

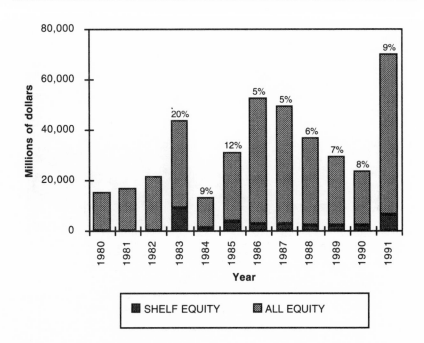

Source: Securities Data Corporation.

underwritings (excluding U.S. government agency securities and certificate of deposit programs). When the debt financing numbers are disaggregated, the growing reliance on shelf registrations is even more
dramatic. By 1991, approximately 80% of the total volume of financings
in both the industrial and utility sectors utilized the shelf registration
procedure (see Figure 6-3 and Figure 6-4).

It has been the finance sector where the greatest variation in shelf
registration use has occurred over the ten year period (see Figure 6-5). A
likely explanation is that in the early years after the introduction of Rule
415, the big auto manufacturers' finance subsidiaries, along with the consumer finance houses and numerous commercial banks, dominated the
shelf debt market. After 1988, however, many banks retreated from the
public markets as a whole because of credit impairment and were in
effect precluded from using the shelf mechanism for holding company
financing. At the same time the auto finance subsidiaries did not increase

Figure 6–3
Shelf Debt+MTN in All Industrial Debt+MTN Issues
1980–1991

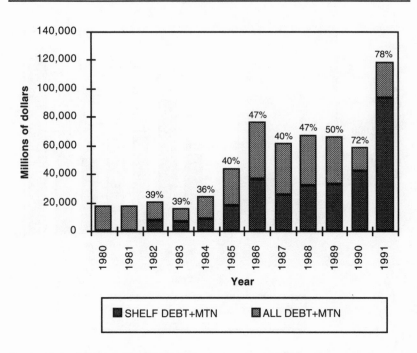

Source: Securities Data Corporation.

total borrowings as fast as the overall growth rate in the debt issue market. Consequently, a smaller proportion of finance-company capital raising involved use of the shelf mechanism at the end of the decade.

Motivations Behind Rule 415

In the SEC's preliminary hearings and in its calls for outsider comment prior to the 1982 introduction of Rule 415, two major arguments favored shelf registration: (1) expected cost savings on the issuance of securities and greater flexibility for issuers in the timing of new financings; and (2) the participation of a broader array of vendors in what would become a de facto competitive bidding market. Enhanced competition was also expected to yield savings to issuing companies, and greater flexibility in timing was expected to permit issuers to tap unusual market "windows" of opportunity, which would promise still more savings.

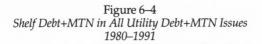

Figure 6–4
Shelf Debt+MTN in All Utility Debt+MTN Issues
1980–1991

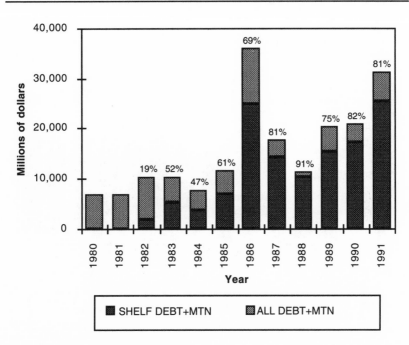

Source: Securities Data Corporation.

Cost Savings

Early studies of costs in the first several years after Rule 415's introduction suggested that there were indeed average savings ranging from 20 to 40 basis points in total issuance costs for debt offerings made via Rule 415 (Kidwell et al., 1984). Later studies, however, cast doubt on both the *size* of the supposed savings and their *attribution* to the shelf registration format (Rogowski and Sorenson, 1985; Fung and Rudd, 1986). One recent paper suggested that data samples analyzed in previous studies had shown an unintended bias toward issuers whose superior credit characteristics would have garnered such savings with or without the introduction of the shelf registration form (Allen et al., 1990). The same study concluded that firms utilizing the shelf option, being predominantly preferred credit risks, had lower issuing costs in the period before Rule 415 was introduced; and indeed the use of shelf registration, once available,

Figure 6–5
Shelf Debt+MTN in All Financial Debt+MTN Issues
1980–1991

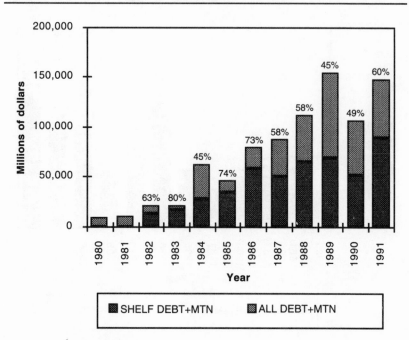

Source: Securities Data Corporation.

had had no incremental effect on reoffering yields. Data generated for this chapter also confirm that, on average, the credit quality of Rule 415 issuers is substantially better than the average for all debt issuers.[4]

The other major advantage attributed to Rule 415 underwritings was that it permitted issuers to capitalize on temporary windows of

4. In 1991, for example, over 81% of all shelf issues—whether measured in terms of dollar volume or number of issues—were rated A- or better by Standard & Poor's, with over 95% rated BBB- or better. This may help account for the absence of significant investor-generated litigation during the first decade of shelf experience, and vindicates to some degree the SEC's move toward a market-based system of regulation and disclosure.

Interestingly, a de facto form of "shelf" registration has also emerged in the municipal finance area, where the credit risks can be substantial. The SEC is barred by law from attaching any preconditions to a new municipal offering, but it *can* require registered broker-dealers to undertake an investigation into the affairs of a municipal issuer to ensure that there are no material misrepresentations to investors. This has effectively put the managing underwriters "on the hook" for the reliability of the issuer information in these deals.

opportunity in the securities markets. But the importance of even that alleged advantage has been questioned in the academic literature. One study concluded that no significant cost savings were in fact realized as a consequence of the timing flexibility provided by shelf registration (Kidwell et al., 1987).

Most studies of shelf offerings evaluate comparative costs of funds over a very brief time frame surrounding a financing. By contrast, market receptiveness to an issuer can decline over time with no deterioration in corporate fundamentals, depending on how the issuer handles its interaction with the market. Vendors and buy-side investors stress the serious long-term impacts on cost-of-capital that can result from "trash deals," overhangs of paper "sloshing around" in the market, poor after-market performance, and "chiseling" for the last basis point. Such impacts are not captured in the various models used by these researchers.

Furthermore, the various studies use comparative data from the period 1977–1982, a generally difficult time economically and an especially tough one in which to sell bonds. Such an environment may have greatly inflated negotiated spreads and reoffering yields as bankers and issuers had to pay up to get investors to swallow debt securities, especially fixed-rate bonds and notes, during a period of historically unprecedented inflation and declining credit quality.

Moreover, the models generally make no allowance for the fact that in contrast to the 1970s, long stretches of the 1980s were marked by lengthy bond-market rallies in which enormous amounts of money could be made by simply "being long" on bonds. This rally was dramatic and extended, and since holding debt paper was the key to participating in it, dealers might have bid with unusual aggressiveness simply to ensure they had bonds to ride the yield curve lower.

In all likelihood the bulk of debt offerings over a lengthy period would not have been offered via Rule 415 unless issuers perceived significant economic advantages to doing so. However, measuring the *extent* of the enhanced economic benefit remains clouded, at least for the present. Conclusive analysis of attributable savings may even be impossible, since many influences—especially those impacting market acceptance of specific issuers over extended time periods—cannot be explicitly captured or represented by proxy within a quantitative model.

Vendor Competition

Whatever the size of cost savings from using Rule 415, the prevailing opinion in the academic literature appears to be that those savings are attributable largely to a climate of increased vendor competition. This leads us to an examination of some of the patterns of competition among vendors during the post–1982 period.

As we noted earlier, the introduction of the shelf registration form was expected to loosen many of the remaining old-school-tie relationships between corporate fund raisers and their traditional investment bankers. This erosion of ties in turn was expected to allow a wider group of securities firms to bid successfully for manager roles in any individual issue of corporate securities. Capital costs would decline in consequence (Kidwell et al., 1987). While in Chapter 5 Crane and Eccles do directly address the broader vendor-client relationship issue, our data on debt issuance suggest that, rather than further broadening the array of participating vendors, Rule 415 has reaffirmed the dominance of the Big Six New York investment banks. Indeed, shelf registration may have fostered even further vendor concentration in the underwriting sector.

This can be seen in Table 6-1 and Table 6-2. From the very introduction of shelfs in 1982, a handful of the traditionally dominant underwriting firms have continued to hold onto the lion's share of the Rule 415 debt business. Table 6-2 shows that over the ten years of experience, the top six firms have held as much as 95% of the shelf market and at the end of 1991 held 88%. To be sure, the market shares of individual firms within this small group have varied somewhat over the period. Several of the six bulge-bracket underwriters took a particularly aggressive stance initially, apparently intending to use the underwriting business won as a wedge to obtain other, more profitable business from the issuing corporations. Certain of these firms subsequently experienced internal difficulties (e.g. Salomon, First Boston, Shearson Lehman) that prompted more conservative approaches. Alternatively, the consistently strong presence of Goldman Sachs and the meteoric rise of Merrill Lynch in recent years are notable.

One possible explanation for the persistent vendor concentration is that debt underwriting has become so price competitive, and the struggle to gain advantage with issuers and investors so intense, that only the largest and most powerful securities firms can afford to sustain an important presence in the business. Because the use of syndicates (to spread risk) in debt shelf deals is very limited—as our research interviews revealed to be the case in most debt underwriting, shelf or conventional—a lead manager needs a large capital base (see Table 6-3).[5] Further, total profitability to the manager cannot be mea-

5. The decline of the syndicate coincided with the rise of the Rule 415 market during the 1980s, and is another barometer of increased concentration in underwriting. In 1980, 80% of all debt and equity underwritings employed a syndicate; by 1988, only 20% used one. Naturally the mix fluctuates in any particular year depending on the amount of equity, and especially initial public offerings, being sold. However, the secular trend is clear: syndicates have become even more uncommon in debt underwriting. Regional firms, generally opponents of both Rule 415 and Rule 144A, have suffered in particular.

Table 6–1
Rule 415 Debt Underwriting Rankings and Market Shares of Top Six Investment Banks
(full credit to book manager only)

	1982	1983	1984	1985	1986	1987	1988	1989	1990	1991
Merrill Lynch	4	6	2	4	5	3	1	1	1	2
	10%	7%	15%	13%	11%	15%	23%	23%	25%	22%
Goldman Sachs	3	2	3	2	2	4	2	3	2	1
	11%	18%	15%	22%	19%	14%	18%	16%	18%	23%
Salomon	2	1	1	1	1	1	3	2	4	4
	19%	24%	35%	26%	21%	22%	16%	16%	15%	11%
First Boston	5	3	4	3	4	5	5	6	5	6
	10%	13%	13%	17%	14%	13%	11%	9%	10%	8%
Morgan Stanley	1	5	6	5	3	2	4	4	3	5
	23%	9%	5%	7%	17%	16%	14%	14%	15%	11%
Shearson Lehman	6	4	5	6	6	6	6	5	NA	3
	7%	10%	6%	6%	9%	10%	9%	10%	NA	13%
Other	20%	19%	11%	9%	9%	10%	9%	12%	14%	12%

Rankings are as indicated; rounding is to nearest percentage.
NA: Figure not available.
Source: Securities Data Corporation.

Table 6–2
Rule 415 Debt Underwriting Market Share Profile for Various Groupings of Top Six Vendors
(full credit to book manager only)

	1982	1983	1984	1985	1986	1987	1988	1989	1990	1991
Leader	23%	24%	35%	26%	21%	22%	23%	23%	25%	23%
Top two firms	42%	42%	50%	48%	40%	38%	41%	39%	43%	45%
Top three firms	53%	55%	65%	65%	57%	53%	57%	55%	58%	58%
Top four firms	63%	65%	78%	78%	71%	67%	71%	68%	73%	69%
Top five firms	73%	74%	84%	85%	82%	80%	82%	79%	83%	80%
Top six firms	80%	81%	89%	91%	91%	90%	91%	88%	86%	88%
Other firms	20%	19%	11%	9%	9%	10%	9%	12%	14%	12%

Source: Securities Data Corporation.

Table 6–3
Securities Industry Concentration*

	1981	1982	1983	1984	1985	1986	1987	1988	1989	1990
Total Revenues (in %)										
Top 10	55.5	57.2	54.3	58.8	57.5	57.3	54.5	54	58.5	56.9
Top 11–25	19.5	18.7	19.6	17.1	19.7	19.8	20.9	20.8	19.3	21.1
Rest of industry	25.0	23.9	26.1	24.1	22.8	22.9	24.6	25.2	22.2	22.0
	100	100	100	100	100	100	100	100	100	100
Industry Revenues (US$ in bn)	19.8	23.2	29.6	31.2	38.6	50.1	50.8	51.8	59.5	54.0
Total Capital (in %)										
Top 10	52.6	54.8	52.9	57.3	63.2	61.9	58.3	57.5	61.8	63.6
Top 11–25	19.6	19.0	18.8	15.7	14.8	16.0	18.5	17.8	16.4	15.9
Rest of industry	27.8	26.2	28.3	27.0	22.0	22.1	23.2	24.7	2 1.8	20.5
	100	100	100	100	100	100	100	100	100	100
Industry Capital (US$ in bn)	8.1	10.7	14.2	16.7	21.9	29.8	35.8	39.1	39.3	35.8

* NYSE member firms doing business with the public.
Source: Securities industry databank.

sured simply by the gross spread earned on an underwriting deal. The benefits that accrue to other dimensions of a firm's business portfolio must also be recognized: the institutional sales side may gain by having a new product as an excuse to call buy-side clients; the firm's traders may glean useful market intelligence from this underwriting activity; and firm-generated market intelligence can be an important value-added product for the corporate finance staff. Each of these conditions bespeaks a large, well-capitalized, diversified vendor.

The vendor group does broaden when the data on shelf managerships is configured to give full credit to all co-managers (rather than just to the lead manager "running the books"). As Table 6-4 shows, Merrill Lynch and Salomon Brothers, in particular, appear to have been popular co-managers on deals they did not themselves control. Drexel, on the other hand, was pretty much a loner until its sudden demise in 1989, not as often being drawn into others' management circles. Kidder, Smith Barney, PaineWebber, and E. F. Hutton, all of whom brought retail as well as wholesale distribution strengths to deals, were active co-managers for shelfs throughout the 1980s. In more recent years Bear, Stearns, Donaldson, Lufkin & Jenrette, and J. P. Morgan have become visible in the Rule 415 market as co-managers. According to our research interviews, each member of this latter group is seen by bulge-bracket vendors as bringing distinctive strengths to a management group: Bear, Stearns for offering specific important relationships; Morgan for both overall financial clout and diversity of issuer relationships; and DLJ for strong secondary trading, research coverage, knowledge of specific sectors, and contacts with certain buy-side accounts.

The scale and operational scope required for bulge-bracket status help explain the concentration observed in debt underwriting data. While shelf registration has increased the level of competition among a small group of already dominant vendors, Rule 415 has also actually raised the barriers to entry for other securities firms. Those barriers have at least three dimensions: financial, informational, and professional. The financial barrier is twofold. *Very large amounts of capital* are the required price of admission even to try the second financial hurdle: the generation and renewal of a *critical mass of business* lines and transactions. Such a portfolio of activities is indispensable if a firm is to represent a comprehensive alternative to the Big Six—and must exist to absorb the annual overhead dues of continued participation. Ongoing participation is the prerequisite to inclusion in the *informational flow of the markets,* the pivot central to matching investor needs and issuer product while trading profitably as principals. Finally, the professional barrier is an issue of *scarcity of skill and culture:* a shortage of people both sufficiently competent to transact business and culturally attuned to a specific firm's mission.

Table 6-4
Rule 415 Debt Underwriting Rankings of Top Six Investment Banks
(full credit to book and co-managers)

	1982	1983	1984	1985	1986	1987	1988	1989	1990	1991
Salomon	1	1	1	1	1	1	1	3	2	1
Goldman Sachs	2	3	2	3	4	5	4	1	3	3
Merrill Lynch	5	2	4	4	2	2	3	5	1	2
First Boston	4	4	3	2	3	3	2	2	5	4
Morgan Stanley	3	—	5	5	5	4	5	6	4	6
Shearson Lehman	6	5	6	6	6	6	6	4	6	5
Kidder Peabody	—	6	—	—	—	—	—	—	—	—

Source: Securities Data Corporation.

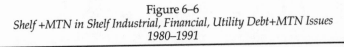

Figure 6–6
*Shelf +MTN in Shelf Industrial, Financial, Utility Debt+MTN Issues
1980–1991*

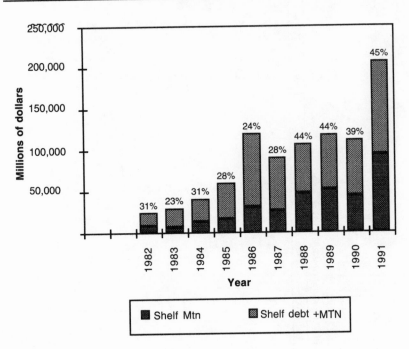

Source: Securities Data Corporation.

Whether new entrants such as American commercial banks or other foreign financial service firms can scale such barriers is open to question.

The Medium Term Note Phenomenon

Rule 415 was undoubtedly responsible for the introduction of the
medium term note (MTN) into the public marketplace. Through the
MTN came a higher order of financial engineering than had been
seen before. So popular was this instrument that by the end of 1991
MTNs had captured almost half of the *total* shelf debt market (see
Figure 6-6).

The MTN market had existed since the early 1970s, but had
remained largely the province of American automobile finance subsidiaries. MTNs had been developed by the captive finance arms of Ford,
Chrysler, and General Motors as an intermediate-term alternative to

commercial paper, which has a maximum maturity of 270 days—too brief for the purposes of most auto financing. The auto subsidiaries had large and recurring appetites for one-to-three-year paper to fund like-term auto loans, but underwriting expenses made conventional short-maturity bonds uneconomic. Thus MTNs in essence became long-dated commercial paper: noncallable, senior, unsecured, fixed-rate obligations sold with some frequency. Until the introduction of shelfs in 1982, issuers sold MTNs directly to investors or into the private placement market. With cumbersome SEC regulations requiring lengthy approval of any amendments to a public offering (even if the change involved only the coupon rates offered) and underwriter support lacking, the MTN could not tap the public markets. At year-end 1981, only about $800 million in MTNs were outstanding (Crabbe, 1992).

The MTN Market After Rule 415

Rule 415 revolutionized the MTN. MTNs now could be publicly issued more or less continuously, without the minimum delay of 48 hours required for nonshelf offerings. The ability to sell continuously meant that issuers could be in the market frequently and for only the amounts immediately needed. Rule 415 also made the use of securities firms as a distribution channel more logical and effective. Investment banks now could be engaged as agents on a best-efforts basis. As directed by the issuer's in-house financial staff, the agent investment bank posted a desired rate scale for a range of maturities, typically nine months to one year, one year to eighteen months, eighteen months to two years, and annually beyond two years. As the agent was not actually underwriting the paper, no proceeds were guaranteed, no underwriting risk was assumed, and no vendor capital exposed. Alternatively, most MTN programs permitted agents "to take down" (i.e., purchase) notes for house accounts and then reoffer them in the same manner as conventional underwritings. As in the pre–1982 efforts, issuers could also bypass the intermediaries altogether and sell MTNs directly to investors, who would often solicit terms directly (or through the agent bank) by a contact known as reverse inquiry.

The much-improved ability to serve as a distribution channel encouraged securities underwriters to commit significant resources to the MTN market after the passage of Rule 415. Beginning in 1982, large investment banks began to staff up MTN sales and trading desks and commit capital to making markets in MTNs. In 1985–1986 alone, the ranks of dealers ready to sell MTNs swelled from half a dozen to more than 25 (*Investment Dealers Digest,* June 1987). This new attention to the market greatly improved secondary market liquidity for the MTN, thus attracting large institutional investors previously absent from the market because of liquidity concerns. Other investors also began to participate in the market with the introduction in 1989–1990 of a book-entry accounting system administered by Depository Trust Company and a companion pricing service offered by Interactive Data Services. By 1991, new issuance volume in the MTN market had reached $72 billion, and outstanding paper exceeded $140 billion (Crabbe, 1992).

During the earlier years of shelf registrations, the MTN market in its new public market form was issuer driven. Through the mid-1980s the majority of paper outstanding was designed to match in term and structure the asset pools, largely auto and consumer loans, being funded. As the decade progressed, Rule 415 filings incorporated ever-more-complicated structural issuer options, including floating rate, callable, putable, extendable, zero coupon, stepdown, inverse floater, foreign currency denominated or foreign currency-indexed, commodity-indexed, and subordinated structures. Asset-backed MTNs were also issued, collateralized by securities ranging from residential mortgages to railway equipment trust certificates to leasing company amortizing notes. By the beginning of the 1990s, very long-dated MTNs (e.g., 20–30 years) became common, as industrial and utility issuers, with their longer-horizoned assets, began to seek a more flexible alternative source of funding to the conventional long-term debt market.

At the same time, the MTN market of more recent years has (along with other financing sectors) become more and more investor driven. Some institutions, especially insurance companies and private pension funds, increasingly have very specifically defined future liabilities because of regulatory and product offering changes (such as the transition to defined benefit plans and the growing popularity of single-premium deferred annuities, guaranteed investment contracts, and similar products). Additionally, shorter-horizon investors such as property-casualty insurers have found themselves stretching for yield in an ever-more-competitive rate environment. MTNs could be tailored to accommodate holes in an investor's asset-liability match, and indeed the role of agents and the process of reverse inquiry were oriented principally toward discovering those holes and designing securities to fill them.

Structured Financings in the MTN Market

Institutional investors also benefited from the enhanced analytical and planning sophistication of microcomputer software and hardware and greatly improved communications systems. This new electronic capacity dovetailed with the development of the derivative markets, including international swap transactions and other structured financing opportunities, enabling investors to dictate to intermediary investment banks the exact type of security desired. MTNs became ideal raw material for structured financings specified by investors to meet their investment needs at a particular moment. For instance, many fixed-income portfolio managers have "natural" hedging needs—against the direction of interest rates, the shape of the yield curve, the trading ranges of specific foreign currencies—that can be cheaply and advantageously satisfied without loss of current yield in the MTN market. Other, smaller portfolio managers might want to establish some limited exposure to a foreign market without having to make a direct purchase of instruments in that market. Still other investors might wish to speculate—perhaps on changes in rates, on the shape of the yield curve, on the convergence or divergence of different currencies, on the prices of commodities, or even on equities, either individually or through an index. Each of these strategies could be accommodated through the MTN market.

By year-end 1991, some market observers estimated that structured financing-driven MTN issuance accounted for about 15% of that market, with the balance comprised of plain vanilla transactions (*Investment Dealers Digest*, January 1992). But the structured segment was certainly the fastest growing, and might have shown an even faster rate of growth in 1991 had general market conditions not been so favorable for plain vanilla shelf debt offerings. Moreover, structured deals are higher value-added than straight deals and therefore more attractive to the vendor-agents. Most issuers now incorporate the ability to do structured transactions into their shelf registration statements. And with good reason: by customizing offerings to specific investor needs, issuers believe they have realized savings of as much as 50–60 basis points over conventional terms (*CFO Magazine*, October 1991).

Structured transactions were not for every issuer and every funding need, however. In general, only the highest rated issuers—AA and above—could participate, since counterparties were unwilling to assume credit risk in addition to all the other risk factors involved. Moreover, the maturities of such transactions tended to be no longer than two or three years. Most market participants were unwilling to speculate on the direction of interest or exchange rates very far into the future.

Many issuers could save significant out-of-pocket expense on an MTN program, sold off a multi-instrument shelf registration over a period of time, compared to a single traditional negotiated deal of equivalent size. Commissions to MTN agents were also generally smaller (as low as 0.125% of principal) than those to underwriters on conventional negotiated deals, if only because no underwriting risk was assumed

(Crabbe, 1992). For issuers with moderate-sized capital needs and an ability to draw down funds intermittently over some period, an MTN structure might result in a lower all-in cost of funds in a flat or declining rate environment.

Other savings accruing to MTN issuers, especially prominent ones, reflected the market share-buying binges periodically afflicting virtually all the bulge-bracket vendors as well as some aspiring dealers. Over the most recent five-year period, virtually every bulge-bracket player had at one time or another "fallen on its sword" in a series of deals, in effect offering issuers below-market financing. Some of this effort could legitimately be described as engaging in loss-leader-type business, either (1) in defense of relationships, or (2) to secure some vague (and usually elusive) goodwill with a nonclient issuer which, it was hoped, might open the door to higher-margin follow-on business in banking or underwriting. Additionally, such activity could add to a firm's fund of market intelligence and improve its buy-side client service through access to greater amounts of merchandise.

Still, much of this "sacrifice" was made as part of attempts to buy more prominent league table positions, which were thought to connote expertise and substance to potential clients. Jockeying for league table prominence could produce almost comical juggling of deals and customers in the final days and hours of the year. And such activity was not confined to the bulge bracket. Our research interviews revealed that in the major bracket, Prudential Securities appears to have indulged in a long period of so-called sword falling in the MTN sector as well as other shelf markets as part of its ill-fated "Project '89" drive to achieve permanent bulge-bracket status.

Despite such gamesmanship, dealer price competitiveness, as in other sectors of the debt market, did not reflect a broadening of the vendor group. The MTN business rapidly came to be dominated by the same Big Six securities firms ascendant in so many other market sectors. Merrill Lynch, for instance, was named as an agent in fully 80% of *all* programs filed in 1991, with Goldman coming in second at almost 60% and Lehman with over 52%. Morgan Stanley, First Boston, and Salomon were all solidly in the mid- to upper 40% range (*Investment Dealers Digest*, January 1992).

Shelf Registration in the Broader Context

The evidence presented thus far confirms that shelf-registered debt placements have captured a large part of the public debt market in the United States. The data also reaffirm the tenacious leadership of half a dozen securities firms within this market, policy makers' hopes notwithstanding. Nonetheless, concentration within the U.S. underwriting sector does not signal the presence of a cartel. Fierce price competition clearly exists among this small group, and the formula for sustaining a position over time is not oligopolistic cooperation but strong capitalization as well as an integrated system of business lines. This interlocking mix of competencies helps extend and retain within the different areas of the firm—sales, trading, banking—as many of the profit opportunities inherent in a debt underwriting as possible, while fostering future follow-on business.

Clearly the debt underwriting business is a line of commerce in which the barriers to entry are quite high. No aspiring major-bracket securities firm has been able to promote itself sustainably into the rarefied bulge group over the past 15 years, despite persistent and costly efforts. Occasional strategic retreats on the debt underwriting front by various of the leading six firms have ultimately been reversed, perhaps on the realization that obtaining a steady supply of product and increasing the contact with current or prospective corporate clients is highly desirable.

This recent impermeability doesn't necessarily secure for the foreseeable future, however, the status quo within the debt financing sector. The dominant firms have to this point withstood insurgencies launched by traditional pretenders, but nontraditional threats may be next. As the NASDAQ national market system has become a powerful counterforce to the New York Stock Exchange, so the private placement market (and the Euromarkets mentioned earlier) have been counterweights to the public debt securities markets in the United States.

The Private Placement Market

By the early 1990s the U.S. private placement market was already huge, having grown boisterously during the 1980s (see Table 6-5). Whereas the Rule 415 debt market expanded at a compound rate exceeding 24% in the 10 years following its inception (1982–1991), the private debt market grew almost as rapidly—at over 21% compounded annually—during a similar period (1981–1990). Many of the strongest credits in the private market did over time migrate opportunistically to the public markets. However, the speed and privacy of the private arena held enduring appeal for many issuers, while naturally secretive dealers appreciated the greater ease with which proprietary financing structures could be protected. The private market was also given a powerful push by billions of privately placed junk debts generated in the LBO boom of the 1980s.[6]

---

6. This flood receded after 1989, of course, but *public* issues of junk bonds made a strong comeback in 1991 and 1992.

Table 6–5
Debt Underwriting Activity in the U.S. Rule 415, U.S. Private Placement, and Euromarkets
(US$ in billions)

	1981	1982	1983	1984	1985	1986	1987	1988	1989	1990	1991
U.S. Rule 415 debt market*	0	23.5	28.5	40.1	59.2	119.2	89.9	106.8	117.2	111.2	207.6
U.S. private debt market**	16.3	25.9	32.7	42.3	70.4	107.1	119.9	172.7	168.5	112.6	81.5
Euromarket debt***	23.5	45.9	45.5	75.3	127.9	154.3	105.9	169.9	206.9	173.2	NA

* Debt underwriting, including medium-term notes, for industrial, financial, and utility issuers.

** Debt only.

*** Includes fixed- and floating-rate debt, but not convertible debt or debt with warrants.

Sources: Securities Data Corporation, *Investment Dealers Digest, Securities Industry Databank.*

The league tables for private placements contained in Table 6-6 reveal many of the same Big Six names in leading positions. But the presence of some large American commercial banks in the rankings should also be noted. Several have achieved prominent positions in this market in recent years, a far cry from their insignificant stature barely a decade earlier. Clearly, some of the leading commercial banks with aspirations to become investment (or even universal) banks have used the private market—which is not formally barred to them by the Glass-Steagall Act because the securities sold there are unregistered—to prove deal-making mettle. Private placements complement natural in-house placing powers, often used to advantage in getting transactions done.

For many investors participating in the private market, the lack of a formal secondary market in privately acquired investments was of minor concern. Such institutions—most notably life insurers—were often acting to "defease" identifiable and contractual liabilities of certain specifications, and as such were "buy-and-hold" investors. For other institutions, the absence of either a secondary market or formal credit-rating updates relieved them of the obligation to "mark to market" on a regular basis.

Most investors, however, actively regarded these attributes as drawbacks of the private placement market and demanded commensurately higher yields on such illiquid investments. In part as a response to this illiquidity risk premium, both regulators and vendors, in concert and alone, have attempted to create de facto or de jure secondary markets for many formerly illiquid financial assets. There are now secondary markets for such financial assets as syndicated bank credits, junk portfolios, LDC debt, and other troubled loans. The popularity of the entire mortgage- and asset-backed sectors—which developed out of both regulatory sanction and vendor ingenuity—clearly reflects a preference for greater liquidity. And the National Association of Insurance Commissioners (NAIC), an industry supervisory body with oversight over insurer investments, has instituted a new credit-rating procedure affecting privately placed loans. In effect the new regimen obliges many investors to "mark" their loan portfolios to what might be seen as a proxy for a secondary market, based on adjustments in the NAIC ratings.

Many (if not most) individuals participate indirectly—like it or not—in the private market through the holdings of their insurers (and increasingly through the portfolios of their pension and mutual fund managers). Nevertheless, the private market remains essentially a wholesale institutional investor marketplace. Caveat emptor seems to be the rule, and the degree of due diligence investigation on many of these nonregistered deals is practically nil. In this sense the private market is

Table 6–6
Top Fifteen Agents in U.S. Private Placement Market

1982	1983	1983	1985	1986
First Boston	Salomon	Salomon	Salomon	Goldman Sachs
Salomon	First Boston	Merrill Lynch	Drexel	Drexel
Merrill Lynch	Goldman Sachs	First Boston	Goldman Sachs	Salomon
Goldman Sachs	Merrill Lynch	Goldman Sachs	Merrill Lynch	First Boston
Lehman	Morgan Stanley	Shearson Lehman	First Boston	Merrill Lynch
PaineWebber	Lehman	Drexel	PaineWebber	Shearson Lehman
Kidder Peabody	A.G. Becker	Morgan Stanley	Shearson Lehman	CITICORP
A.G. Becker	PaineWebber	BANKERS TRUST	Morgan Stanley	PaineWebber
Morgan Stanley	Drexel	PaineWebber	CITICORP	J.P. MORGAN
Dean Witter	Kidder Peabody	Kidder Peabody	Kidder Peabody	BANKERS TRUST
Drexel	E.F. Hutton	E.F. Hutton	J.P. MORGAN	Morgan Stanley
Smith Barney	CITICORP	Smith Barney	BANKERS TRUST	Pru-Bache
NA	Dean Witter	CITICORP	BANK OF AMERICA	FIRST CHICAGO
BANKERS TRUST	Smith Barney	J.P. MORGAN	FIRST CHICAGO	CHASE BANK
NA	BANKERS TRUST	Dean Witter	Dillon Read	Kidder Peabody

Table 6-6 (cont.)
Top Fifteen Agents in U.S. Private Placement Market

1987	1988	1989	1990	1991
Salomon	First Boston	Goldman Sachs	Goldman Sachs	Golman Sachs
First Boston	Goldman Sachs	First Boston	First Boston	First Boston
Drexel	Merrill Lynch	Salomon	J.P. MORGAN	Merrill Lynch
Goldman Sachs	Drexel	J.P. MORGAN	Salomon	Salomon
Shearson Lehman	Salomon	Drexel	Merrill Lynch	Morgan Stanley
Merrill Lynch	Shearson Lehman	Shearson Lehman	Shearson Lehman	J.P. MORGAN
BANKERS TRUST	Morgan Stanley	Merrill Lynch	CITICORP	CHEMICAL BANK
Morgan Stanley	J.P.MORGAN	BANKERS TRUST	CHEMICAL BANK	Shearson Lehman
PaineWebber	PaineWebber	CITICORP	Morgan Stanley	CITICORP
J.P. MORGAN	BANKERS TRUST	Morgan Stanley	CHASE BANK	Kidder Peabody
CITICORP	CITICORP	FIRST CHICAGO	BANKERS TRUST	CHASE BANK
Kidder Peabody	CHEMICAL BANK	CHASE BANK	Kidder Peabody	FIRST CHICAGO
Pru-Bache	Kidder Peabody	BANK OF AMERICA	PaineWebber	CONTINENTAL BK
CHEMICAL BANK	BANK OF AMERICA	PaineWebber	CONTINENTAL BK	PaineWebber
FIRST CHICAGO	Pru-Bache	CHEMICAL BANK	FIRST CHICAGO	BANKERS TRUST

Commercial banks entered in uppercase.
NA: Not Available
Source: Investment Dealers Digest, various issues.

in sympathy with the thrust of public policy, which is toward a market-based system of regulation and control conducted almost entirely among sophisticated institutional investors.

The private market could be a barometer for future developments in what would be an altered public debt market. The new competitors surfacing in the leadership ranks of the private placement market could become more important factors in the public debt markets should the two sectors continue to converge. Such convergence has already occurred in the case of the MTN market. And it is well under way in the private market, as manifested in the recent flurry of issues sold under the new SEC Rule 144A.

The Rule 144A Market

Rule 144A was designed to bring greatly enhanced liquidity to the private placement market. Adopted by the SEC in April 1990, Rule 144A, like Rule 415, was an addition to the Securities Act of 1933. The SEC's stated intent in promulgating 144A was to bolster the competitiveness of the American capital markets—especially in light of the European cooperation planned after 1992—by attracting foreign issuers and retaining American companies increasingly attracted to the highly flexible Euromarkets (*Investment Dealers Digest*, February 1989). Rule 144A was also conceived to increase the efficiency and liquidity of the rapidly growing private placement market by qualifying more buyers to invest in private placements and easing resale restrictions for those buyers. In short, 144A was written to liberalize investing and trading in privately placed unregistered securities.

To date, utilization of this new market—positioned somewhere between a bona fide public offering and a conventional private placement—has been relatively modest. Among the few large American companies that have undertaken high-profile deals are Delta, BFI, Federal Express, and American Airlines. Many of these transactions involved structured debt—especially lease-related—financings and often included heavy foreign participation on the buy side. Use of 144A by American equity issuers has been negligible. The most frequent 144A issuers have been foreign companies and sovereign entities, many previously discouraged from accessing the U.S. markets by the heavy disclosure requirements on registered offerings and the perception of weak liquidity in the private placement secondary market. British, Swedish, Spanish, Dutch, French, and Mexican multinationals and state institutions have been especially heavy issuers, either via discrete offerings wholly into the 144A market or the sale of tranches of Euro- or global offerings to American investors through 144A.

The goal of enhanced secondary market liquidity in the 144A market remains elusive, however. Most deals are distributed by one vendor, rather than by a syndicate. Hence only one firm, at most, is likely to have an active, ongoing commitment to after-sale support of any specific 144A issue. In view of the minimal disclosure obligations and consequent poor information flows, competing securities firms have even less inducement than usual to make a market in such securities of issuers that are not already clients.

Rule 144A deals have tended to be done in a quasi-public style. Usually such offerings do not incorporate customized documentation or typical unregistered covenant features such as sinking funds. Most of the debt issues sold as 144A issues have had uncomplicated structures, with bullet maturities, and the issuers have most often been highly rated companies. Partly as a result, pricing has been very tight to the public markets for comparable securities. These trends have led market participants to conclude that the 144A market will be confined to the higher-quality end of the traditional private placement market, with a lot of plain vanilla debt being sold by investment grade issuers. Needless to say, such a market would be uninteresting to the traditional private placement buyer, commonly a sophisticated buy-and-hold investor requiring more complicated structures and higher yields to reflect those characteristics.

Underwritten 144A Deals

The incipient convergence of the top-rated, plain vanilla 144A market with the public market is best illustrated by the emergence of the "underwritten" 144A deal. Before 144A, it was of course illegal to underwrite a private placement—that is, to purchase unregistered securities for immediate, broad reoffering. Under 144A, an investment bank can execute such a transaction: a private placement in which the bank takes down an entire issue of unregistered securities from an issuer on a firm commitment basis, and turns around and resells the paper to qualified institutional buyers. In effect such an offering is underwritten, rather than agented, as a conventional private placement must be. Most of these so-called underwritten 144As are sold off the vendors' public desks, "talked up" by the existing fixed-income sales force, tightly priced to the public market, and circled (i.e., spoken for) within a matter of hours. Covenants and terms are simple and standardized, and documentation is limited: instead of a conventional prospectus, a "wraparound" containing a page of terms and covenants is attached to an issuer's existing financial data (sometimes merely a copy of the most recent annual report). Investors are offered the deal

on a "take-it-or-leave-it" basis, with no opportunity for input on covenants or other features as in a traditional private placement. From
issuer authorization to placed deal, the whole process often occurs
within four to seven days.

In order to avoid prosecution for underwriting unregistered securities, the investment bank orchestrating an underwritten 144A signs a
purchasing agreement rather than an underwriting agreement. Legal
niceties aside, however, the convergence of the public and private markets is clear to many industry participants. For example, the Morgan
Stanley 144A team quite openly and forthrightly emphasizes its purpose: to "make sure our private deals smell, feel and trade like a public
offering," in the words of Vikram Pandit, managing director. Accom-
plishing this, in his view, involves four steps that together constitute the
four principal characteristics of any public offering: committing a firm's
capital to the deal; pricing the issue on a par with comparable public
market prices; acting as a market maker in the issue after the sale; and
assembling a group of satisfied buyers—in this case, "qualified investment buyers" or "QIBs"—for future transactions (*Investment Dealers
Digest*, April 1992).

Innovation or Smoke and Mirrors?

The convergence of public and private market under 144A is not without its critics. Such skeptics, buy-side investors and corporate issuers
alike, think Street vendors are merely selling the same package—an
agented, and not underwritten, private placement—for a higher price.
These critics contend that whether a 144A deal is underwritten or not,
the underwriting risk is illusory because such deals are presold before
the underwriting price is set; therefore underwriting fees are unjustified.
Moreover, the disparagers claim, the public-style pricing and distribution in such 144A deals make it inappropriate to attach fee structures
based on more highly engineered conventional private transactions; as
suggested previously, underwritten 144A issues are standardized, non-
negotiable, and shopped to a mix of public and private buyers, with
pricing much closer to public market equivalents than traditional private issues. Instead, the convergence of the private and public
markets—the underwritten 144A deal—is considered merely a marketing gimmick sold by investment banks to differentiate themselves (especially from commercial banks lacking underwriting capabilities) and to
extract higher fees. Cynics identify foreign companies as especially vulnerable to this "pitch." These issuers are persuaded to place part of their
financings in the American market—either through direct debt deals or
through placement of tranches of Euro-equity offerings—to diversify
their funding sources.

Investment banker enthusiasts, on the other hand, claim that their work with 144A transactions has in effect created a new "U.S. Euromarket." In this new market, foreign issuers can sell financings, untrammeled by SEC disclosure requirements, to sophisticated investors. Buy-side skeptics see the distinction between a pre-sold, formally underwritten deal and a pre-sold, "best-efforts" placement as minor at best. Executives of John Hancock, for example, have characterized 144A as a "non-event," merely a "codifying of the status quo" (*Investment Dealers Digest*, March 1992).

Certainly the 144A market in its infancy has provided some interesting results from a vendor competition perspective. For the first full calendar year in which 144A placements could be sold (January 1991–December 1991), the new market constituted a beachhead for firms outside the bulge bracket. True, four of the Big Six did finish on top (Merrill, Goldman, Morgan Stanley, Lehman), managing over 55% of 144A private placements. However, First Boston found itself relegated to the eighth position, and Salomon finished out of the top ten, which was filled out with such names as Chemical Bank (fifth), Bankers Trust (sixth), Bear, Stearns (seventh), DLJ (ninth), and J.P. Morgan (tenth) (*Investment Dealers Digest*, April 1992).

End Running the Street

The contention that Street vendors may not be adding much value on 144A deals has not entirely escaped buy-side investors. In 1990, Prudential Capital, the investment banking arm of the Prudential, set up Pru-Shelf, a program designed to eliminate the investment banker middleman in 144A-eligible private placement deals. Pru-Shelf borrowers would avoid SEC registration costs, rating agency fees, and outside legal expenses, because Prudential planned to maintain in-house lawyers to prepare documentation. As for banking fees, Prudential estimated its charges to be 75% less than customary Street bills. This cost differential largely reflected the disparities in compensation levels between Wall Street and the insurance world—even in its investment banking incarnation—and Prudential's proclaimed focus on generating quality assets rather than large fees. Although the success enjoyed by Prudential—and other in-house insurance-company syndication units—has been limited, the very creation of such entities is tangible evidence of a changing buy-side attitude toward the vendor community.

Conclusions

Viewing recent developments in the American securities underwriting terrain from a distance, one can make several observations. While the volume of new financings has grown dramatically, the apparent importance of underwriting to the P&Ls of the leading securities vendors has diminished substantially (both from a spread and a percentage-of-total-revenues point of view) on a secular basis. Nevertheless, despite this decline and the much greater breadth of their lines of business, the bulge-bracket securities firms have tenaciously held onto their leadership in the U.S. primary financing sectors. Vendor response to the Rule 415 phenomenon is but another manifestation of that behavioral pattern.

Despite some vendor disclaimers to the contrary, we hypothesize that the exercise of leadership and control over the corporate financing sector has been and is seen as pivotal to primacy in other market and product categories where higher profit margins prevail. In that sense, primary corporate financing leadership is viewed as a "hub" from which a number of "spokes"—i.e., lines of business—radiate. The leading securities vendors implicitly recognize this and act accordingly. Either consciously or unconsciously they have created formidable barriers to entry for other securities vendors aiming to attain a similar position in financing U.S. corporations.

In the near future it is unlikely that any traditional vendor will displace, or even expand, the bulge group dominating the U.S. public markets. However, the developments driving the convergence of the private placement and public offering markets could become disruptive to the status quo. Motivated by opportunism as well as by a sense of competitive imperative, some of the largest and strongest commercial banks might pose a significant competitive challenge to these dominant securities firms, at least in selected markets. Large institutional investors, forsaking their historic buy-side purview for a broader role, could also be wild cards in the more distant future.

Appendix

Table 6A-1
Debt and Medium-term Note Underwriting Record, 1982-1991

	1982		1983		1984		1985		1986		1987		1988		1989		1990		1991	
	Issues	$mill	Issues	$mill	Issues	$mill	Issues	$mill	Issues	$mill	Issues	$mill	Issues	$mill	Issues	$mill	Issues	$mill	Issues	$mill
Industrial Issuers (I)																				
Debt and MTNs	249	20,107	253	16,167	230	24,069	418	43,936	644	76,879	497	61,596	356	67,329	348	65,811	276	58,358	479	118,910
Shelf Debt and MTNs (2)	72	7,808	67	6,275	74	8,675	135	17,428	232	35,973	169	24,807	167	31,597	167	32,760	177	41,827	356	93,020
% Shelf (2)/(I)	28.9	38.8	26.5	38.8	32.2	36.0	32.3	39.7	36.0	46.8	34.0	40.3	46.9	46.9	48.0	49.8	64.1	71.7	74.3	78.2
Financial Issuers																				
Debt and MTNs (I)	179	21,820	180	21,018	249	62,126	326	46,769	455	80,231	473	87,502	453	111,483	495	154,054	407	106,872	639	147,595
Shelf Debt and MTNs (2)	101	13,760	115	16,837	168	27,860	197	34,724	262	58,423	241	50,825	253	64,760	248	69,182	200	52,283	316	89,218
% Shelf (2)/(I)	56.4	63.1	63.9	80.1	67.5	44.8	60.4	74.2	57.6	72.8	51.0	58.1	55.8	58.1	50.1	44.9	49.1	48.9	49.5	60.4
Utility Issuers																				
Debt and MTNs (I)	122	10,307	99	10,280	66	7,680	107	11,533	273	36,028	140	17,746	108	11,500	136	20,334	131	20,953	189	31,283
Shelf Debt and MTNs (2)	25	1,930	65	5,350	38	3,605	62	7,015	188	24,803	110	14,324	94	10,458	101	15,261	112	17,136	162	25,387
% Shelf(2)/(I)	20.5	18.7	65.7	52.0	57.6	46.9	57.9	60.8	68.9	68.8	78.6	80.7	87.0	90.9	74.3	75.1	85.5	81.8	85.7	81.2
Ind'l/Fin'l/Util.																				
Debt and MTNs (I)	550	52,234	532	47,464	545	93,875	851	102,237	1372	193,138	1110	166,844	917	190,312	979	240,199	814	186,183	1307	297,788
Shelf Debt and MTNs (2)	198	23,498	247	28,462	280	40,141	394	59,167	682	119,198	520	89,955	514	106,815	516	117,204	489	111,245	834	207,625
% Shelf(2)/(I)	36.0	45.0	46.4	60.0	51.4	42.8	46.3	57.9	49.7	61.7	46.8	53.9	56.1	56.1	52.7	48.8	60.1	59.8	63.8	69.7

Note: Medium-Term Notes figures include only domestic issues.

Table 6A-2
Debt and Medium-term Note Underwriting, 1982-1991: Breakdown by Issuer Type

	1982		1983		1984		1985		1986		1987		1988		1989		1990		1991	
	Issues	$mill	Issues	$mill	Issues	$mill	Issues	$mill	Issues	$mill	Issues	$mill	Issues	$mill	Issues	$mill	Issues	$mill	Issues	$mill
Industrial Issuers																				
Debt	242	19,109	252	16,152	222	23,262	405	41,463	624	73,041	468	56,640	309	56,452	302	54,031	211	38,228	383	75,895
MTNs	7	998	1	15	8	807	13	2,473	20	3,838	29	4,956	47	10,877	46	11,780	65	20,129	96	43,015
Debt and MTNs	249	20,107	253	16,167	230	24,069	418	43,936	644	76,879	497	61,596	356	67,329	348	65,811	276	58,358	479	118,910
Shelf Debt	65	6,810	66	6,260	67	7,969	124	15,103	212	32,135	143	20,276	120	20,720	125	21,891	129	26,247	262	52,255
Shelf MTNs	7	998	1	15	7	707	11	2,325	20	3,838	26	4,531	47	10,877	42	10,870	48	15,580	94	40,765
Shelf Debt and MTNs	72	7,808	67	6,275	74	8,675	135	17,428	232	35,973	169	24,807	167	31,597	167	32,760	177	41,827	356	93,020
% Shelf	28.9	38.8	26.5	38.8	32.2	36.0	32.3	39.7	36.0	46.8	34.0	40.3	46.9	46.9	48.0	49.8	64.1	71.7	74.3	78.2
Financial Issuers																				
Debt	164	15,585	160	14,555	211	50,106	284	31,638	383	49,131	386	51,831	329	54,213	375	63,405	323	51,537	547	86,353
MTNs	15	6,235	20	6,462	38	12,020	42	15,131	72	31,100	87	35,671	124	57,271	120	90,649	84	55,335	92	61,242
Debt and MTNs	179	21,820	180	21,018	249	62,126	326	46,769	455	80,231	473	87,502	453	111,483	495	154,054	407	106,872	639	147,595
Shelf Debt	86	7,525	95	10,375	132	16,180	160	20,744	206	32,423	198	31,743	174	30,606	189	33,824	153	28,740	240	42,676
Shelf MTNs	15	6,235	20	6,462	36	11,680	37	13,981	56	26,000	43	19,081	79	34,155	59	35,359	47	23,543	76	46,542
Shelf Debt and MTNs	101	13,760	115	16,837	168	27,860	197	34,724	262	58,423	241	50,825	253	64,760	248	69,182	200	52,283	316	89,218
% Shelf	56.4	63.1	63.9	80.1	67.5	44.8	60.4	74.2	57.6	72.8	51.0	58.1	55.8	58.1	50.1	44.9	49.1	48.9	49.5	60.4

Table 6A-2 (cont.)
Debt and Medium-term Note Underwriting, 1982–1991: Breakdown by Issuer Type

	1982 Issues	1982 $mill	1983 Issues	1983 $mill	1984 Issues	1984 $mill	1985 Issues	1985 $mill	1986 Issues	1986 $mill	1987 Issues	1987 $mill	1988 Issues	1988 $mill	1989 Issues	1989 $mill	1990 Issues	1990 $mill	1991 Issues	1991 $mill
Utility Issuers																				
Debt	122	10,307	99	10,280	66	7,680	106	11,333	268	35,258	133	15,976	93	9,050	106	14,365	106	14,767	152	24,824
MTNs	0	0	0	0	0	0	1	200	5	770	7	1,770	15	2,450	30	5,969	25	6,186	37	6,459
Debt and MTNs	122	10,307	99	10,280	66	7,680	107	11,533	273	36,028	140	17,746	108	11,500	136	20,334	131	20,953	189	31,283
Shelf Debt	25	1,930	65	5,350	38	3,605	61	6,815	183	24,033	103	12,554	79	8,008	76	10,386	95	13,076	125	18,928
Shelf MTNs	0	0	0	0	0	0	1	200	5	770	7	1,770	15	2,450	25	4,875	17	4,060	37	6,459
Shelf Debt and MTNs	25	1,930	65	5,350	38	3,605	62	7,015	188	24,803	110	14,324	94	10,458	101	15,261	112	17,136	162	25,387
% Shelf	20.5	18.7	65.7	52.0	57.6	46.9	57.9	60.8	68.9	68.8	78.6	80.7	87.0	90.9	74.3	75.1	85.5	81.8	85.7	81.2
Ind'l/Fin'l/Util																				
Debt	528	45,001	511	40,987	499	81,048	795	84,434	1275	157,430	987	124,447	731	119,715	783	131,802	640	104,532	1082	187,072
MTNs	22	7,233	21	6,477	46	12,827	56	17,803	97	35,708	123	42,397	186	70,598	196	108,397	174	81,651	225	110,716
Debt and MTNs	550	52,234	532	47,464	545	93,875	851	102,237	1372	193,138	1110	166,844	917	190,312	979	240,199	814	186,183	1307	297,788
Shelf Debt	176	16,264	226	21,985	237	27,754	345	42,662	601	88,590	444	64,573	373	59,334	390	66,100	377	68,063	627	113,859
Shelf MTNs	22	7,233	21	6,477	43	12,387	49	16,506	81	30,608	76	25,382	141	47,482	126	51,103	112	43,183	207	93,766
Shelf Debt and MTNs	198	23,498	247	28,462	280	40,141	394	59,167	682	119,198	520	89,955	514	106,815	516	117,204	489	111,245	834	207,625
% Shelf	36.0	45.0	46.4	60.0	51.4	42.8	46.3	57.9	49.7	61.7	46.8	53.9	56.1	56.1	52.7	48.8	60.1	59.8	63.8	69.7

Table 6A–3
Medium-term Note Underwriting, 1982–1991

	1982 Issues	1982 $mill	1983 Issues	1983 $mill	1984 Issues	1984 $mill	1985 Issues	1985 $mill	1986 Issues	1986 $mill	1987 Issues	1987 $mill	1988 Issues	1988 $mill	1989 Issues	1989 $mill	1990 Issues	1990 $mill	1991 Issues	1991 $mill
Industrial Issuers																				
All MTNs																				
Domestic	7	998	1	15	8	807	13	2,473	20	3,838	29	4,956	47	10,877	46	11,780	65	20,129	96	43,015
Global					0	0	0	0	0	0	0	0	3	3,500	2	920	4	1,800	2	1,350
Euro					0	0	0	0	3	1,200	1	100	4	2,048	6	2,100	3	2,100	7	3,350
Private					1	75	0	0	3	300	3	550	3	1,400	10	2,875	7	1,875	0	0
Total	7	998	1	15	9	882	13	2,473	26	5,338	33	5,606	57	17,825	64	17,675	79	25,904	105	47,715
Shelf MTNs																				
Domestic	7	998	1	15	7	707	11	2,325	20	3,838	26	4,531	47	10,877	42	10,870	48	15,580	94	40,765
Global					0	0	0	0	0	0	0	0	3	3,500	2	920	4	1,800	0	0
Euro					0	0	0	0	1	3,839	0	0	0	0	0	0	0	0	0	0
Private					0	0	0	0	0	0	0	0	0	0	0	0	0	0	0	0
Total	7	998	1	15	7	707	11	2,325	21	7,677	26	4,531	50	14,377	44	11,790	52	17,380	94	40,765
% Shelf	100.0	100.0	100.0	100.0	77.8	80.2	84.6	94.0	80.8	143.8	78.8	80.8	87.7	80.7	68.8	66.7	65.8	67.1	89.5	85.4
Financial Issuers																				
All MTNs																				
Domestic	15	6,235	20	6,462	38	12,020	42	15,131	72	31,100	87	35,671	124	57,271	120	90,649	84	55,335	92	61,242
Global	0	0	0	0	0	0	0	0	0	0	9	5,770	8	5,000	9	5,915	8	12,315	8	26,075
Euro	0	0	0	0	0	0	0	0	2	512	4	1,707	8	2,700	20	7,833	9	13,760	31	36,467
Private	0	0	0	0	0	0	0	0	0	0	0	0	2	1,250	8	6,237	8	1,023	14	9,725
Total	15	6,235	20	6,462	38	12,020	42	15,131	74	31,612	100	43,148	142	66,221	157	110,634	109	82,433	145	133,509
Shelf MTNs																				
Domestic	15	6,235	20	6,462	36	11,680	37	13,981	56	26,000	43	19,081	79	34,155	59	35,359	47	23,543	76	46,542
Global	0	0	0	0	0	0	0	0	0	0	0	0	0	0	0	0	0	0	0	0
Euro	0	0	0	0	0	0	0	0	1	12	3	4,250	6	2,050	8	6,942	9	14,315	0	0
Private	0	0	0	0	0	0	0	0	0	0	1	300	1	3,000	0	0	0	0	0	0
Total	15	6,235	20	6,462	36	11,680	37	13,981	57	26,012	47	23,631	86	39,205	67	42,301	56	37,858	76	46,542
% Shelf	100.0	100.0	100.0	100.0	94.7	97.2	88.1	92.4	77.0	82.3	47.0	54.8	60.6	59.2	42.7	38.2	51.4	45.9	52.4	34.9

Table 6A-3 (cont.)
Medium-term Note Underwriting, 1982-1991

	1982		1983		1984		1985		1986		1987		1988		1989		1990		1991	
	Issues	$mill	Issues	$mill	Issues	$mill	Issues	$mill	Issues	$mill	Issues	$mill	Issues	$mill	Issues	$mill	Issues	$mill	Issues	$mill
MTN–Ind'l/Fin'l/Util																				
Domestic	22	7,233	21	6,477	46	12,827	56	17,803	97	35,708	123	42,397	186	70,598	196	108,397	174	81,651	225	110,716
Global	0	0	0	0	0	0	0	0	0	0	1	300	9	8,500	10	7,290	13	14,115	11	27,725
Euro	0	0	0	0	0	0	0	0	5	1,712	12	7,027	11	4,748	17	8,015	11	9,933	38	39,817
Private	0	0			1	75	0	0	3	300	4	800	9	2,775	29	11,175	16	8,975	24	13,055
Total	22	7,233	21	6,477	47	12,902	56	17,803	105	37,720	140	50,524	215	86,621	252	134,877	214	114,674	298	191,312
Shelf MTNs																				
Domestic	22	7,233	21	6,477	46	12,387	49	16,506	81	30,608	76	25,382	141	47,482	126	51,103	112	43,183	207	93,766
Global	0	0	0	0	0	0	0	0	0	0	1	300	8	8,100	9	6,290	12	13,115	1	300
Euro	0	0	0	0	0	0	0	0	2	512	3	4,250	2	450	2	2,172	1	3,000	0	0
Private	0	0	0	0	0	0	0	0	0	0	0	0	0	0	0	0	0	0	0	0
Total	22	7,233	21	6,477	43	12,387	49	16,506	83	31,120	80	29,932	151	56,032	137	59,565	125	59,298	208	94,066
% Shelf	100.0	100.0	100.0	100.0	91.5	96.0	87.5	92.7	79.0	82.5	57.1	59.2	70.2	64.7	54.4	44.2	58.4	51.7	69.8	49.2

References

Allen, David S., Robert E. Lamy, and Rodney G. Thompson (1990). "The Shelf Registration of Debt and Self-Selection Bias," *The Journal of Finance*, vol. XLV, no. 1 (March), pp. 275–287.

CFO Magazine, October 1991, p. 74.

Crabbe, Leland (1992). "Corporate Medium-Term Notes," *Journal of Applied Corporate Finance*, vol. 4, no. 4 (Winter), p. 90.

Crane II, Dwight B., and Robert G. Eccles (1993). "Customer Relationships in the 1990s," Chapter 5, this volume.

Fung, W.K.H., and Andrew Rudd (1986). "Pricing New Corporate Bond Issues: An Analysis of Issue Cost and Seasoning Effects," *The Journal of Finance*, vol. XLI, no. 3 (July), pp. 633–644.

Investment Dealers Digest, June 12, 1987, p. 44; February 2, 1989, p. 18; June 17, 1991, pp. 21–22; January 20, 1992, pp. 18, 22; March 9, 1992, p. 21; April 9, 1992, p. 21.

Kidwell, David, M. Wayne Marr, and G. Rodney Thompson (1984). "SEC Rule 415: The Ultimate Competitive Bid," *The Journal of Financial and Quantitative Analysis*, vol. 19, no. 2 (June), pp. 183–195.

——— (1987). "Shelf Registration: Competition and Market Flexibility," *Journal of Law and Economics*, vol. XXX, no. 1 (April), pp. 181–206.

CHAPTER 7

COMPETITION AND CHANGE IN THE MUTUAL FUND INDUSTRY

Erik R. Sirri and Peter Tufano

Introduction

During the past two decades, mutual funds have become an important investment vehicle for individuals. In 1970, the U.S. mutual fund industry managed assets of roughly $50 billion, but by 1990 this figure had grown to $1.1 trillion, a twentyfold increase.[1] By any measure, mutual funds have become a major force in the United States and global financial economies.[2] As an example, Figure 7-1 shows that in the United States, money market funds have captured a material share of the deposit market, and equity mutual funds have grown large relative to households' direct holdings of common stock. The growth took place as literally thousands of funds, offered by hundreds of different firms, competed among one another and against all of the other investments available to consumers.

This chapter examines the ways in which funds have competed in the past and how competition is likely to change in the future. In particular, we describe a variety of strategies that funds have employed in their battle for consumers' monies, and we comment on the apparent effectiveness of the strategies. We also identify the effects of these competitive strategies on the structure of the industry. Finally, we discuss possible scenarios for competition in the future, not only narrowly within the mutual fund industry but also broadly within the entire financial services sector.

---

1. Investment Company Institute (ICI), *Mutual Fund Fact Book* (Washington, D.C.: ICI, 1991), p. 74.
2. It is interesting to note that 1991 was the first year in which total net assets of mutual funds owned and operated outside the United States exceeded those of U.S.-operated funds. See ICI, 1991, p. 57.

Figure 7-1
Consumer holdings of mutual funds relative to their direct alternatives. Each series represents the ratio of the household sector's holdings of mutual funds compared to their holdings of non-mutual fund substitutes.

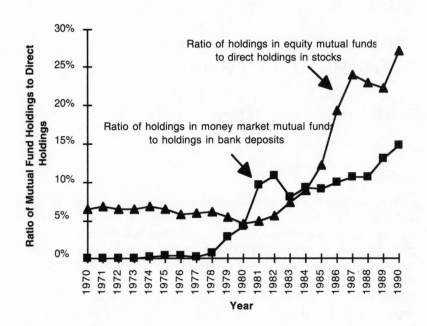

Source: Federal Reserve Board Flow of Funds data.

At one level, mutual funds are simple and transparent financial intermediaries. Participants pool their resources, each owning a share in the pool, and empower a management company to make investment decisions within broad guidelines. Though simple in concept, mutual funds as configured in practice are complex, even from the perspective of a reasonably sophisticated investor. The Investment Company Institute has classified more than 21 types of funds offered by mutual fund families; they range from growth funds to precious metals funds to single-state municipal bond funds. Funds are promoted through advertisements, direct mailings, dedicated sales forces, telephone solicitation, and defined-contribution pension plans. A variety of fee structures are used to charge customers for fund services. Finally, even after the fact, measuring how well a fund has performed may seem to many consumers a mystical science.

Figure 7-2
Elements of the Value Chain for a Mutual Fund

Part of the confusion the mutual fund consumer faces is the result of funds' efforts to differentiate themselves from one another. In its basic form, a mutual fund has characteristics of a commodity product; within regulatory bounds, almost any financial services firm can aggregate a group of traded securities and sell shares in the pool. If the product is marketed as a commodity, funds must compete on the basis of price. If it is marketed as a differentiated product, however, price competition tends to be less severe. As a result, most funds attempt to differentiate themselves on the basis of non-price factors.

We begin by discussing two frameworks through which to view the mutual fund industry. One divides the industry into a set of activities, whereas the other reduces it to the economic functions it serves. The two views provide structures to organize our thoughts about how funds can and do compete and about where future threats and opportunities lie.

Two Definitions of Mutual Funds

An Institutional, or Activity-Based, View

As a business organization, a mutual fund management company or fund complex (firm) undertakes a series of activities designed to generate value for its customers. By arraying a firm's strategically important activities, one can construct a firm's value chain representation. This analytic tool has been advanced by Michael Porter.[3] In grouping a firm's activities the analyst must consider the manner in which the economics of various activities differ and how rivals distinguish themselves on the basis of these activities. We identify five links in the value chain for a typical mutual fund, as shown in Figure 7-2.

The first activity is the *investment selection*. Mutual funds implement their investment strategy through their selection of security holdings.

3. Michael E. Porter, *Competitive Advantage* (New York: The Free Press, 1985).

Funds vary in the amount of latitude they grant to portfolio managers. Investments may be dictated completely by fund charter, as is done in an S&P 500 index fund, or security selection may be left completely to the fund manager's discretion, as in a growth fund. To support this function, funds require research which may be conducted in-house or purchased from vendors either with cash or with soft-dollar payment from brokers.

The next activity is *trading and execution*. Once the decision has been made to buy or sell a particular security, a trade must be executed in the capital markets. This process involves not only getting the best price for the security, but also administering back-office functions such as custodial services. Though this particular link in the chain may seem minor at first glance, trading and execution expertise are increasingly being recognized as critical activities. For instance, for index products in which a performance benchmark is perfectly observable, mutual funds will try to minimize the drag on fund performance caused by positive cash balances through use of futures contracts, thereby obtaining portfolio returns that closely match the benchmark's value.

The third item in the chain is *customer record keeping and reporting*. This refers to the tasks performed by transfer agents and to the activities and resources required to produce periodic statements for fund shareholders. Like trading and execution, they are what Porter refers to as indirect activities and therefore may seem to be minor functions for funds. However, fund complexes do differentiate themselves along this dimension, especially in the defined-contribution retirement market, and failure to manage this activity can damage consumer satisfaction.

The fourth activity, *marketing and distribution*, describes how the funds communicate with potential customers and sell their products. Traditionally, open-end mutual funds were categorized as either no-load or load funds, and the distinction was relatively simple: no-load funds used print and electronic media, word of mouth, and mailings to appeal to consumers directly, whereas load funds hired salespeople to market and sell their products. To pay the salespeople, load funds charged customers one-time fees, called "loads."[4] Brokerage firms are the biggest vendors of load funds, although banks, insurance companies, and financial planners also sell them. In a reference to their different distribution channels and clienteles, it is often remarked that no-load funds are "bought" while load funds are "sold."

---

4. Sales charges traditionally were levied at the time a consumer first bought a fund; however, more recent pricing strategies have levied the equivalent of sales charges throughout the life of the consumer's holding, or at the termination of the investment.

Today, the traditional relationship between distribution method and fee structure has broken down. A fund complex may sell directly to consumers or may use a sales force to call on potential customers. Funds that use direct sales techniques may or may not charge a load or other selling commission. We will use the terms "direct" and "brokered" to denote different distribution methods, reserving the load/no-load distinction for funds that do or do not charge one-time sales fees.

The final activity in our value chain is *investor liquidity services.* By this we mean the activities funds undertake to permit investors to switch among various investments or to liquidate their portfolios. For example, the open-end mutual fund provides an important liquidity service by offering to redeem shares at any time at the fund's current net asset value. Fund complexes provide liquidity services by offering investors a broad range of investment alternatives, including money market funds, and convenient telephone transfers among these alternatives.

Having broken down a mutual fund into a set of activities, one could in principle identify for each activity how a firm might differentiate its product or achieve a low-cost position. With appropriate data, the relative costs of each of the activities can be estimated for each firm.[5] Although we lack specific data to conduct this cost breakdown, we attempt to estimate the relative magnitude of the costs of various activities using raw industry data averages (see Figure 7-3). We identify four related equity-investment products—institutional money management, 401(k) plan management, no-load funds, and load funds—each of which provides a slightly different bundle of activities. Although all four perform comparable investment management, trading, and execution functions, they differ in the extent to which they provide costly customer record keeping and marketing. For example, the primary difference between institutional money managers and 401(k) plan managers is that the 401(k) manager provides extensive record keeping for each of the thousands of individual participants. The difference between 401(k) plans and no-load funds lies primarily in marketing: retail no-loads sell directly to consumers, and 401(k) vendors sell to businesses, which in turn make the funds available to their employees through defined contribution plans. Comparing no-load and load funds, we find the apparent primary cost difference to be that load funds still rely on brokered distribution.

---

5. Activity-based analyses of firms have recently proved to be powerful tools in management accounting in which cost allocations are made on the basis of firm activities. See Robert Kaplan and Robin Cooper, *The Design of Cost Management Systems* (Englewood Cliffs, N.J.: Prentice Hall, 1991).

Figure 7-3
Functions Served and Fees Charged for Managed Equity Investment Products

	Institutional Money Manager	401(k) Manager	Average No-Load Fund	Average Load Fund
Investment Advice, Trading, and Execution	●	●	●	●
		same		
Customer Record Keeping and Reporting	○	●	●	●
	few accounts	many accounts		
Marketing and Distribution	○	○	●	●
	business to business		consumer marketing	
Estimate of Average Annual Fees Charged, in basis points	50[a]	100+[b]	100+[c]	200+[d]

Key: ● = many services provided   ○ = few services provided

Sources:
[a] Median fees charges for $50 million account in actively managed equities from Josef Lakonishok, Andrei Shleifer, and Robert W. Vishny, "The Structure and Performance of the Money Management Industry," in *Microeconomics 1992*, edited by Martin Neil Baily and Clifford Winston (Washington, D.C.: The Brookings Institution, 1991), pp. 339–392.
[b] 401(k) fees from *CFO Magazine*, May 1992.
[c] Average fees of no-load equity funds in 1990, calculated by authors.
[d] Average fees of load equity funds in 1990, calculated by authors. Investors assumed to hold load funds for seven years.

If the differences in fees charged for these products are proportional to the costs of the marginal activities provided, then we can roughly estimate the relative magnitudes of the costs of various activities. Based on the data in Figure 7-3, the breakdown in fee differences for equity products translates into 50 basis points for investment management, 50 basis points for record keeping, and up to 100 basis points for person-to-person marketing. If fees are related to costs, the findings suggest that for a load fund, costs might be split 25% for investment management, 25% for record keeping, and 50% for marketing.

A Functional View

An activity view is most useful in identifying where a firm can lower its costs and differentiate its product. Where the value chain concept breaks a firm into a set of activities, functional analysis proposed by Robert C. Merton and Zvi Bodie[6] considers the most basic functions that a financial system, financial institution, or financial product satisfies. By focusing on functions common across countries and over time, they encourage the analyst to go beyond institutional analyses, which might fail to recognize competition from very different institutions. Merton and Bodie identify six functions that can be used to characterize any financial product, institution, or system:[7]

- A payments system for the exchange of goods and services
- A mechanism for the pooling of funds to undertake large-scale indivisible enterprises
- A way to transfer economic resources through time and across geographic regions and industries
- A way of managing uncertainty and controlling risk, as through selling, hedging, or diversifying
- A body of price information to help coordinate decentralized decision making in various sectors of the economy
- A way of dealing with the agency problems created by asymmetric information

In aggregate, the mutual fund industry provides many of these functions. For example, by providing investment liquidity, especially check-writing services, the industry permits individuals to buy goods and services. Funds that invest in large-denomination instruments (such as commercial paper) and sell shares to consumers in small denominations provide pooling of funds. By buying securities from various parts of the world, international equity funds facilitate the transfer of resources across geographic regions. With large holdings in individual firms, subject to regulatory constraints,[8] mutual funds could in principle satisfy a desire to control agency problems (caused by the separation of ownership and control of the modern corporation) by actively monitoring the actions of managers and boards of firms in which they invest.

Of the functions satisfied by mutual funds, perhaps the most obvious is helping households to manage risk efficiently. Modern financial

---

6. Robert C. Merton and Zvi Bodie, "A Framework for Analyzing the Financial System," unpublished manuscript, 1992.
7. The following discussion draws heavily from Merton and Bodie, 1992.
8. However, mutual funds are subject to regulatory constraints that inhibit their ability to monitor the firms in which they have holdings. See Mark Roe, "Political and Legal Restraints on Ownership and Control of Public Companies," *Journal of Financial Economics* 27 (1990), pp. 1–42.

theory, pioneered by Markowitz, Sharpe, Lintner, Treynor, Mossin, and others, suggests that individuals should hold well-diversified investment portfolios. Mutual funds, which are able to buy and sell securities much more cheaply than individuals can, provide diversified portfolios at low cost. As institutions transacting in large lots, mutual funds pay lower commissions, approximately $.08 per share of common stock as compared with $.54 a share for a consumer buying 100 shares of a $40 stock through a retail broker. Funds can also spread fixed costs of research over a larger block of securities. As a result, the individual acting alone and attempting to create a diversified portfolio would face excessive costs and inconvenience. For example, an individual wishing to invest $10,000 in the S&P 500 index, an amount roughly equal to the average mutual fund account,[9] would invest approximately $20 per firm, buying one-half of one share on average. Even if the individual purchased $100,000 worth of the S&P stocks, he or she would not only pay exceptionally high commissions on odd-lot trades, but also face the task of reinvesting small dividends and rebalancing the portfolio with changes in the market value of the 500 stocks, making this direct attempt at diversification infeasible.

Competition: Past and Present

Mutual funds can compete with one another either by satisfying different economic functions or by configuring the activities in the value chain so as to produce either a low-cost or a differentiated product. In this section, we analyze how funds and fund complexes have chosen to compete and the apparent success and failure of their competitive strategies.

Competitive Alternatives

Generically, a firm can compete either by charging lower prices sustained by its low cost or by differentiating its offering. If an industry's products are perfect substitutes or commodities, a low-cost strategy may be a firm's only viable option. A firm may lower its costs by investing in technology, achieving scale economies by increasing output or spreading costs over a broad product line through scope economies. Decomposing a firm into a set of value chain activities is useful in implementing low-cost strategies because the value chain identifies the individual cost elements by which a firm can achieve a cost advantage over its rivals.

9. ICI, 1991, p. 70.

In an industry selling products that are near but imperfect substitutes, firms engage in what economists call monopolistic competition. To avoid price competition, they strive to distinguish themselves by differentiating their products from those offered by rivals, thereby allowing themselves to set prices or act like monopolists within a market niche. To pursue a product differentiation strategy, a firm must determine some dimension along which it can set itself apart from its rivals. Either a functional or value chain analysis can identify the choices available.

In most products, competition takes place at more than one level. For example, in the breakfast cereal business, individual brands (e.g., Cheerios, Wheaties) compete for consumers, but the firms that offer these products (e.g., Kellogg's, General Mills) market multiple brands and compete against one another for supermarket shelf space. Similarly, in the mutual fund business, both brands (funds) and firms (complexes) compete. Complex-level competition is especially critical in the mutual fund business because one function, or value chain element, satisfied by mutual funds is what we have called investor liquidity. A complex delivers these services to consumers by offering a variety of funds, liquidity services (in the form of check writing and a money market fund), and easy transfer privileges to other investments.

In the breakfast cereal business, we observe the coexistence of firms pursuing low-cost strategies (with generic or private-label brands) and differentiated product strategies (with brand-name cereals). The mutual fund industry also supports both low-cost and high-differentiation strategies. The low-cost strategies have focused on selling the most commodity-like products, especially indexed products, with low fees. Differentiation strategies have been more varied, with firms setting themselves apart along at least three dimensions: fund performance, marketing efforts, and new-product development. In the late 1980s, no single dominant strategy appeared, at least when measured by growth in assets under management. In the following section, we examine the strategic decisions taken by complexes and funds and their impacts on the amount of assets under management.

Performance-based Differentiation Strategies

In the investment selection dimension, funds may attempt to differentiate themselves on the basis of their investment performance. Beginning with Michael Jensen,[10] academic studies of more than two decades have failed to demonstrate that fund managers can consistently earn superior risk-adjusted returns. Nevertheless, funds that realize exceptional historical

10. Michael Jensen, "The Performance of Mutual Funds in the Period 1945–1964," *Journal of Finance,* May 1968, pp. 389–416.

returns use this performance record in their marketing to try to differentiate themselves from their rivals.[11]

In other research, we examine the impact of historical performance
on fund growth by studying the returns and growth rates of 632 equity
mutual funds (partitioned by investment objective into funds with similar goals) from 1970 to 1990.[12] Specifically, we explore the effect of high
relative performance on the inflows of new money into the fund. Our
results are somewhat surprising. Briefly, we find that performance matters, but only for star performers. Top-performing mutual funds receive
net inflows of new money, yet funds that perform poorly do not lose
very many assets. This asymmetry between consumers' reactions to
very high performance and very low performance suggests a possible
"heads I win, tails I don't lose" strategy: manage funds for high dispersion in returns. Once a fund does well and captures assets, it does not
appear to lose them through subsequent poor performance.

At least in the equity sector, these findings suggest that fund complexes that strategically encourage higher-risk investment strategies
may be able to grow faster than complexes encouraging more conservative bets. Note that we do not advocate this strategy, nor do we suggest
it would work for nonequity funds. Furthermore, performance differences among funds explain only a modest portion of the growth rates of
equity mutual funds, leading us to consider how other strategic choices
affect funds' assets and profitability.

New-Product Differentiation Strategies

New-product introductions could enable a complex to benefit in two
ways. First, given the asymmetric response of consumers to high- and
low-performing funds, introducing many new funds with varying performance is the complex-level analog of a fund making higher-risk
investments. The high-performance fund will attract money, but the los-
ers will not necessarily be penalized. Second, by offering a wide variety
of funds, a complex can deliver greater investor liquidity services.

However, introducing new products is not costless. A complex
must incur the direct costs of lawyers and accountants plus its time and
expense to educate salespeople and consumers. In addition, new funds
may cannibalize existing complex accounts. Finally, brand extensions

---

11. Anecdotal evidence suggests that complexes do indeed follow this strategy. In a recent
    issue of *Money* magazine (May 1992), nearly 75% of the advertisements for equity
    mutual funds prominently displayed the historical performance of the fund for some
    time period, either in absolute terms or relative to a selected benchmark.
12. Erik R. Sirri and Peter Tufano, "Buying and Selling Mutual Funds: Flows, Performance,
    Fees and Services." Working paper, Harvard Business School, 1992.

may attenuate the value of the consumer franchise. One senior mutual-fund executive expressed his fear that a new fund that performed disastrously and received media attention could harm the sales of existing funds.

Nevertheless, the top 20 mutual-fund complexes introduced more than 500 new funds in the period from 1985 to 1990, although not all firms engaged in product innovation at the same pace. On average, independent load fund complexes introduced about half as many new products as no-load and captive-broker complexes, and the five largest complexes in 1985 introduced about twice as many funds per complex as did the next fifteen firms (see Figure 7-4).

In the aggregate, products introduced from 1985 to 1990 accounted for one-third of the dollar growth in total net assets (TNA) of the top 20 complexes from 1985 to 1990. The most prolific complexes that created the most new products grew faster on average, but we must be careful not to infer causality. One cannot distinguish whether faster growing fund complexes added products or whether complexes that added products grew more rapidly. However, there is a strong positive association between growth and a strategy of differentiation through new-product introductions.

We find no evidence from the past 10 years that new products dramatically cannibalize existing products. If new funds cannibalize older funds, then complexes introducing many new products should slow the growth of their older funds relative to the growth rate of complexes that introduce fewer new funds. Figure 7-5 fails to show this pattern. Older funds in complexes introducing more new products grow no more slowly than older funds in complexes offering fewer new products.

Distribution Method Differentiation Strategies

Load and no-load funds offer similar investment management, record-keeping, and investor liquidity services. Complexes in the higher-fee load sector typically differentiate their fund products from those offered in the no-load sector by bundling costly person-to-person selling and investment advice. As a result, the fees that funds charge consumers vary dramatically for relatively similar investment products sold through varied distribution channels. For example, among aggressive growth equity funds, no-load funds charged annual expenses averaging 1.32% of TNA (or assets under management) in 1990, but load funds charged annual expense ratios of 1.12% in addition to loads of 4.07%. *Ignoring discounting, a consumer would have to hold a load fund for more than 20 years for it to have the same total annual fees as the no-load.*

Figure 7–4
Number of new mutual funds introduced from 1985–1990 by the largest 20 mutual fund complexes. Complexes are ranked on the basis of total net assets in 1985.

New Funds Introduced	
Total	518
Maximum for one complex	85
Minimum for one complex	2
Average per complex	26
Median per complex	21

Mean number of new funds introduced in 1985–1990 by type of mutual fund complex.

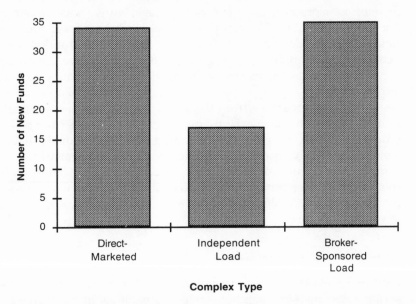

Complexes were grouped according to categories defined by Michael Goldstein and Lili Linton in "The Future of the Money Management Industry," Bernstein Research, 1992. Direct-marketing complexes sell funds directly to investors without a broker. They tend to sell no-load funds, although many funds in such a complex may carry loads. Examples include Fidelity and Vanguard. Independent load complexes rely on brokers to sell their mutual funds but are not themselves a unit of brokerage. Examples include Franklin and Kemper. Broker-sponsored load complexes are units of brokerage firms and tend to sell load funds through brokers. Examples include Merrill Lynch and Prudential-Bache.

Figure 7–4 (cont.)
Mean number of new fund introductions by complexes of different size. Complexes are ranked on the basis of total net assets in 1985.

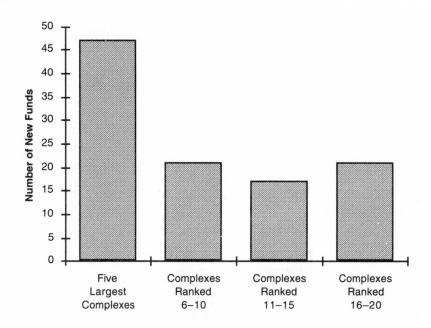

Source: Authors' estimates.

This difference in fees may explain why the no-load sector grew from 5.7% of mutual fund assets in 1960 to 28.6% in 1990. Although a large number of mutual fund buyers are willing to forego costly direct marketing for lower fees, many consumers still appear to value the services provided by load funds. These services include marketing that reduces consumer need to search for funds, advice that simplifies buying decisions, and possibly nonmutual fund services also offered by brokers and financial planners.[13]

13. Consumer preference for these services is evident in the ICI survey of mutual fund buyers, summarized in its 1990 *Mutual Fund Fact Book*. For instance, "personal-guidance-oriented consumers" account for 13% of those surveyed, and they seek "personal contact in making investments." In contrast, "fee-sensitive independent consumers" account for 11% of those surveyed and presumably are the predominant purchasers of no-load funds.

Figure 7–5

Source of growth for the 20 largest fund complexes, 1985–1990. The growth in total net assets is decomposed into two categories: growth due to products introduced prior to 1985, and growth due to funds offered first in 1985–1990.

Category	(in $ billions)	Share
Total	381.3	100%
Due to funds introduced prior to 1985	252.3	66%
Due to funds introduced subsequent to 1985	129.0	34%

Growth in "old" funds as a function of new-product introductions. This chart shows the mean growth in total net assets from 1985 to 1990 of funds introduced prior to 1985, broken down by the number of new products introduced by the complex in the period 1985–1990. Growth rate of all funds is shown for comparison.

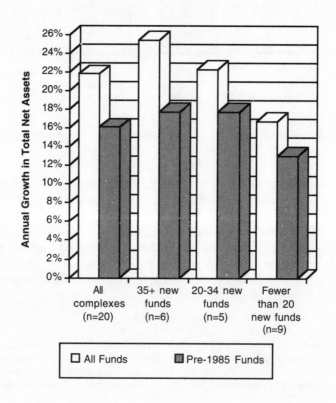

Source: Authors' estimates.

Complexes employing these different distribution strategies—funds bundled with and without direct marketing—coexist and have thrived in the mutual fund industry. Of the five complexes that gained the greatest share of the mutual fund industry from 1985 to 1990, three employed direct distribution and two were distributed primarily by brokers. Overall during the five-year period, complexes using these two distribution methods grew at roughly equal rates. Thus no one distribution strategy has proved dominant.

Low-Fee Strategies

Even *within* the load and no-load sectors, complexes charge different fees for comparable funds. If funds can convince consumers that they offer highly differentiated products, then consumers may tolerate paying higher prices. If not, firms charging lower fees should dominate and grow faster than funds charging higher fees.

A firm selling an otherwise equal but lower-fee product must enjoy a cost advantage that may stem from economies in any or all of the value chain activities as shown in Figure 7-6. Mutual funds may achieve economies of scale in record keeping/reporting and marketing/distribution, and economies of scope in marketing/distribution and liquidity services. Below a relatively small, minimally efficient scale, funds may also enjoy economies in investment selection.[14] Both our own study of fund growth and the research of others support the notion that complexes can achieve scale and scope economies, and that fees charged are statistically related to proxies that measure these economies.[15]

If some complexes enjoy economies and pass their savings on to consumers in the form of lower fees, low-price strategies should be successful. One might expect to find that *after holding constant* fund type, distribution method, and variables measuring services provided, lower-fee funds should gain share at the expense of higher-fee funds. Our work on 632 equity mutual funds from 1979 to 1990 supports this hypothesis. Mutual fund consumers are slightly cost sensitive. In our work on equity mutual funds, we find that funds charging fees 10% higher than the mean fee (or approximately 15 basis points higher),

14. André Perold and Robert Salomon, "The Right Amount of Assets Under Management," *Financial Analysts Journal*, May/June 1991.
15. J. Dermine and L. Röller, "Economies of Scale and Scope in the French Mutual Funds (SICAV) Industry," *Journal of Financial Intermediation*, vol. 2 (1992), pp. 83–93, documented scale and scope economies in the mutual fund industry. Our unpublished work provides additional evidence supporting the existence of scale and scope economies at the account, fund, and fund complex level.

Figure 7-6
Strategies for Mutual Fund Rivals

This figure identifies the value chain elements, and for each, how low cost or differentiation strategies could be implemented.

Value Chain Element	Cost-Based Strategies	Differentiation-Based Strategies
Investment Selection	Scale—assets under management over a narrow region (fund)	Superior performance (fund) Product choice—passive strategies (fund)
Trading and Execution	Economies at large-scale (complex)	Superior trading skills translating into higher performance
Customer Record Keeping and Reporting	Scale—number of accounts (complex)	Superior technology—quicker reports, fewer mistakes (complex)
Marketing and Distribution	Scale—national advertising economies (complex) Scope—spread costs over many funds (complex)	Superior marketing and advertising (complex)
Investor Liquidity Services	Scope—economies in new-product development (complex)	Wide selection of funds, exchange privileges, related financial services, check writing (complex)

experience a growth rate 1.2 percentage points lower than do funds charging the average fee.

Figure 7-7 shows a similar analysis for mutual fund complexes. We compare the gain or loss in market share from 1985 to 1990 among the top 20 complexes with the average fees they charged for equity products. A complex's market share and fees are compared with other complexes employing a similar distribution method. Complexes gaining market share in their sector appear above the horizontal line, and complexes with below-average fees appear to the left of the horizontal line.

Figure 7-7 shows that complexes that gained the greatest market share followed very different pricing strategies. Among directly dis-

Figure 7-7
*Change in market share and total fees charged relative to sector average from 1985–1990.
Sample includes 20 largest mutual fund complexes, on the basis of total
net assets in 1990.**

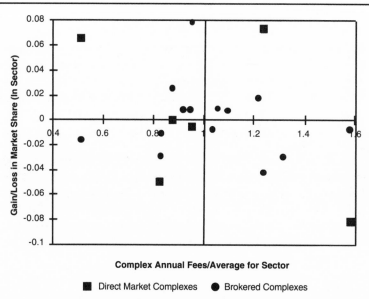

Complex Annual Fees/Average for Sector

■ Direct Market Complexes   ● Brokered Complexes

* The 20 largest mutual fund complexes in 1990 were separated by method of distribution
into two sectors: direct marketing or brokered. See Figure 7-4 for a fuller description of
the criteria used to separate complexes. Within each sector, the change in each complex's
market share from 1985 to 1990 was calculated and is shown along the vertical axis.
Along the horizontal axis is shown each complex's average total fees charged per dollar
of total net assets using equity fund fees as a benchmark. This measure is calculated by
adding the expense ratio to the load annualized over a seven-year holding period
(ignoring discounting) and dividing by the mean total fees for the appropriate sector.

tributed complexes, one top gainer charged fees nearly half of the average, whereas another charged fees 20% above the average for the
group. These two complexes, with very different pricing strategies,
gained roughly comparable share among the largest no-loads. In the
brokered sector, the complex with the greatest gain in market share
charged fees very close to the load fund average. Perhaps the results
are most remarkable for what we do *not* observe: there is no strong
downward-sloping mass of points. These results suggest that the
industry has been successful in communicating a message of differentiation to many consumers. It appears that firms have successfully convinced many consumers to pay for marketing, a major component of

costs for a fund complex.[16] However, the rapid growth of a large low-fee, no-load product suggests that at least some consumers are not convinced of this message.

Industry Implications of Complex-level Strategies

We may each act to advance our own self-interest, but our joint actions can leave everyone worse off. For example, on a hot summer day, we may all start off for the beach in our cars, looking forward to a refreshing swim. However, as any New Englander can attest, if everyone acts on this impulse at the same time, we all spend more time on the highway or searching for parking places than enjoying the beach, and we may wish we had stayed home.

This example reminds us that it is important to examine the collective impacts of individual actions. In the mutual fund industry, the competitive choices of low-cost and differentiation strategies must be studied in the aggregate. We examine the impact on the mutual fund industry structure of different strategies adopted by fund complexes: offering many new products, marketing extensively, and offering funds with low fees.

Consumer Confusion

As a group, mutual fund complexes have introduced more than 2,500 new funds during the past 15 years. When compared with the total number of securities listed on the New York and American Stock Exchanges and the NASDAQ, this sheer increase in the number of funds offered is staggering (see Table 7-1). At this rate, in a few years there would be more mutual funds than listed securities to choose from.

The potential mutual fund purchaser must not only cope with an exploding set of alternatives, but also track funds that change names, merge out of existence, or merely liquidate. For example, there were 1,882 long-term mutual funds in 1989, as reported by IBC/Donoghue. Of these, 102 changed names, 44 were merged out of existence, and 17 dissolved by year-end. Thus 163, or nearly 9%, of the old funds changed status during the year. In addition, 147 new long-term funds were added, or 7.5% of the total funds as of 1990.[17]

Although mutual fund complexes attempt to compete against one another by launching new products or repositioning old ones, in aggre-

---

16. This assertion is borne out in the no-load sector, where we find a positive relationship between advertising expenses and total fees charged.
17. IBC/Donoghue, *Mutual Fund Almanac 1991*. Long-term funds exclude money market mutual funds and short-term tax-exempt funds.

Table 7–1
*Number of mutual funds versus the number of publicly listed securities on the NYSE,
AMEX, and NASDAQ.*

	1975	1980	1985	1990
Number of mutual funds	423	564	1,528	3,108
Number of listed securities on NYSE, AMEX, and NASDAQ	5,957	6,251	8,022	8,053

Sources: ICI *Mutual Fund Fact Book, NYSE Fact Book; AMEX Fact Book; NASDAQ Fact
Book,* 1991.

gate they may be heightening consumer confusion. Reaching consumers, let alone communicating a message, is more difficult and costly in an increasingly crowded marketplace. Consistent with this conjecture, we observe large increases in marketing expenditures among no-load funds. In the second half of the 1980s, no-load TNA rose by 19% annually, and magazine advertising grew 30% per year.[18]

The advertising content of such no-load funds may also produce confusion. Earlier, we commented on a sample of equity fund advertisements taken from a recent issue of *Money* magazine. With nearly three-quarters emphasizing performance claims, the average consumer may find it difficult to understand how so many funds can claim to be top performers (albeit during different time periods and relative to different groups). If the various claims are difficult to interpret—and even more difficult to reconcile—then the advertising itself may merely confuse consumers.

Confusion, whatever its source, may make consumers seek advice or seek simpler products. Such a step would make the bundled marketing and advising services provided by brokers of load funds more valuable. Alternatively, it could force directly distributed funds to provide advice to consumers. We conjecture that, in the aggregate, extensive product development and advertising by no-load complexes that brings in new monies may have inadvertently caused at least some of the slowdown in the growth of this sector. Furthermore, heightened consumer confusion may increase the need for even costlier marketing. Lastly, the conflicting claims and product proliferation may have hastened the acceptance of index funds, whose investment strategy is easy to communicate.

Aggregate Price Competition and Economies

No-load complexes' increased marketing expenditures raise their costs and the fees they charge consumers. We find that fees charged

---

18. Leading National Advertisers, *Ad $ Summary* and *Class Brand Report,* 1980, 1985, 1990.

Figure 7-8
Total mean annual fees charged by equity mutual funds, 1970–1990. Total annual fees equal expense ratios plus the load amortized over seven years. These fees are weighted by fund assets under management in each year.

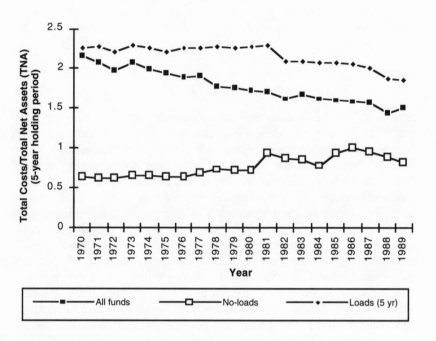

Source: Authors' estimates.

by no-load funds have risen markedly during the past 20 years[19] despite the aggressive efforts by some no-load mutual fund complexes to differentiate themselves by offering extremely low-fee products (see Figure 7-8).

Although fees on equity no-load funds have risen, as a group they remain lower priced than equity load funds, making it reasonable to assume that no-loads exert pressure on the load sector to reduce fees. Consistent with this conjecture, we find that total fees charged in the load sector have fallen in the past two decades, especially in the 1980s. Whereas loads charged by load funds have fallen, the expense ratios of load funds have risen. Using reasonable assumptions about how long consumers hold equity load funds, we estimate that total annualized fees

19. The analysis of fees in this section refers to fees for equity mutual funds with investment objectives including aggressive growth, growth and income, and long-term growth.

Figure 7-9

The growth of no-load equity mutual funds as a percentage of all equity mutual funds (asset weighted), and the difference in total costs between no-load and load equity mutual funds. Total fees are defined as the expense ratio plus the load amortized over seven years.

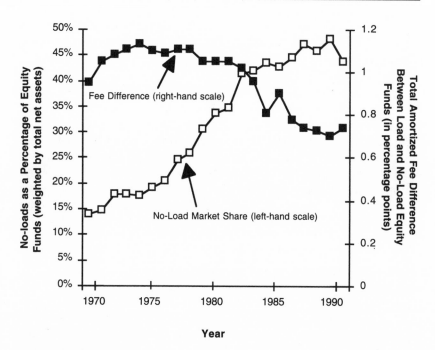

Year

Source: Authors' estimates.

per dollar invested—including annual expenses plus loads—appear to have fallen in the past two decades in the load sector.[20] (See Figure 7-8.)

Thus even though fees are rising in the no-load sector, they are falling in the load sector. Figure 7-9 shows that as the gap has narrowed and the relative benefit of no-load over load funds has been reduced, the no-load sectors' gains have moderated. If no-loads continue to market heavily and introduce many new products, the price differences between load and no-load funds will shrink even more, and no-load funds may find it more difficult to capture greater share from the load sector. As we have noted, rising consumer confusion may also moderate the growth of the no-load sector.

20. Ideally, to calculate the true annualized fees paid by load customers, we would need information on the length of their average holdings. In 1990, the ICI reported that for the three classes of equity funds we are studying, redemptions averaged 14% per annum, implying on average a seven-year holding period horizon in aggregate.

Given the changing mix of load and no-load funds and their different fees, competition has benefited the consumer; in aggregate, consumers of all equity mutual funds have enjoyed lower total fees over time
(see Figure 7-8). This conclusion is somewhat at odds with those recently
reported in the popular press that discuss only the rise in expense ratios,
without considering either the changing level of loads or the mix of load
and no-load funds. However, our calculations suggest that consumers of
equity funds as a group paid less for mutual fund services in 1990 than
they did in 1970.[21]

While competition may encourage complexes to reduce their fees,
falling costs permit them to sustain lower fees. In this regard, the growth
of large fund complexes that can reap benefits of cost economies may
permit the industry to continue to lower its fees. The industry is becoming more concentrated as the largest complexes capture an increasing
share of the market.[22] Not only have these large firms gained more retail
mutual fund business, but they also have been able to capture scale
economies in investment management and record keeping by selling
their services to 401(k) plans.

Summary: Competition in the Aggregate

Like the New Englanders sitting in traffic on a beautiful July weekend
when they had thought they would be enjoying the beach, mutual fund
complexes must consider the impacts of their collective actions. New-
product strategies may promise to differentiate a complex, but if rivals
follow similar strategies, no one will appear distinctive and consumers
may merely be confused. A no-load fund's high marketing strategy may
gain customer accounts, but if other complexes respond in kind, an

21. This conclusion must be qualified somewhat in that the equity fund product has actu-
    ally changed over time, because indexed products—with reportedly small investment
    management costs—were not offered in the early 1970s. Vanguard claims to have
    introduced in 1976 the first retail mutual fund that contractually aimed to track a broad
    market index. By 1990, we calculate that broad-based index funds (excluding gold-
    index funds, single-state index funds, and sectoral-index funds) accounted for approxi-
    mately 2.6% of the total net assets of the equity mutual fund sector. Given the relatively
    small size of broad-based indexed-equity products in the aggregate, this change in
    product mix cannot account for the fall in total fees.
22. In 1985, the top four complexes accounted for 17.5% of industry TNA; but by 1990, their
    share had risen to 25.5%. During the same period, the share of the top 12 complexes
    rose from 38% to 49% of TNA. This increase in concentration halted the downward
    slide in concentration throughout the 1970s and early 1980s. In this earlier period, mas-
    sive entry in the business apparently reduced the concentration of the largest com-
    plexes. For example, the top four complexes held more than one-third of industry
    assets in 1970 before falling to 17.5% in 1985. All of these concentration figures were cal-
    culated using aggregate data from the Investment Company Institute (ICI) and the
    Investment Company Data Institute (ICDI).

advertising war may leave all firms worse off. Finally, responses to price competition may leave the low-price firm with a smaller price advantage.

In the absence of cost economies, these forces drive prices down and costs of new-product development and marketing up. However, at the same time, economies may reduce costs so that the total impact on profit is not clear. Whether the profitability of the industry in the aggregate rises or falls will depend on the rate at which revenues fall relative to costs.[23]

The Future of Mutual Fund Competition

The previous sections discussed the current structure of the mutual fund industry and the nature of the competition between funds and fund complexes over the last two decades. In this section, we analyze possible threats and opportunities that vendors of mutual funds may face in the years ahead. If impenetrable walls separate the mutual fund industry from the rest of the financial services sector, or if boundaries clearly partition different niches within the industry, we would need to consider only rivalry among existing firms selling existing products. However, it is likely that the industry will find traditional boundaries increasingly blurred.

The load/no-load distinction has been compromised as no-load complexes offer funds with sales commissions and 12b-1 fees. Recent SEC proposals will allow other traditional boundaries to become much more porous. Funds historically classified themselves as either open end or closed end, but the SEC proposes approving a hybrid of the two: an interval fund. Interval funds would permit shareholder redemptions, much as an open-end fund would, except that the redemptions could take place only at specific times—for example, one day a month or even once a year. Between these redemption dates, the fund would effectively be closed, blurring the traditional open/closed distinction. Another SEC proposal would place mutual funds and hedge funds in greater competition. Traditionally, retail mutual funds have been somewhat distinct from hedge funds—which have greater flexibility in their investment charters—in that the latter could have no more than 99 investors and were exempt from SEC oversight. The SEC proposes that funds with unlimited numbers of "qualified investors" have latitude similar to that of hedge funds. Thus the SEC proposal would create a class of products

23. At least one analyst has predicted that margins in the money management industry will continue to fall over time due to forces similar to those discussed in this chapter. See Michael L. Goldstein and Lili Linton, "The Future of the Money Management Industry," Bernstein Research, March 1992.

falling somewhere between mass-marketed mutual funds and boutique investment management services.

As boundaries shift or are erased completely, merely focusing on yesterday's threats and opportunities will leave a firm at risk. Similarly, remaining fixated on one potential threat may leave a firm exposed to many others. Therefore the goal of this section is not to outline a single scenario for the future, but to point to some directions in which competition may develop. We liberally draw on our analyses of the activities funds perform and the functions they satisfy to identify the most likely competitive threats and opportunities to the existing competitive structure of the fund industry.

To organize this discussion, we will divide likely competitive developments into one of four categories, as shown in Table 7-2. First, we discuss existing rivals selling traditional fund products (box I). Here we focus on the ways in which competition among existing mutual fund vendors might unfold, briefly discussing competition involving new distribution channels, technology, pricing, and scale economies. Second, we recognize that mutual funds can be and are sold by organizations other than traditional fund rivals (box II); we discuss the competition from organizations such as banks or other service firms. Third, competition may change as current mutual fund vendors continue to expand their product lines beyond traditional mutual fund services (box III).

Table 7–2
Future Competitive Structure of the Mutual Fund Industry

Organization/Institution

		Existing Fund Rival	Other Rivals
Product	Traditional fund product	I	II
	Other products	III	IV

Finally, we recognize the competitive threats and opportunities arising from nontraditional mutual fund products, perhaps sold by nontraditional rivals (box IV). When reduced to the basic consumer needs or economic functions they satisfy, mutual funds, both now and in the future, will compete with a broad range of alternatives.

Rivalry among Existing Mutual Fund Complexes

New distribution channels.   The preceding discussion demonstrates the important role played by marketing and distribution. Distribution-based differentiation is likely to continue, if not intensify. For example, mutual fund complexes also have tapped into organizations such as the American Medical Association (AMA) and the American Association of Retired Persons (AARP) as conduits to reach consumers. These targeted distribution attempts offer lower costs of simply reaching potential buyers. Furthermore, funds may be able to appeal more to these targets by receiving informal certification by groups like AARP and by tailoring their products to the particular needs of the target niche. For instance, because of the age and risk profile of AARP members, fixed-income or high-yielding funds may be particularly attractive. Targeted distribution of this type is likely to continue.

In a similar fashion, funds are likely to continue to leverage existing group distribution returns by extending their employer-targeted marketing efforts beyond 401(k) tax-advantaged investing for retirement. Employers who provide 401(k) or 403(b) plans typically select a handful of funds in which tax-advantaged contributions can be made as part of a self-directed, defined-contribution retirement program. Apart from its tax advantages, this type of plan is attractive to consumers because its administrator narrows the choices from which the employee may select, thereby providing an informal certification function, not of the likelihood of favorable investment returns, but of the soundness of the complex's offerings and policies. For each successful marketing call, the 401(k) vendor receives the benefit of a large inflow of dollars from a large number of individuals. Provision of 401(k) services also allows the vendor to supply employees with non tax-advantaged investment vehicles. It can pass some of these same reductions in marketing costs along to the employees. The corporation could provide its employees with the same investment management advice available through a retail-marketed fund, but at a lower cost.[24]

These and other attempts to distribute similar investment management services simultaneously through varied distribution channels would be facilitated through a proposed investment-company organizational form called hub and spoke, which broadens the notion of a commingled fund.[25] Shares in a central or "hub" fund are purchased by a collection of other unique "spoke" funds, shares of which in turn are purchased by consumers. The advantage is that each spoke fund can be

---

24. We recognize that corporations might be unwilling to participate because of fears of *implied* liability if the employees lose money in a non-tax-advantaged savings plan in which the investment alternatives were in some sense screened by the corporation. Current SEC proposals, which would permit funds greater flexibility in charging different consumers different fees, might facilitate this type of marketing program.
25. See Christopher P. Harvey and Richard M. Tardiff, "Hub and Spoke: An Alternative to Multiple Class Distribution," *FACS of the Week*, April 20, 1992, pp. 6, 7, 12.

distributed, marketed, and priced differently because it is sold to a distinct consumer group. For instance, one spoke may be a no-load 401(k) plan, and another may be a load fund distributed through a bank. The manager of the hub may benefit by eliminating redundant overhead and administrative costs. Such a flexible structure would completely sever the link between investment management and the marketing/distribution activity, enabling complexes to capitalize on a variety of distribution opportunities.

Trading and execution.   Trading and execution are activities in which technology plays an important role. By investing in the latest information-gathering and data-processing technologies, a fund complex may engage in both a differentiation and a cost-reduction strategy. Funds can use technology to speed order processing, eliminate personnel from customer interactions, and streamline back-office operations. Furthermore, quantitative management styles frequently require investment in sophisticated computer hardware and software to run complex portfolio or security models. However, because of the long lead time for new activities derived from technology, funds may be uncertain as to whether they are investing enough for the future. The temptation to reduce technology spending in favor of boosting current profits is powerful, but in the long run may be costly. Undercapitalized fund complexes may be especially disadvantaged if the failure to invest places them at a cost or quality disadvantage.

Pricing.   The industry's current experimentation with "A" and "B" funds, otherwise identical funds with different fee structures (no-load and high annual fees versus load and low annual fees), along with the SEC proposal to allow different fees to be charged to different customers, may ultimately lead to other innovative pricing plans. For instance, funds could unbundle their services and charge consumers for the services they value most highly. This pricing practice is common in the software industry. Whereas virtually all software companies offer technical assistance, some provide it completely free of charge, others charge users for the telephone call, and still others permit users to buy service contracts. In the same fashion, mutual funds could charge consumers for exactly those services they demand and receive.

Even if regulation forced funds to charge consumers the same fees, funds could effectively set differential prices by providing consumers with customized bundles of services. As an analogy, institutional investors that trade through certain brokers earn soft-dollar credits that can be used to purchase research and trading hardware from third-party vendors. In a similar fashion, a fund complex could allow customers to earn credits that could be spent on services such as independent financial planning, data services, or tax preparation, offered either within or outside the fund complex. By effectively charging different prices for different quantities of mutual fund services purchased, the rebate structure would allow funds to set prices closer to value perceived by the consumer.

Scale economies.   Record keeping and distribution are activities for which complex-level scale economies exist, placing smaller complexes at a disadvantage. However, the unbundling of activities permits smaller complexes to gain some economies of scale at a cost. Historically, small load complexes have unbundled distribution activities by engaging brokers to sell their products, but they must pay dearly for this customer access. In a similar fashion, smaller fund complexes providing mainly investment advice have joined forces with independent turnkey 401(k) service providers that deliver record-keeping services. Even if smaller complexes can tap into larger firms' distribution and record-keeping skills *at cost*, this development would not ensure parity, let alone success. Especially in a crowded market, a low structure cost and lower fees do not guarantee success. Smaller complexes are more and more likely to be overpowered by the increasingly expensive marketing of large complexes with established brand franchises.

Entry by Mutual Funds into Other Businesses

The most notable recent example of the entry of mutual funds into another line of business is the 401(k) market. This class of defined-contribution plans is the perfect client from the viewpoint of the fund's management. The owner base is steady and does not withdraw funds. The marketing and distribution effort is centralized and emphasizes a single employer rather than many employees. Moreover, retail products do not need to be retailored to fit this class of user. In fact, some of the funds most in demand are brand-name products that can be bought outside of any 401(k) plan.

It is also a feature of this market that success in entering the business hinges on reliable and thorough shareholder reporting. The 401(k) system places requirements on record keeping above those for a normal fund product. If these functions are not handled seamlessly, the fund sponsor will suffer the cost of pacifying thousands of irate employees who receive erroneous periodic statements. Yet the defined-contribution nature of the plan means that employees bear the risks of performance, so that at the margin there may be incentives for sponsors to select a 401(k) vendor with better reporting than investment skills. This in turn intensifies the competition on the record-keeping activity in the value chain and makes this aspect of differentiation important for success in this growing market.

Mutual funds do more than repackage investment advice; they also sell nonfund financial products to their existing retail customers. Examples include large fund complexes that offer check-writing services (through money market mutual funds), credit cards, brokerage services, and insurance. Such strategies explicitly recognize that a complex's distinctive competence may be its brand- name and customer base, not necessarily its investment management skills. Brokerage firms, which distribute a variety of independently managed load funds as well as captive mutual fund offerings, have always offered a wide variety of financial products to their customers. In fact, their entry into the captive-fund management business did not come until the 1970s, when they recognized the growing importance of mutual funds as a vehicle for the small investor. Until that time, the wire houses distributed only other independent firms' offerings.

As we look forward, the interesting questions continue to center on the viability of some version of the financial supermarket. While some past attempts to create one-stop shopping for financial services have been unsuccessful, the distinctive trend seems to be for firms to offer more, rather than fewer, services. As that trend continues, the question becomes this: From what basic product or basic clientele is extension into other product areas more feasible? As vendors offer more financial products, we must define much more precisely what "product" a mutual fund or retail financial services vendor sells.

Merton and Bodie's perspective suggests that investors demand intertemporal wealth shifting, diversification, and hedging attributes in their investments. Interestingly, mutual funds are particularly good at the first and second functions and noticeably lacking in the third. While the needs of an investor change predictably over time as he or she progresses through the life cycle, mutual funds as *final products* do little to help investors meet their hedging or life cycle needs. Rather, mutual funds provide consumers with the raw materials they can use to fashion investments that satisfy these hedging or life cycle needs.

This customizing function has been satisfied by financial planners or by full-service brokers who offer investment advice in exchange for a fee. Yet mutual funds could more aggressively serve these consumer needs for customizing. One recent attempt at giving customized advice was introduced by Fidelity Investments.[26] Consumers fill out a short questionnaire that they submit to Fidelity; then they receive a recommended portfolio that can be constructed from Fidelity products. The

26. Jonathan Clements, "Fidelity Investments Plans to Move Into Advice-Giving," *The Wall Street Journal*, December 9, 1992, p. C1.

existence of the program is both a response to consumer confusion and an attempt by a no-load fund complex to encroach on the province of broker-distributed funds. This latter class of funds often bundles the investment advisory function with the mutual fund through the selling efforts of the agent or broker.

Fund complexes also have the basic building blocks with which to develop products to satisfy investors' life cycle needs. As an example, consider a young couple currently renting an apartment. Likely to be saving money toward the purchase of their own house, they are particularly exposed to changes in housing prices and financing costs. Mutual fund complexes or other financial services vendors could easily tailor an investment vehicle designed to hedge such a risk. The product may consist of traded securities, derivatives written on an underlying housing index, or both. It could be offered on an agency or a principal basis (with a regulatory change), according to the fund's ability to sell off or hedge the resulting net position. Such a fund offering would solve a particular investment problem many consumers face in their lifetime. If the product can be offered at lower cost than investment advice, it will dominate and allow the fund complex to gain market share at the expense of investment advisers. In such a case, a financial product supplants a service in the marketplace, where both are capable of fulfilling the same function for investors.

Near-Term Threats from New Rivals

Even if mutual fund complexes stay within the narrow bounds of producing and marketing what we call mutual funds, they are likely to face increasing competition from other firms. Because marketing and distribution constitute not only a major cost but also a key method of differentiation, successful new mutual fund entrants are likely to be firms with broad consumer franchises that can merely purchase investment management skills.

Although the most obvious candidates are financial services firms such as banks and insurance companies, it would be myopic to limit a scan of potential entrants to existing financial services vendors. Perhaps the best analogy is the credit-card business. Banks were the traditional vendors of credit cards, building on their other consumer credit activities. However, today's fastest-growing cards are Discover, sold by a subsidiary of Sears, and the AT&T Universal Card. Sears and AT&T used their distribution power aggressively to succeed in the credit card business.

The potential rivals most frequently mentioned are commercial banks. Banks maintain ties to consumers through both their lending and deposit activities and, in the wake of declining profitability, are aggressively seeking to enter new businesses. It would be imprudent to dismiss the will and capacity of banks—such as Citicorp, with its consumer banking and brokerage business—to enter the mutual fund business, whether as a distributor of its own or others' funds.[27]

Even though banks seek greater fee income, doubts remain about their effectiveness in entering the mutual fund business. Their relatively high-cost structures could confer a significant disadvantage in price-sensitive segments of the mutual fund business. Furthermore, it remains to be tested whether most banks and their staffs can sell noninsured, nondeposit products as well as they are able to sell commodity-like insured bank deposits. Finally, we speculate that although banks have long customer lists, the most valuable of these customers are already served by mutual funds or brokers who offer mutual funds. If so, the banks' only competitive distribution advantage may be in reaching smaller, less-profitable mutual fund accounts.

If not traditional financial services providers, who might enter this industry? Firms that quickly come to mind are those with strong consumer franchises and distribution networks such as AT&T and Sears. Still other rivals may be drawn from industrial firms, where pension fund managers may seek to parlay their investment-manager-picking skills into profits. It seems unlikely that these skills alone—absent strong distribution and record-keeping skills—will permit them to succeed broadly in the mutual fund business.

Threats from Substitutes

The mutual fund industry may encounter increasing competition from substitute products—that is, products that provide many of the same economic functions as mutual funds but are not narrowly mutual funds. The institutions that deliver such products may be existing fund rivals or firms that seem quite distant and nonthreatening at present.

Consider imminent threats to sellers of indexed mutual funds products. As a group these passive funds, the returns of which are designed to track the performance of a broad index, all provide roughly equal security selection services to consumers. Because of their commodity nature and the ease with which performance can be measured, price competition is likely to be intense, and the lowest-cost providers of this service will prevail.

In the very near future, mutual funds may compete with exchanges offering indexed products. Consider the recent proposal by the American Stock Exchange to list S&P 500 Depository Receipts, or SPIDERS. These

---

27. Goldstein and Linton (p. 49) report that currently 87% of the banks with more $1 billion in assets sell mutual funds.

securities will represent an interest in a trust holding shares of stock in the S&P 500 Index and will provide investors with returns of that portfolio. SPIDERS are expected to compete directly against mutual fund index funds, and, according to some observers, their low fee structure may enable them to capture share against all but the lowest-fee index funds.[28]

In a similar fashion, mutual funds have recently succeeded in marketing sector funds that invest exclusively in defined classes of firms (e.g., biotechnology and high technology). Recent exchange-traded securities (bearing service marks like TIPS, STEPS, and STAIRS) also allow consumers to make bets on specific sectors of the economy.[29] Although no one of this menagerie of branded products poses a current threat to the mutual fund industry, as a class they provide consumers with an alternative to sector funds.

Mass-produced, exchange-listed products may chip away at the passive end of the mutual fund industry, but the more actively managed funds may face competition from another set of rivals. As noted at the beginning of this section, the SEC proposes to let funds with any number of "qualified" buyers have wide latitude in their investment decisions, thus allowing sellers of hedge funds to broaden their clienteles and market more aggressively against retail mutual funds. We note also that plans to create an active market in traditional partnerships, including investment partnerships, may make this traditionally illiquid investment much more attractive to potential mutual fund buyers who also demand liquidity services.[30]

Perhaps the most interesting long-run threats and opportunities may arise from a more fundamental redefinition of the mutual fund and the other investment vehicles with which it competes. The mutual fund industry self-categorizes its offerings crudely by the type of securities a fund holds—aggressive growth equity funds, single-state municipal bond funds, money market funds, and so on—forcing consumers to determine which portfolio of investments will solve their *real* problems: saving for children's education, planning for retirement, or generating current cash flow to meet living expenses.[31]

28. See Robert Steiner, "New Amex 'Spiders' Mimic S&P Index," *The Wall Street Journal,* March 12, 1992, p. C1.
29. For example, see Tom Pratt, "Goldman on Bandwagon with Another Steps Clone," *Investment Dealers Digest,* March 23, 1992, p. 21. These products offer capped appreciation and, in essence, are covered call-writing strategies.
30. Karen Slater Damato, "Investors to Find It Easier to Sell Partnership Stakes," *The Wall Street Journal,* December 2, 1992, p. C1.
31. Some have suggested that even as guides to what the fund invests in, these labels are uninformative or misleading. See Barbara Donnelly, "What's in a Name? Some Mutual Funds Make It Difficult for Investors to Judge," *The Wall Street Journal,* May 5, 1992, p. C1.

Such consumer needs have not fundamentally changed over time. However, the mutual fund industry—and the financial services sector more broadly—seems content to deliver an increasing number of new products, few of which address these needs *directly*. There are a few obvious exceptions. Insurers, having long recognized consumers' desires to hedge against death, illness, and disability, accordingly created contracts with payoffs contingent on these unfortunate events. One savings institution has patented a product that promises to deliver consumers a payoff indexed to college tuition costs, thus attempting to meet a common consumer requirement.[32] This product is structured as a certificate of deposit, but it could have been set up as a mutual fund.

As we have argued earlier, a mutual fund could offer consumers a limited set of investment vehicles, each targeted at a well-defined set of consumers with common investing needs determined by their age, family circumstances, and wealth—that is, by their life cycle. This small set of what could be called "cycle funds" would not be defined by what they held, but rather by what need they really satisfied. One might seek to deliver a return producing a constant standard of living over time. Another might be indexed to college costs. A third might be indexed to health care costs. Such products could be structured as mutual funds, CDs, insurance contracts, or other financial claims.

By drawing on its investing and marketing expertise, a financial institution might be able to appeal both to the timeless needs of consumers and to the current confusion faced by investors who need to sift among thousands of varied and increasingly complicated financial products. If successful, the organization selling these claims could capture market share from a variety of broadly competing investment alternatives, including mutual funds.

Conclusions

Over the past two decades, the open-end mutual fund industry has become an increasingly important component of the financial services sector. Consumers have entrusted the industry with more than a trillion dollars. Mutual funds have siphoned short-term funds away from bank and thrift deposits, and long-term funds have supplanted consumers' direct equity holdings. Within the industry, rivalry has been intense as firms struggle to differentiate themselves. As a result, today's consumer enjoys lower prices and more investment choices—but likely faces greater confusion. This confusion allows funds to divide and conquer

---

32. See Ellen Schultz, "CDs Pegged to College Costs Look Good to Parents, but Do They Make the Grade?," *The Wall Street Journal*, March 29, 1992, p. C1.

the market, conferring a comparative advantage to distribution methods that provide consumers with either credible advice or a prescreened yet comprehensive set of alternatives.

In pondering the industry's future prospects, we find it useful to look beyond the mutual fund to consider the activities a fund undertakes and the economic needs it satisfies. Activity-based analyses highlight how vendors can succeed by capitalizing on distribution strength and low costs arising from the scale of their businesses. Functional analyses of the industry lead us to consider the threat of substitutes in the form of non-mutual fund products.

Although predicting the future is a task best left to mystics and consultants, it seems likely that rivalry will continue to be intense, marketing and distribution will be critical, and natural economies will tend to favor larger competitors. The mutual fund industry will continue to attract new rivals—banks, insurance companies, exchanges, and possibly non-financial services sector distributors—that seek the growth and profitability that characterizes the industry. At the same time, mutual fund complexes will look beyond their traditional offerings and seek to capitalize on their distribution capability by offering insurance products, credit cards, check-writing services, and perhaps services that currently appear to be only distantly related.

The result is that the mutual fund industry may cease to exist *as an industry* and may simply become a class of products sold by different types of institutions or, more broadly, a set of economic needs satisfied through a variety of seemingly dissimilar alternatives. The lines between different financial services firms—and between different products— will become increasingly blurred. Ultimately, all of these firms seek the same goal: to capture consumers' dollars. To meet their need to pay bills, reduce risk, and save for retirement or for college, consumers are forced to choose from among thousands of different mutual funds, 401(k) investments, variable rate annuities, insurance products, certificates of deposit, stocks, bonds, limited partnerships, and exotic financial instruments. In this market it is no surprise that even sophisticated consumers have surrendered, letting professionals make and execute their investment choices.[33]

A marketer advising anyone who hopes to sell to these already overloaded consumers would tell them, "Listen to the customer." Merton and Bodie might phrase it differently, but they would convey a similar message. Whereas mutual fund firms think of themselves as

---

33. See Jay O. Light and André Perold, "The Institutionalization of Wealth: Changing Patterns of Investment Decision Making," in *Wall Street and Regulation,* edited by Samuel L. Hayes, III (Boston: Harvard Business School Press, 1987), pp. 97–126.

competing *against* one another, the most successful rivals will remember that they are competing *for* consumers. This suggests that both managers of financial services firms and academics studying these firms would be well advised to spend more time thinking not about exotic solutions but about fundamental consumer needs.

CHAPTER 8

MANAGEMENT OF RISK CAPITAL IN FINANCIAL FIRMS

Robert C. Merton and André F. Perold

Introduction

This chapter develops a concept of risk capital that can be applied to the financing, capital budgeting, and risk-management decisions of financial firms. The development focuses particularly on firms that act as principals in the ordinary course of business. Principal activity can be asset related, as in lending and block positioning; liability related, as in deposit taking and writing of guarantees (including insurance, letters of credit, and other contingent commitments); or both, as in issuing swaps and other derivatives to customers.

For the purposes of this chapter, principal financial firms have three important distinguishing features. First, their customers can be major liability holders—for example, policy holders, depositors, and swap counterparties. By definition, customers strictly prefer to have the pay-offs on their contracts as unaffected as possible by the fortunes of the issuing firm; hence they strongly prefer firms of high credit quality. Investors, in contrast, expect their returns to be affected by the profits and losses of the firm; hence they are less credit sensitive, provided that they are compensated appropriately for risk. This means that A-rated firms, for example, usually can raise the funds they need to operate, but are at a disadvantage competing with AAA-rated firms in businesses such as underwriting insurance or issuing swaps. The presence of credit-sensitive customers therefore greatly increases the importance of risk control of the overall balance sheet.[1]

---

1. For an elaboration on the difference between "customers" and "investors" of the financial services firm as a core concept, see Merton, 1992a, b; and Merton and Bodie, 1992.

A second distinguishing feature of principal firms is their opaqueness to customers and investors.[2] That is, the detailed asset holdings and business activities of a firm are not publicly disclosed (or else are disclosed only after a considerable time lag). Furthermore, principal financial firms typically have relatively liquid balance sheets that in the course of only weeks can and often do undergo a substantial change in size and risk.[3] Unlike manufacturing firms, principal financial firms can enter, exit, expand, or contract individual businesses quickly at relatively low cost. These are changes that customers and investors cannot easily monitor. Moreover, financial businesses—even nonprincipal businesses such as mutual fund management—are susceptible to potentially enormous event risk in areas not easily predictable or understood by outsiders.[4] All of this implies that principal firms will generally experience high agency and information costs in raising equity capital and in executing various types of customer transactions.[5] We will refer to these "dissipative" or "deadweight" costs collectively as *economic costs of risk capital,* in a manner to be made more precise. Risk management by the firm is an important element in controlling these costs.

A third distinguishing feature of principal financial firms is that they operate in competitive financial markets. Thus their profitability is highly sensitive to their cost of capital, especially to their cost of risk capital. Expensive risk capital is a problem for organizations that operate in a more or less decentralized fashion if they try to allocate these costs to individual businesses or projects. As we shall discuss, there is no simple way to do so. Moreover, any allocation must necessarily be imputed, if only because principal transactions often require little or no up-front expenditure of cash but are nevertheless risky. For example, an underwriting commitment can be executed with no immediate cash expenditure, but the customer counterparty will not enter into the agreement if it does not believe that the underwriting commitment will be met. The commitment made by the underwriting business is backed by the entire firm. Therefore, the strength of this guarantee is measured by the overall

2. Ross, 1989, develops the notion of "opaqueness" of financial institutions. See Merton, 1992b, for further discussion.

3. As reported in *The Wall Street Journal,* October 24, 1991, the investment bank of Salomon Brothers reduced its total assets or "footings" by $50 billion in a period of approximately 40 days.

4. For example, consider the potentially large exposures from the so-called scandals at E.F. Hutton (check writing), Merrill Lynch (ticket in drawer), Salomon Brothers (Treasury auction), Drexel Burnham Lambert (FIRREA/collapse of high-yield debt market), and T. Rowe Price Associates (money market fund credit loss).

5. For detailed development and review of the literature on asymmetric information and agency theory in a financial market context, see Barnea, Haugen, and Senbet, 1985; Jensen, 1986; and especially Strong and Walker, 1987.

credit standing of the firm. In effect the problem of capital allocation within the firm is the problem of charging correctly for the guarantees provided by the firm to its constituent businesses.

These distinctive features of principal financial firms—credit-sensitivity of customers, high costs of risk capital that result from being opaque, and high sensitivity of profitability to the cost of risk capital—are important to include explicitly in analyzing the financing, capital budgeting, and risk-management decisions within the principal financial firm. We now prepare for that analysis by developing the concept of risk capital.

Risk capital is defined as *the smallest amount that can be invested to insure the value of the firm's net assets against a loss in value relative to a risk-free investment.* By net assets, we mean gross assets minus customer liabilities, valued as if these liabilities are default free. Customer liabilities can be simple fixed liabilities such as guaranteed insurance contracts (GICs) or complex contingent liabilities such as property and casualty insurance policies. With fixed customer liabilities, the riskiness of net assets (as measured, for example, by the standard deviation of their change in value) is the same as the riskiness of gross assets. However, with contingent customer liabilities, the riskiness of net assets depends not only on the riskiness of gross assets, but also on the riskiness of customer liabilities and the covariance between changes in the value of gross assets and changes in the value of customer liabilities. The volatility of the change in the value of net assets is the most important determinant of the amount of risk capital.

As defined, risk capital differs from other types of capital, such as *regulatory capital,* which attempts to measure risk capital according to a particular accounting standard, and *cash capital,* which represents the upfront cash required to execute a transaction. Cash capital is a component of *working capital,* which includes the financing of operating expenses such as salaries and rent. Cash capital can be large, as with the purchase of physical securities, or small, as with futures contracts and repurchase agreements; or even negative, as with the writing of insurance.

The organization of our chapter is as follows. In the next section we present a series of examples to show that the amount of risk capital depends only on the riskiness of net assets and is invariant to the form of financing of the net assets. These examples further establish how risk capital funds on the one hand are provided by the firm's shareholders (except in the case of extremely highly leveraged firms) and on the other hand are implicitly or explicitly used to purchase asset insurance. Potential issuers of asset insurance to the firm are third-party guarantors and the firm's stakeholders, including customers, debtholders, and shareholders. Following that, we discuss how standard methods of accounting can fail to account correctly for risk capital in the calculation of firm profitability and how this can lead to an overstatement of profitability. Thereafter we examine the economic costs of risk capital to the firm. We show that these costs are the spreads on the price of asset insurance induced by information costs (adverse selection and moral hazard) and agency costs. We then use this framework to establish the implications for hedging and risk-management decisions. Finally, for multibusiness firms, we discuss the problems that arise in trying to allocate a firm's risk capital among its individual businesses. We show that for a given configuration, the risk capital of a multibusiness firm is less than the aggregate risk capital of the businesses on a stand-alone basis. Therefore full allocation of risk capital across the individual businesses of the firm is generally not feasible, and attempts at full allocation can distort the true profitability of individual businesses significantly.

Risk Capital

To explain and further motivate our definition of risk capital, we now turn to a series of hypothetical but concrete examples. In the first set of examples there are no customer liabilities, and so gross assets equal net assets. After that, we consider two cases with customer liabilities, one with fixed liabilities and the other with contingent liabilities.

Consider the hypothetical newly formed firm of Merchant Bank, Inc., a wholly owned subsidiary of a large AAAA-rated[6] conglomerate. The firm currently has no assets. Merchant Bank's one and only deal this year will be a $100 million participation in a one-year bridge loan promising 20% interest ($120 million total payment at maturity). It does not plan to issue any customer liabilities. Merchant Bank's net assets will thus comprise this single bridge loan.

The bridge loan is a risky asset. We assume in particular that there are only three possible scenarios: a likely "anticipated" scenario in which the loan pays off in full the promised $120 million; an unlikely "disaster" scenario in which the borrower defaults but at maturity the lender recovers 50 cents on the dollar—that is, collects $60 million; and a rare "catastrophe" scenario in which the lender recovers nothing.

To invest in the bridge loan requires $100 million of cash capital. Because this asset is risky, the firm also needs risk capital.

Merchant Bank wants to finance the cash capital by means of a one-year note issued to an outside investor. The firm wants the note to be default free. If these terms can be arranged, then at the current riskless rate of 10%, $110 million would be owed the noteholder at maturity.

6. By AAAA-rated, we mean a firm with default-free liabilities that without question will stay that way.

In general, a firm has two ways to eliminate the default risk of its debt liabilities. Both involve the purchase of insurance: the first is to eliminate risk indirectly through the purchase of insurance on its *assets;* the second and more direct method is to purchase insurance on its (debt) *liabilities*. (Combinations of these would also work.) As we shall see, the two are economically equivalent. The risk capital of the firm is equal to the smallest investment that can be made to obtain complete default-free financing of its net assets.

Risk Capital and Asset Guarantees

Suppose that Merchant Bank buys insurance on the bridge loan from a AAAA-rated bond insurer. Suppose further that for $5 million Merchant Bank can obtain insurance just sufficient to guarantee a return of $110 million on the bridge loan.[7] With this asset insurance in place, the value of Merchant Bank's assets at the end of the year will equal or exceed $110 million. The noteholders of Merchant Bank are thus assured to receive the full payment of their interest and principal. The note will be default free.

It follows from the definition of risk capital that the price of the loan insurance ($5 million) is precisely the amount of risk capital Merchant Bank requires if it holds the bridge loan. Merchant Bank would need to fund it with a $5 million cash equity investment from its parent. Once these transactions have been completed, Merchant Bank's accounting balance sheet will be as follows:

Accounting Balance Sheet A

Bridge loan	$100	Note (default free)	$100
Loan insurance			
(from insurance company)	5	Shareholder equity	5

If, at the end of the year, the bridge loan pays off as promised, Merchant Bank will be able to return a total of $10 million pre-tax to its parent ($20 million in interest income less $10 million in interest expense). If the bridge loan defaults, the asset insurance covers any shortfall up to $110 million, and Merchant Bank will just be able to meet its note obligations. There will be nothing to return to the parent. The risk capital used to purchase the insurance will have been just sufficient to protect the firm from any loss on the underlying asset (including financing expense of the cash capital). And of course, the risk capital itself will have been

---

7. That is, *full insurance*. The insurance would take the form of paying Merchant Bank the difference between the promised debt payments and actually received cash flows on the bridge loan.

lost. In this arrangement, the insurance company bears the risk of the asset; Merchant Bank's parent as shareholder bears the risk of loss of the risk capital itself.

The payoffs (cash flows) at maturity to the various stakeholders in Merchant Bank can be summarized in the following table:

Table A. Payoff Structure

Scenario	Bridge Loan	Loan Insurance	Bridge Loan + Insurance	Firm Stakeholders	
				Note	Shareholder
Anticipated	120	0	120	110	10
Disaster	60	50	110	110	0
Catastrophe	0	110	110	110	0

Note that in this example, Merchant Bank's accounting balance sheet corresponds to what we will call the firm's *risk-capital balance sheet:*

Risk-Capital Balance Sheet A

Bridge loan	$100	Note (default free)	$100
Loan insurance	5	Risk capital	5
(from insurance company)			

By inspection of the two balance sheets, "shareholder equity" is equal to the firm's risk capital, and the nonequity liabilities are default free. We shall see, however, that the accounting and risk-capital balance sheets are in general quite different.

Risk Capital and Liability Guarantees

A parent guarantee of the note is an alternative and perhaps the most common form of credit enhancement for the debt of a subsidiary such as Merchant Bank.[8] This way, the parent makes no cash equity investment

---

8. This insurance could take the form of the parent either paying the noteholder the $110 million promised payment in the event of default and then seizing Merchant Bank's assets, or paying the noteholder the difference between the promised payment and actual payments Merchant Bank is able to make. The parent guarantee avoids outside lenders becoming involved in any bankruptcy of the subsidiary and gives the parent some "choice"; but for our purposes here, we can abstract from such details of structure.

in Merchant Bank. At the outset, the firm's accounting balance sheet is as follows:

Accounting Balance Sheet B

Bridge loan	$100	Note (default free)	$100
		Shareholder equity	0

Here, Merchant Bank again obtains the necessary $100 million in cash capital through issuance of a default-free note. However, all asset risk is now borne by the parent. Thus the risk capital is merely taking the form of the parent guarantee of the note. This guarantee is an additional asset of the subsidiary which does not appear on its balance sheet. Suppose that the value of this guarantee is worth $G million. Then the parent's (off balance-sheet) equity investment in Merchant Bank is worth $G million, and Merchant Bank's balance sheet can be restated in terms of its risk-capital balance sheet as:[9]

Risk-Capital Balance Sheet B

Bridge loan	$100	Note (default free)	$100
Note guarantee (from parent)	G	Risk capital	G

As in the previous example, if the bridge loan pays off as promised, Merchant Bank will be able to return a total of $10 million pretax to its parent ($20 million in interest income less $10 million in interest expense). If the bridge loan defaults, so too will Merchant Bank on its note, and the noteholder will either collect any unpaid amount from the parent, or the parent will pay out the promised $110 million and receive the value of the bridge-loan asset seized; either way the economic effect is the same. Merchant Bank, of course, will have nothing to return to its parent, as equity holder. In this arrangement, the parent bears the risk of the asset as guarantor of its subsidiary's debt; the parent also bears the risk of loss of the risk capital as

---

9. See Merton, 1983, for a real-world application of this "extended" balance-sheet approach to capture the "hidden" asset and corresponding equity investment arising from parent guarantees of its subsidiary's debt. Bodie, 1990, uses a similar approach to analyze corporate pension assets and liabilities and the firm's guarantee of any shortfall on the pension plan.

shareholder of Merchant Bank. Table B summarizes in terms of pay-offs at maturity:

Table B. Payoff Structure

Scenario	Bridge Loan	Note sans Guarantee	Note Guarantee	Note + Guarantee	Shareholder
Anticipated	120	110	0	110	10
Disaster	60	60	50	110	0
Catastrophe	0	0	110	110	0

A comparison of Table A and Table B demonstrates the economic equivalence between liability insurance and asset insurance.[10] In both, the noteholder bears no risk, and the parent, solely in its capacity as shareholder of Merchant Bank, obtains the same cash flows: $10 million in the "anticipated" scenario and zero otherwise. Moreover, the note guarantee has the same cash flows as the bridge-loan insurance. The note guarantee therefore is also worth $G = \$5$ million. Thus risk capital is once again $5 million.[11]

Liabilities with Default Risk

We now turn to the more typical case in which our hypothetical firm, Merchant Bank, is willing to issue liabilities with some default risk. Suppose it issues the same 10% note (promising $110 million at maturity), but without any of the credit enhancements of the previous case. This now-risky note will sell at a discount $D to par (at a promised yield to maturity higher than 10%[12]), leaving Merchant Bank $D short of its need for $100 million cash capital. The shortfall in initial funding must be supplied in the form of a cash equity investment. Merchant Bank's beginning balance sheet is as follows:

Accounting Balance Sheet C

Bridge loan	$100	Note (risky)	$100−D
		Shareholder equity	D

10. This equivalence may not apply exactly if one takes account of the various bankruptcy costs and delays in payments which could occur, for example, if Merchant Bank sought Chapter 11 bankruptcy protection.
11. The assumption that economically equivalent cash flows have the same value is made only for expositional convenience in this part of the chapter. Later in the discussion of the management of risk capital, the assumption is relaxed to take account of differences in information and agency costs among alternative guarantors.
12. Since the coupon is 10%, the *promised* yield to maturity must exceed 10% if the bond price is below par.

Once again, if the bridge loan pays off as promised, Merchant Bank will be able to pay a total of $10 million pre-tax to its parent.[13] If the bridge loan defaults, so too will Merchant Bank default on its note, and the noteholder will be at risk for any shortfall on the bridge loan under $110 million. Merchant Bank will have nothing to return to its parent.

Merchant Bank's shareholder here receives the same payoffs as it did in the previous examples (see Table C). This economic equivalence implies that the firm's equity must be worth $D = \$5$ million initially. Correspondingly, the risky note will have an initial value of $95 million (with a *promised* yield to maturity of $15 on $95, or 15.8%).

To see where risk capital enters, consider the position of the debtholder. The debtholder can interpret its purchase of the risky note as equivalent to the following three-step transaction: (1) the purchase of default-free debt from Merchant Bank for $100 million; (2) the sale to Merchant Bank of debt insurance for $5 million; and (3) the netting of payments owed the debtholder on the default-free debt against payments owed the firm if the insurance is triggered. It is perhaps easiest to see this by observing the economic identity:[14]

$$\text{Risky note} + \text{note insurance} = \text{Default-free note}$$

so that

$$\text{Risky note} = \text{Default-free note} - \text{note insurance.}$$

As already shown, note insurance is economically equivalent to asset insurance (compare Tables A and B). Thus the debtholder can interpret its purchase of the risky note as equivalent to the purchase of default-free debt coupled with the *sale* to Merchant Bank of *asset* insurance (on the bridge loan) for $5 million. In other words:

$$\text{Risky note} = \text{Default-free note} - \text{asset insurance.}$$

This relation allows the restatement of accounting balance sheet C in its risk-capital form:

Risk-Capital Balance Sheet C

Bridge loan	$100	Note (default free)	$100
Asset insurance (from noteholder)	5	Risk capital	5

13. $20 million in interest income less $15 million in cash plus amortized interest expense plus $5 million return of capital.

14. See Merton, 1990, and Merton and Bodie, 1992, for a full development and applications of this identity.

The payoffs at maturity associated with this risk-capital balance sheet are shown in Table C.

Table C. Payoff Structure

Scenario	Bridge Loan	Asset Insurance	Default-free Note	Risky Note = Default-free Note – Asset Insurance	Shareholder
Anticipated	120	0	110	110	10
Disaster	60	50	110	60	0
Catastrophe	0	110	110	0	0

Each of the examples (A, B, C) has a different accounting balance sheet. Yet all have very similar risk-capital balance sheets. They have the same amount of risk capital—because the underlying asset requiring the risk capital is the same in all cases—and they differ only in which parties bear the risk of insuring the asset: the insurance company (example A), the parent (example B), or the noteholder (example C).

A More General Case

The concept of risk capital is now further expanded by analyzing a more general balance sheet. The goals here are to illustrate the case of fixed customer liabilities and the purchase of asset insurance from multiple sources.

Consider a firm with an investment portfolio of risky assets worth $2.5 billion.

The firm has customer liabilities outstanding in the form of one-year guaranteed investment contracts (GICs) promising 10% on their face value of $1 billion. Because the riskless rate is also 10%, the *default-free* value of these customer liabilities is $1 billion. The net assets—equal to assets minus the default-free value of customer liabilities—are thus worth $1.5 billion.

The riskiness of the portfolio is assumed to be such that the price of insurance to permit the portfolio to be financed risklessly for a year is $500 million. Since the customer liabilities are fixed, it follows that the price of insurance to permit the *net* assets to be financed risklessly for a year is also $500 million.[15] Therefore, $500 million is the required risk capital based on a one-year horizon.

15. By the end of the year, the *gross* assets will have experienced a loss relative to a risk-free investment if they fall below $2,750 million (110% of $2,500 million). The *net* assets will have experienced a loss relative to a risk-free investment if they fall below $1,650 million (110% of $1,500 million). Since year-end net assets always equal year-end gross assets minus $1,100 million, any shortfall in year-end *gross* assets is exactly equal to the shortfall in year-end *net* assets, and vice versa. Therefore the loss to the insurer of gross assets is identical to the loss to the insurer of net assets, and the prices of the two policies are the same.

The firm's investor financings are in two forms: one-year junior debt promising 10% on its face value of $1 billion, and shareholder equity. Thus the total promised payment on fixed liabilities at the end of the year is $2.2 billion, comprised of $1.1 billion of GICs and $1.1 billion of debt that is junior to the GICs.

Suppose that the firm has formally obtained *partial* insurance on its investment portfolio, arbitrarily chosen to cover the *first* $300 million of decline of value of portfolio value below $2.5 billion. The insurance is thus structured to guarantee the portfolio value at $2.5 billion at year-end, but is capped at a maximum payout of $300 million. The cap will be reached if the portfolio value falls below $2.2 billion ($2.5 – $0.3 billion) as shown in Figure 8-2A. Call this formally purchased insurance "third-party" insurance, and assume that its value is $200 million. The value of the policy appears as an additional asset on the firm's accounting balance sheet.

Figure 8-1 shows the payoffs on the various liabilities of the firm depending on the value of the investment portfolio at year-end. Because the portfolio is only partially protected from loss by the firm-owned insurance policy, the junior debt and the customer liabilities are both potentially at risk to receive less than their promised payments. As the senior liability, the GICs are most protected against a decline in the firm's asset values. As shown in Figure 8-1, customers holding the GICs are at risk only if the value of the firm's portfolio has fallen below $800 million at year-end, a decline in value of more than 68%. Accordingly, the GICs trade at only a small percentage discount to par. In our example we assume that the discount is 1% for a price of $990 million, with a promised yield to maturity of 11% ($110 on $990). The junior debt is considerably riskier: the holders are exposed to loss if the value of the firm's portfolio falls below $1,900 million by year-end, a decline of about 24% (Figure 8-1). This debt therefore will trade at a larger discount to par. In our example we assume that the discount is 10% for a price of $900 million, with a promised yield to maturity of 22.2% ($200 on $900). The value of the firm's equity is equal to $810 million, the difference between the value of total assets ($2,700) and the market value of customer- and investor-held liabilities ($990 + $900). The accounting balance sheet (valuing assets and liabilities at market) is thus as follows:

Accounting Balance Sheet D

Investment portfolio	$2,500	GICs (par $1,000)	$990
Third-party insurance	200	Debt (par $1,000)	900
(insurance company)		Equity	810
Total assets	2,700	Total liabilities	2,700

Figure 8–1
Payoffs to Firm Capital Providers

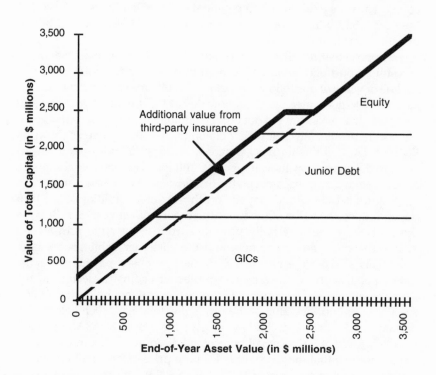

We now proceed to construct the risk-capital balance sheet for this firm. As in our earlier discussion of liabilities with default risk, the economic interpretation of the GIC holders is as if they have purchased default-free GICs and simultaneously *sold* some asset insurance to the firm, with the two transactions netted against each other. GIC holders are at risk only in the least likely of circumstances, and so they provide a kind of "catastrophe" insurance. As shown in Figures 8-2A and 8-2B, the catastrophe insurance pays off only if the portfolio value falls by more than 68%. The (implicit) price of this insurance is the discount from the default-free value of the GICs, or $10 million ($1,000 million – $990 million). Similarly, the debtholders' position is as if they purchased default-free debt and simultaneously sold the firm asset insurance with a value of $100 million ($1,000 million – $900 million). This insurance pays off if the firm's portfolio falls below $1,900 million, but the maximum payoff

Figure 8–2A
Components of Asset Insurance

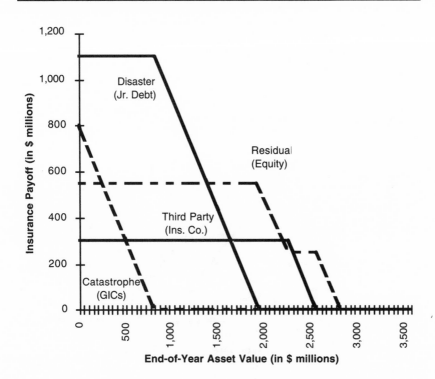

is capped at $1,100 million. The risk to the debtholders is greater than the risk to the GIC holders, but is still relatively small. It is a kind of "disaster" insurance. See Figures 8-2A and 8-2B.

So far we have accounted for total premiums of $310 million for asset insurance (third party + catastrophe + disaster). But we know that it takes $500 million in premiums to fully insure the portfolio. Hence the balance of the insurance, representing $190 million in premiums, must be provided by the equityholders. This insurance covers all the risks not covered by the other kinds of insurance. Therefore we call it "residual" insurance.

Figure 8-2B shows the combination of all sources of asset insurance. The total insurance has the same payoff structure as a put option on the portfolio with an exercise price equal to the current value of the portfolio ($2.5 billion) plus one year of interest at the riskless rate ($250 million),

Figure 8–2B
Components of Asset Insurance

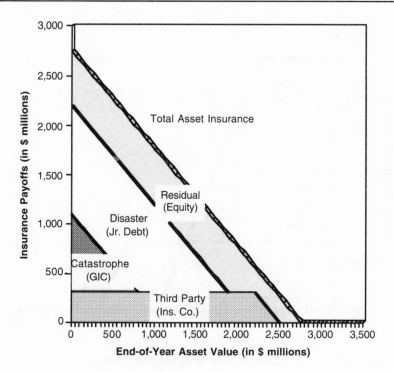

or $2.75 billion. The aggregate value of this asset insurance or put option ($500 million) equals the risk capital of the firm.[16]

16. An alternative interpretation of the coverage provided by the four sources of insurance is as follows: the equityholders fully insure the gross assets at a level of $2,750 million by year-end, but purchase reinsurance from the insurance company that insures the assets to a level of $2,500 million by year-end. The insurance company in turn purchases reinsurance from the debtholders that insures the gross assets to a level of $1,900 million by year-end. The debtholders then purchase reinsurance from the firm's GIC customers that insures the gross assets to a level of $1,100 by year-end. Equivalently, this can be expressed in terms of *put options:* the equityholders sell to the firm, for $500 million, a put option on the gross assets with exercise price $2,750 million. They in turn spend $310 million of the $500 million proceeds to buy a put option from the insurance company with exercise price $2,500 million. The insurance company then spends $110 million to buy a put option from the debtholders with exercise price $1,900 million. Finally, the debtholders spend $10 million to purchase a put option from the GIC customers with exercise price $1,100 million. The equityholders, insurance company, and debtholders have each sold a put option on the gross assets at one exercise price and purchased reinsurance in the form of a second put option at a lower exercise price. See Merton, 1977, 1992a, b, for the formal development of the correspondence between loan guarantees and put options.

The equityholders can think of their $810 million investment as serving three functions: providing $500 million of default-free cash-capital financing (bringing the total cash capital to $2.5 billion), providing $500 million of risk capital to pay for asset insurance, and selling to the firm a portion of that asset insurance worth $190 million. The equityholders' net cash contribution is $500 + $500 − $190 million, which equals $810 million.

The risk-capital balance sheet of the firm is as follows:

Risk-Capital Balance Sheet D

Asset portfolio	$2,500	Cash capital (default free)	
		Customers (GICs)	$1,000
Asset insurance		Debtholders	1,000
Equityholders	190	Equityholders	500
(residual insurance)		Total cash capital	2,500
Insurance Co.	200		
(third-party insurance)			
Debtholders	100		
(disaster insurance)			
Customers	10	Risk capital	500
(catastrophe insurance)		(equityholders)	
Total insurance	500		
Total assets	3,000	Total capital	3,000

This balance sheet encapsulates three basic functions of capital providers. First, *all provide cash capital*. Second, *all are sellers of asset insurance* to the firm, although in varying degrees. Customers and other senior providers of cash capital are typically sellers of catastrophe-type insurance—the kind that is called upon to pay in only the rarest of instances. This level of exposure is typical because customers prefer to have their contract payoffs insensitive to the fortunes of the issuing firm. Customers will buy contracts from the firm only if they perceive the risk of default on those contracts to be very low. "Mezzanine" debtholders and equityholders are investors who provide cash capital and sell to the firm almost all the insurance not purchased from third-party providers.

The third function is the provision of risk capital, which is the cash required for the purchase of asset insurance. It is almost always performed by equityholders, as in all our illustrations. (Nonequity liability-holders and other stakeholders in the firm will also be providers of risk capital if the market value of the underlying assets is less than the value of promised liabilities, capitalized at the riskless rate.)

A comparison of the risk-capital balance sheet with the accounting balance sheet thus illustrates that the debt and equity of the firm need not, and usually will not, equal the firm's cash capital and risk capital, respectively. Cash capital is determined by the assets of the firm. Risk capital is determined by the riskiness of the net assets of the firm. Debt and equity, defined in the institutional sense, represent the netting of asset insurance against the provision of riskless cash capital and risk capital.

Contingent Customer Liabilities

As we noted earlier, with contingent customer liabilities, the riskiness of net assets will in general differ from the riskiness of gross assets. The following example illustrates this difference.[17]

Consider again a principal financial firm with no equity, but with liabilities that are fully guaranteed by an AAAA parent. Suppose the firm issues a contingent liability in the form of a one-year S&P 500 index-linked note; in this example the note promises to pay $100 million times the total return per dollar on the S&P index over the year. The purchaser of the note is a customer—for instance, a pension fund—that wants the return on its $100 million portfolio to exactly match that of the S&P 500 stock index. The customer has chosen this method of investing as an alternative to investing in an S&P 500 index fund. At the instant the transaction is consummated, the firm's accounting balance sheet is as follows:

Accounting Balance Sheet E		
Cash	$100	Index-linked note	$100
		Shareholder equity	0

How the firm chooses to invest the $100 million will determine its risk capital. For instance, the firm might invest in one-year U.S. Treasury bills paying 10%. If it does so, the *gross* assets are riskless, but the *net* assets are extremely risky. In fact, the net assets are equivalent to a short position in the S&P 500.[18] By year-end, the parent as guarantor will have to make up a shortfall that is equal to the total return on $100 million worth of the S&P 500 minus $10 million, the return on U.S. Treasury bills, if this amount is positive. This shortfall payment is the same payoff as obtainable with a European call option on $100 million worth of the S&P 500 with a strike price of $110 million.[19,20] The risk capital of the

---

17. See Bodie, 1990, for an illustration of this point in the case of gross and net assets of a corporate pension plan.
18. Assuming the firm receives full use of the proceeds of the short sale.
19. The option must be protected from dividend payouts.
20. We saw previously that the purchase of insurance was economically equivalent to the purchase of a put option on the net assets. That is also the case here because a European call option on the S&P 500 is equivalent to a European put option on a *short* position in the S&P 500—that is, a put option on the net assets.

firm—the smallest amount that can be invested to insure the value of its net assets—is thus equal to the value of this call option.

As an alternative to U.S. Treasury bills, the firm might invest in the actual portfolio of stocks comprising the S&P 500. Assume it can do so costlessly. In this case, the *gross* assets are risky, but they exactly match the liabilities, so that the *net* assets are *riskless*. When the assets are invested this way, the firm's risk capital is zero.

As another alternative, the firm might invest in a customized portfolio of stocks that tracks fairly closely the S&P 500 but omits companies the firm believes will underperform the S&P 500 index. In this case, the riskiness of the net assets is determined by the potential deviations in performance between the customized portfolio and the index. The risk capital of the firm will equal the value of a guarantee that pays the amount by which the customized portfolio underperforms the index, if it does so at all.[21]

These examples illustrate how the riskiness of the net assets can be significantly less than or greater than the riskiness of the gross assets. The examples also show that it is the riskiness of *net* assets that determines the type of insurance required to permit default-free financing for the firm, and hence it is the riskiness of net assets that determines the amount of the firm's risk capital.

Accounting for Risk Capital in the Calculation of Profits

As we have discussed, risk capital is implicitly or explicitly used to purchase insurance on the net assets of the firm from a variety of potential providers. Insurance is a financial asset, and the gains or losses on this asset should be included along with the gains or losses on all other assets in the calculation of profitability. Standard methods of accounting often fail to do this, however. For example, as we discussed earlier, when a parent guarantees the performance of a subsidiary, the guarantee is not usually accounted for as an asset on the balance sheet of the subsidiary.

To illustrate, consider a securities underwriting subsidiary of a principal financial firm. The subsidiary anticipates deriving $50 million in revenues from underwriting spreads over the next year. It anticipates customary expenses of $30 million, so that its profit before tax is anticipated to be $20 million. This profit figure assumes no mishaps such as occurred, for example, in the underwriting of British Petroleum shares in

---

21. Thus the value of *perfect* stock-selection skills equals the value of the risk capital of the portfolio because *with such skills,* the portfolio *never* underperforms the index and its risk capital is thus reduced to zero. See Merton, 1981, for a theory that equates the value of market timing to the value of a portfolio guarantee.

1986.[22] The subsidiary has an ongoing net working-capital requirement of $10 million. It has no other formal assets or liabilities and so its equity capital is $10 million. Its pre-tax return on equity is anticipated to be 200% for the year. Therefore the subsidiary's accounting balance sheet and income statement are as follows:

Accounting Balance Sheet F

Net working capital	$10	Shareholder equity	$10

Accounting Income Statement F

Revenues (underwriting spreads)	$50
Customary expenses	(30)
Profit before tax	20
Pre-tax ROE	200%

However, this accounting analysis ignores risk capital, which here is the price of insurance (implicitly provided by the parent) needed to ensure that the subsidiary can perform its underwriting commitments. Suppose the insurance would cost $15 million in premiums. Then the risk capital balance sheet of the subsidiary would include the insurance as an asset, and total shareholder equity would be $25 million, consisting of $10 million of cash capital and $15 million of risk capital.

Risk-Capital Balance Sheet F

Net working capital	$10	Cash capital	$10
Underwriting guarantee	15	Risk capital	15
(from parent)		Shareholder equity	25

After the fact, if the underwriting business does indeed perform as anticipated, the parent guarantee will not have been needed. Thus the insurance that enabled the subsidiary to get the business in the first place will have expired worthless. Including the loss on this insurance in the income statement results in an anticipated net profit of $5 million, or

22. In October 1987, prior to the stock market crash, the British government arranged to sell its $12.2 billion stake in British Petroleum to the public. The underwriting firms agreed to pay $65 per share, a full month before the offering would come to market. The shares fell to $53 post crash. According to the *New York Times*, October 30, 1987, the four U.S. underwriters collectively stood to lose in excess of $500 million. A subsequent price guarantee from the Bank of England reduced these losses to an estimated $200 million after tax.

a pre-tax return of 20% on *economic* equity of $25 million, as shown in Table F:

Table F. Anticipated Net Profit
Including Risk Capital

Revenues	$50
(underwriting spreads)	
Customary expenses	(30)
Underwriting insurance	(15)
Profit before tax	5
Pre-tax ROE	20%

Obviously, it makes a difference if the risk capital expended on insurance is omitted in the calculation of profits. In particular, omitting risk capital overstates profits when the underlying assets perform well (because the insurance expires worthless) and omitting risk capital understates profits when the underlying assets perform poorly (because the insurance becomes valuable).

The Economic Cost of Risk Capital

Accounting for risk capital in the calculation of actual after-the-fact profits is important for reporting and other purposes such as profit-related compensation. For the purposes of decision making before the fact, however, *expected* profits must be estimated. This requires estimation of the expected or economic cost of risk capital. Since risk capital is used to purchase insurance, and insurance is a financial asset, risk capital will not be costly in the economic sense if the insurance can be purchased at fair market value. For example, the purchase of $100 worth of IBM stock is not costly in this sense if it can be purchased for $100.

Usually, however, transacting is not costless. Typically, a spread is paid over fair market value. These spread costs are deadweight losses to the firm. In terms of traditional use of bid-ask spread, the bid price from the firm's perspective is the fair value and the ask price is the amount the firm must actually pay for the insurance. Thus the economic cost of risk capital to the firm is the spread it pays in the purchase of this insurance.

The reasons for such spreads in insurance contracts vary by type of risk coverage, but the largest component for the type discussed here usually relates to the insurer's need for protection against various forms of information risks and agency costs.[23]

23. See Borch, 1990, for a general discussion of these risks and costs in the context of insurance contracts.

- *Adverse selection* is the risk insurers face in not being able to distinguish good risks from bad risks. Unable to fully discriminate, they limit amounts of coverage and set prices based on an intermediate quality of risk, and try to do so to profit enough from the good risks to offset losses incurred in the underpricing of bad risks.
- *Moral hazard* is the risk insurers face if they are not able to monitor the actions of the insured. Once covered, those insured have an incentive to increase their asset risk.
- *Agency costs* are the dissipation of asset values through inefficiency or mismanagement. As residual claimants with few contractual controls over the actions of the firm, equityholders bear the brunt of these costs.

Because principal financial firms are typically opaque in their structure, insurers of such firms—capital providers included—are especially exposed to these information and agency risks. Spreads for providing asset insurance to these types of firms—and hence their economic cost of risk capital—will therefore be relatively higher than for more transparent institutions.

It is unlikely that the cost of risk capital will be independent of the form in which the insurance is purchased. The spreads on each form of insurance are determined differently. For example, in an all-equity firm, the required asset insurance is sold to the firm by its shareholders. The cost of risk capital so obtained will tend to reflect high agency costs (given the extensive leeway afforded to management by this structure), but little in the way of moral-hazard costs because there is no benefit to management or the firm's shareholders from increasing risk for its own sake. Debt financing, on the other hand, can impose a discipline on management that reduces agency costs. But then moral-hazard spreads can be high, especially in highly leveraged firms, if debtholders perceive an incentive for management to "roll the dice." The task for management is to weigh the spread costs of the different sources of asset insurance to find the most efficient way of spending the firm's risk capital.

Managing the firm most efficiently does not necessarily imply obtaining the lowest cost of risk capital. Consider the case of *signaling costs*. Firms faced with high spread charges can try to obtain lower spreads by making themselves more transparent, signaling that they are "good" firms. For example, "good" firms can report on a mark-to-market basis knowing that the cost of doing so would be prohibitive to "bad" firms (they would be seized by creditors and/or lose their customers). Transparency can have its costs, however. For example, increasing transparency could lead to greater disclosure of proprietary strategies or reductions in flexibility to take advantage of transiently available business opportunities. Thus the principal firm has to trade off between paying higher spread costs of risk capital for opaqueness and paying signaling costs and losing competitive advantages for transparency.

In calculating expected profitability for the overall firm, risk-capital costs are an expense item along with cash-capital costs. To illustrate, consider the last example (D) in which the firm required $2.5 billion of cash capital and $500 million of risk capital. Being riskless, the cost of cash capital is the AAAA rate (a little less than LIBOR) assumed to be 10% per annum. Suppose that the spread or economic cost of one-year risk capital is $30 million.[24] That is, the fair-value bid price of the insurance provided by risk capital is $470 million, and the ask price is $500 million. Thus the spread is 6% of the ask price. Then total capital costs for the firm will be:

Cash-capital costs:	$250 (10% of $2.5 billion)
Risk-capital costs:	30 (6% of $500 million)

The rate paid for cash capital is the same for all firms, 10%. Risk-capital costs could vary considerably among firms, and in very special cases could be as low as zero.[25]

We next apply our risk-capital concept to two important areas of firm management.

Hedging and Risk Management

The implications of our framework for hedging and risk-management decisions are straightforward. Exposures to broad market risk—such as stock market risk, interest rate risk, or foreign-exchange rate risk—usually can be hedged with derivatives such as futures, forwards, swaps, and options. By definition, hedging away these risk exposures reduces asset risk. Thus hedging market exposure reduces the required risk capital.

---

24. See Merton, 1992b, for an explicit model of these spread costs.

25. For example, an open-end mutual fund is highly transparent. Moreover, the liability holders are principally customers who can redeem shares daily. Enforced by the securities laws, the selection of assets matches the promised contingent payments on customer liabilities, as expressed in the fund's prospectus. Hence *net* assets are virtually riskless.

Firms that speculate on the direction of the market and therefore maintain a market exposure will require more risk capital. By purchasing put options on these market risks, the firm can maintain its desired exposures with the least amount of risk capital.

If there were no spread costs for risk capital, larger amounts of risky capital would impose no additional costs on the firm. In this case, firms may well be indifferent to hedging or not.[26] But if there are spread costs, and if these costs depend on the amount of risk capital, then a reduction in risk capital from hedging will lead to lower costs of risk capital if the hedges can be acquired at relatively small spreads.[27] That will usually be the case with hedging instruments for broad market risks where significant informational advantages among market participants are unlikely.[28]

Capital Allocation and Capital Budgeting

Financial firms frequently need to consider entering new businesses or exiting existing businesses. The cost of risk capital can be an important influence on these decisions. As always, the marginal benefit must be traded off against the marginal cost. But to evaluate the net marginal benefit of a decision is difficult, for in principle it requires a comparison of total firm values under the alternatives being considered. One simplifying assumption is that the economic cost of risk capital is not very sensitive to the decision in question. This might be reasonable, for example, if the decision does not lead to disclosures that materially change the degree of transparency or opaqueness of the firm. In this case, the incremental cost of risk capital is proportional to the incremental *amount* of risk capital, which must then be calculated.

A second instance in which it may be desirable to calculate the risk capital applicable to a particular business is, as we have already noted, for the calculation of actual after-the-fact profits to determine profit-related compensation. In either of these instances it can be tempting to try to allocate the risk capital of the firm to individual businesses in order to determine the amount of risk capital for each business. We now discuss a major problem that arises in such approaches to the allocation of risk capital.

If the risk capital for the firm were just the *sum* of the risk capital required for each of its businesses, then the incremental risk capital

---

26. Except if it changes the transparency or opaqueness of the firm, as discussed previously.
27. Merton, 1992b, provides a model of spread costs that produces this result.
28. For example, see Gammill and Perold, 1989, for an explanation of the very narrow observed spreads on stock-index futures relative to the spreads on individual stocks.

could be determined on the basis of a stand-alone analysis of each business. However, there are diversification effects that can dramatically reduce the firm's risk capital. The importance of these effects depends on the correlations among the profits of the firm's various businesses.

We illustrate with a three-business example. Table 1 shows the current gross assets, customer liabilities, net assets (investor capital), and one-year risk-capital requirements of each business on a stand-alone basis. The businesses have the same amounts of gross assets, but different amounts of net assets because they have different amounts of customer liabilities. Business 1 requires substantial amounts of investor capital but relatively little stand-alone risk capital. Business 3 is the riskiest, requiring the most stand-alone risk capital. However, it has the least investor capital. Business 2 is fairly risky, and requires a moderate amount of investor capital.

Table 1
($ millions)

	Gross Assets	Customer Liabilities	Investor Capital	Stand-Alone Risk Capital[29]
Business 1	$1,000	$500	$500	$150
Business 2	1,000	600	400	200
Business 3	1,000	700	300	250
Total	$3,000	$1,800	$1,200	$600

Table 2 shows how the profits of the three businesses are correlated. At .5, Business 1 and Business 2 are fairly highly correlated. Business 3 is uncorrelated with Businesses 1 and 2.

Table 2
Correlation Among Businesses

	Business 1	Business 2
Business 2	.5	
Business 3	0	0

29. Risk capital in this example is computed using the loan guarantee model in Merton, 1977, which is based on the Black-Scholes option-pricing model. Risk capital for this model will be roughly proportional to the standard deviation of profits. See the Technical Appendix for the precise calculations. See Merton, 1992b, and Merton and Bodie, 1992, for an extensive bibliography of more general models for valuing loan guarantees.

Because the businesses are not perfectly correlated with one another, there will be a diversification benefit: the risk of the portfolio of businesses will be less than the sum of the stand-alone risks of the businesses. Risk capital—the value of insurance on the portfolio of assets—will therefore mirror this effect, and the risk capital for the total firm will be less than the sum of the (stand-alone) risk capital for each of the three businesses. Based on the posited correlations in Table 2, the risk capital of the firm evaluates to $394 million, a 34% reduction relative to the aggregate risk capital on a stand-alone basis.

The reduction in risk capital derives from the interaction among the risks of the individual businesses. Being less than perfectly correlated leaves room for one business to do well while another does poorly. In effect, the businesses in the portfolio coinsure one another, thus requiring less external asset insurance.

An important implication of this risk-reduction effect is that businesses that would be unprofitable on a stand-alone basis because of high risk-capital requirements might be profitable within a firm that has other businesses with offsetting risks. Thus the true profitability of individual businesses within the multibusiness firm will be distorted if calculated on the basis of stand-alone risk capital. A decision-making process based on this approach will forego profitable opportunities and "leave money on the table."

The alternative approach of allocating the risk capital of the combined firm across individual businesses also suffers from this problem. To show why, we examine the *marginal* risk capital required by a business. This can be done by calculating the risk capital required for the firm without this business and subtracting it from the risk capital required for the full portfolio of businesses. Doing so for the three businesses in our example produces the results in Table 3:

Table 3

Combination of Businesses	Required Risk Capital for Combination	Marginal Business	Marginal Risk Capital
1+2+3	$394		
2+3	320	1	$74
1+3	292	2	102
1+2	304	3	90
	Summation of marginals:		$266

The first line of Table 3 shows the required risk capital for the combination of all three businesses, taking into account the less-than-perfect correlations among the businesses. As already noted, this amounts to $394 million. The next three lines of Table 3 show the calculation of the marginal risk capital of each business. For example, in the second line we calculate the required risk capital for a firm composed only of Businesses 2 and 3, taking into account the zero correlation between these businesses. It amounts to $320 million. The difference between $320 million and the required risk capital for all three businesses is $74 million. This is the marginal risk capital for Business 1. It is the reduction in risk capital that a firm in Businesses 1, 2, and 3 would achieve by exiting Business 1; or it is the additional risk capital required for a firm in Businesses 2 and 3 to enter Business 1.

For the purposes of making the marginal decision, the cost of marginal risk capital should be used. As shown in the last line of Table 3, however, the summation of marginal risk capital, $266 million, is only two-thirds of the full risk capital of $394 million required for the firm. Thus if marginal risk capital is used for allocation among businesses, $128 million (32% of total risk capital) will not be allocated to any business.[30]

The discrepancy between the total risk capital of the firm and the sum of the marginal risk capital of its businesses will of course depend on the specifics of those businesses, but it can be very large. Using the aggregate of marginal risk capital, Figure 8-3 illustrates how much of the firm's total risk capital goes unallocated as a function of the number of businesses in the firm, and the correlation among their profits. The analysis assumes that all businesses are the same size (in terms of stand-alone risk capital) and are symmetrically correlated. As shown in Figure 8-3, the unallocated capital is larger at lower correlations. Only at the extreme of perfect correlation among the businesses is all of the capital allocated. In all other cases, at least some is not allocated. In the case of no correlation among the businesses, for example, the marginal risk capital of the individual businesses can account for as little as 50% of firm risk capital, so that as much as 50% can (and should) go unallocated.

These conclusions hold quite generally. Full allocation of the firm's risk capital overstates the marginal amount of risk capital. And the risk capital of a business evaluated on a stand-alone basis overstates the marginal risk capital by an even greater amount.[31]

---

30. "Grossing up" the marginal allocations (by 32% in the example) to fully allocate the firm's risk capital does not solve the problem. Instead, it overstates the benefits of reductions in risk capital from dropping businesses or not starting new ones.

31. See the Technical Appendix for a formal proof of these propositions. Merton, 1992b, provides another extensive example. The fact that risk capital cannot be allocated stems from the "externality" arising out of the less-than-perfect correlations among the profits of individual businesses and the asymmetric risk faced by providers of insurance: limited upside, and potentially large downside.

Figure 8–3
*Unallocated Risk Capital**

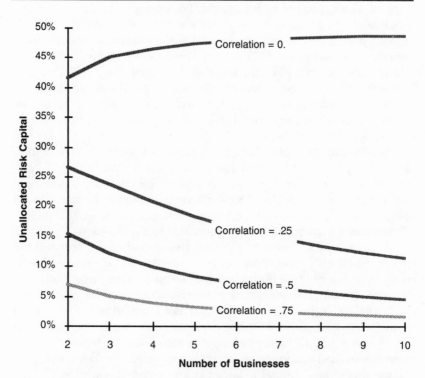

Number of Businesses

* Percentage of total firm risk capital not accounted for by the marginal risk
  capital of the individual businesses; calculations assume businesses are symmetrically correlated and have the same stand-alone risk capital.

Summary and Conclusions

Financial firms that act as principals in the ordinary course of business
do so in terms of asset- as well as liability-related activities. Liability-
related activities (e.g., deposit taking and issuing guarantees such as
insurance and letters of credit) are mostly customer driven, which
makes such businesses credit sensitive. Principal activities create a special set of financing, capital budgeting, and risk-management decisions
for the firm.

We have developed a framework for analyzing those decisions
within the principal financial firm. The framework is built around a concept of risk capital that is defined as the smallest amount that can be

invested to insure the *net* assets of the firm against loss in value relative to a risk-free investment. Using this definition of risk capital, the chapter develops a number of important conclusions:

The amount of risk capital is uniquely determined and depends only on the riskiness of the net assets. It is invariant to the form of financing of the net assets.

Risk-capital funds are provided by the firm's residual claimants, usually shareholders (except in the case of extremely highly leveraged firms). Implicitly or explicitly, this capital is used to purchase asset insurance. Potential issuers of asset insurance to the firm are third-party guarantors and the firm's stakeholders, including customers, debtholders, and shareholders.

The economic costs of risk capital to the firm are the spreads on the price of asset insurance induced by information costs (adverse selection and moral hazard) and agency costs.

For a given configuration, the risk capital of a multibusiness firm is less than the aggregate risk capital of the businesses on a stand-alone basis. Full allocation of risk capital across the individual businesses of the firm therefore is generally not feasible. Attempts at such a full allocation can significantly distort the true profitability of individual businesses.

Technical Appendix

Calculation of Risk Capital in Table 1 and Table 3

For a given business, let the value of gross assets at time t be denoted by A_t, and the default-free value of customer liabilities be denoted by L_t, for $0 \le t \le T$. Gross assets and customer liabilities may both have uncertain, contingent payoffs. The value of the net assets at time t is $A_t - L_t$. If the net assets were invested risklessly, they would amount to $(A_0 - L_0)\exp(rT)$ at time T, where r is the continuously compounded riskless rate of interest. The shortfall in net assets relative to a riskless return is thus $(A_0 - L_0)\exp(rT) - (A_T - L_T)$, so that insurance to permit default-free financing of the net assets must pay $\max\{(A_0 - L_0)\exp(rT) - (A_T - L_T), 0\}$ at time T. This is the same payoff structure as a European put option on the net assets with exercise price $(A_0 - L_0)\exp(rT)$. Under the assumption that the gross assets and customer liabilities both follow geometric Brownian motions, the value of this put option, and hence the amount of risk capital, is given by:

$$\text{Risk Capital} = A_0 F(1,1,0,T,\sigma),$$

where $F(S,E,r,T,\sigma)$ is the Black-Scholes (1973) formula for a European call option on a stock with initial value S, exercise price E, riskless rate r, expiration date T, and volatility σ.[32] Here, σ is the volatility of profits as measured by the volatility of percentage changes in the ratio of gross assets to customer liabilities A_t/L_t (or simply the percent volatility of gross assets if customer liabilities are fixed or are nonexistent). As shown by Taylor's expansion for $\sigma\sqrt{T}$ not too large, the formula for risk capital is closely approximated by:

$$\text{Risk Capital} \approx .4A_0\sigma\sqrt{T}.$$

The formula used here for the variance rate of profits for a combination of N businesses is given by $\Sigma\Sigma w_iw_j\rho_{ij}\sigma_i\sigma_j$, where ρ_{ij} is the correlation between the profits of businesses i and j, and w_i is the fraction of gross assets in business i. The formula is an approximation that applies exactly only if investments in the businesses are continuously rebalanced so that the volatilities of the profits of the individual businesses maintain their relative proportions over the interval 0 to T. For the purposes here, this approximation has no material effect.

In Table 1, the volatility of business profits was assumed to be 37.5%, 50%, and 62.5% per annum, respectively. Using the preceding variance formula, the volatility of the profits of the combination of three businesses evaluates to 32.8% per annum. This low percentage volatility of the three businesses combined stems directly from the diversification effect. The pairwise combinations show a similar effect.

Table AA shows that for the range of parameter values used here the approximation $.4A_0\sigma\sqrt{T}$ is very close to the exact Black-Scholes option value:

Table AA
($ millions)

	Gross Assets	Standard Deviation (σ)	Approximate Risk Capital ($.4A_0\sigma\sqrt{T}$)	"Exact" Risk Capital (Black-Scholes)
Business 1	$1,000	37.5%	$150	$148.7
Business 2	1,000	50.0%	200	197.4
Business 3	1,000	62.5%	250	245.3
1+2	2,000	38.0%	304	301.4
1+3	2,000	36.4%	292	288.8
2+3	2,000	40.0%	320	317.0
1+2+3	3,000	32.8%	394	390.8

32. See Fischer, 1978, Margrabe, 1978, and especially Stulz, 1982. $\sigma^2 = \sigma^2_A + \sigma^2_L - \sigma_A\sigma_L\rho_{AL}$, where σ_A is the volatility of gross asset returns, σ_L is the volatility of customer liability returns, and ρ_{AL} is the correlation between gross asset returns and customer returns.

The Relationship of Marginal Risk Capital to Combined and Stand-Alone Risk Capital

This section establishes the general propositions that (a) the sum of the risk capital of stand-alone businesses exceeds the risk capital of the businesses combined in one firm, and (b) the risk capital of a combination of businesses exceeds the sum of the marginal risk capital of each of those businesses.

As in the first part of this Appendix, let $X = (A_0 - L_0)\exp(rT) - (A_T - L_T)$ be the shortfall (or surplus if it is negative) in the net assets of a business at time T. Let there be N individual businesses, and let X_i be the shortfall for business i. From the preceding, insurance to permit default-free financing of the net assets of business i must pay $f(X_i) = \max\{X_i, 0\}$ at time T. Note that the function $f(.)$ is convex and satisfies $f(0) = 0$.

The sum of the insurance payoffs to the stand-alone businesses is $\sum f(X_i)$, and the insurance payoff to the combined businesses is $f(\sum X_i)$. Since $f(.)$ is convex, we can apply Jensen's inequality to obtain:

$$\sum f(X_i) \geq f(\sum X_i),$$

which establishes the first proposition.[33]

To establish the second proposition, we note that $f(\sum_{j \neq i} X_i)$ is the insurance payoff to the firm consisting of all businesses except i. Thus the marginal insurance payoff is

$$f(\sum X_i) - f(\sum_{j \neq i} X_j).$$

We now observe the identity

$$\sum X_i = \sum_i (\sum_{j \neq i} X_j) / (N-1).$$

Therefore, by Jensen's inequality,

$$f(\sum X_i) \leq \sum_i f((\sum_{j \neq i} X_j) / (N-1)).$$

Applying Jensen's inequality a second time and using the fact that $f(0) = 0$, we obtain

$$(N-1)f(\sum X_i) \leq \sum_i f(\sum_{j \neq i} X_j),$$

from which it follows that

$$Nf(\sum X_i) - \sum_i f(\sum_{j \neq i} X_j) \leq f(\sum X_i)$$

or

$$\sum_k \{f(\sum X_i) - f(\sum_{j \neq k} X_j)\} \leq f(\sum X_i).$$

---

33. This is the well-known proposition that a portfolio of options always returns at least as much as the corresponding option on a portfolio of underlying securities.

This proves that the sum of the marginal insurance payoffs is at most the insurance payoff to the combined firm. Therefore the risk capital of a combination of businesses exceeds the sum of the marginal risk capital of each of those businesses.

References

Barnea, A., R.A. Haugen, and L.W. Senbet, 1985. *Agency Problems and Financial Contracting.* Englewood Cliffs, N. J.: Prentice Hall.

Black, F., and M. Scholes, 1973. "The Pricing of Options and Corporate Liabilities," *Journal of Political Economy* 81 (May–June), pp. 637–654.

Bodie, Z., 1990. "The ABO, the PBO, and Pension Investment Policy," *Financial Analysts Journal* 46 (September/October), pp. 27–34.

Borch, K.H., 1990. *Economics of Insurance.* Amsterdam: North-Holland.

Fischer, S., 1978. "Call Option Pricing When the Exercise Price Is Uncertain, and the Valuation of Index Bonds," *Journal of Finance* 33 (March), pp. 169–176.

Gammill, J. F., and A. F. Perold, 1989. "The Changing Character of Stock Market Liquidity," *The Journal of Portfolio Management* 15 (Spring), pp. 13–18.

Jensen, M. C., 1986. "Agency Costs of Free Cash Flow, Corporate Finance, and Takeovers," *American Economic Review* 76 (May), pp. 323–329.

Margrabe, W., 1978. "The Value of an Option to Exchange One Asset for Another," *Journal of Finance* 33 (March), pp. 177–186.

Merton, R. C., 1977. "An Analytical Derivation of the Cost of Deposit Insurance and Loan Guarantees: An Application of Modern Option Pricing Theory," *Journal of Banking and Finance* 1(June), pp. 3–11.

—— 1981. "On Market Timing and Investment Performance Part I: An Equilibrium Theory of Value for Market Forecasts," *Journal of Business* 54 (July), pp. 363–406.

—— 1983. "Prepared Direct Testimony of Robert C. Merton on Behalf of ARCO Pipe Line Company." Federal Energy Regulatory Commission, Washington, D.C., Docket No. OR78-1-011 (Phase II), Exhibits II N-C-34-0-34-4 (November 28).

———— 1990. "The Financial System and Economic Performance," *Journal of Financial Services Research* 4 (December), pp. 263–300.

———— 1992a. *Continuous-Time Finance,* rev. ed. Oxford: Basil Blackwell.

———— 1992b. "Operation and Regulation in Financial Intermediation: A Functional Perspective." Working Paper # 93-020, Harvard Business School.

Merton, R. C., and Z. Bodie, 1992. "On the Management of Financial Guarantees," *Financial Management* 21 (Winter), pp. 87–109.

Ross, S. A., 1989. "Institutional Markets, Financial Marketing, and Financial Innovation," *Journal of Finance* 44 (July), pp. 541–556.

Strong, N., and M. Walker, 1987. *Information and Capital Markets.* Oxford: Basil Blackwell.

Stulz, R. M., 1982. "Options on the Minimum or the Maximum of Two Risky Assets: Analysis and Applications," *Journal of Financial Economics* 10 (July), pp. 161–185.

CHAPTER 9

SOME IMPLICATIONS AND CONCLUSIONS

Samuel L. Hayes, III

Twenty years ago the world of financial services was relatively uncomplicated, with a few distinct alternative products proffered by a limited group of competitors, both circumscribed by heavy regulation. As we approach the twenty-first century, a mind-boggling array of financial products and services are offered by a much wider set of vendors acting as intermediaries and principals. In the words of Professor Warren Law, the keynote speaker at the Harvard Business School colloquium where these chapters were first presented: "In the financial markets the age of innocence is behind us!"

In this new age of sophistication the relationships between financial services vendors, corporate "clients" (issuers) and institutional "customers" (investors), have been dramatically redrawn. Sophisticated institutional investors have displaced individuals as prime consumers of financial products, and their demands for liquidity have forced vendors to alter their own business practices dramatically. Adaptations include a radical recapitalization of the entire industry, the extension of operating hours and compression of commissions and other compensation, the creation and support of many new products and markets, acceleration in the process of bringing new products and conventional issues to market, and a huge increase in the scale of resources needed to compete effectively. Corporate clients, the issuers of securities and recipients of credit and other products, are also increasingly sophisticated and have exploited the shift in the industry's balance of power to receive more favorable prices and accelerated underwriting time frames.

Of course, the financial industry has not evolved in an economic and political vacuum. Economic fluctuations, particularly in interest, exchange, and inflation rates, have become the oxygen that financial players breathe. Innovation has turned volatility, the traditional scourge of the marketplace, into the most profitable friend that many financial firms have ever had. Interest-rate swaps, portfolio insurance, and other concoctions of financial alchemy have created fortunes for vendors on Wall Street and transformed the industry from a club of well-spoken gentlemen to a profession that includes crack mathematicians, statisticians, and technical experts. The impact of technology on the pace, complexity, and cohesion of the financial markets has been a revolutionary influence, and a sine qua non for much of the more evolutionary change. The political context that determines regulations and conventions has also influenced the strategies and fortunes of various financial sectors in substantial ways. And the increasing interdependencies among national markets, products, and players has made global sophistication indispensable.

Financial services vendors, the central focus of this book, are surrounded by the various constituencies and interest groups. Investors, capital raisers, and new competitors are all part of the story that has been addressed. Further, the chapters in this book have addressed important contemporary issues, including organizational structure and the management of a firm's capital position. Finally, there is the all-important influence of the regulatory skein that surrounds the entire industry.

Investors

There is much evidence in this book and elsewhere of the shift in power and influence toward professionally managed pools of capital in the United States and around the world. Certainly strong retail franchises were (and are) the raison d'etre of such vendors as Bank of America (Chapter 1) and the U.S. savings and loans sector (Chapter 2). Nevertheless, in the United States today, institutional investors clearly hold the purse strings of purchasing power and trading volume that have attracted the attention of financial intermediaries like moths to a bright light. The U.S. mutual fund phenomenon discussed by Sirri and Tufano in Chapter 7 is a reflection of perceptions and reactions to that accumulating power.

Individual investors view the contemporary financial marketplace with increasing trepidation. Many see a playing field tilted against them and are seeking the shelter of professionally managed portfolios. Indeed, by 1990 individual ownership of all outstanding publicly quoted U.S. equities fell below 50% to 46.7%—down from 77% in 1955—for the first time.[1] Once individual investors have been corralled

1. SEC Chairman Richard C. Breeden before a Senate subcommittee, *The American Banker*, October 15, 1992, p. 8.

into a specific mutual fund or mutual fund complex, Sirri and Tufano find that they tend to stay, giving that institutional player both long-term clout in the marketplace and a relatively stable annuity of management and other fees. The premium prices paid in recent changes of ownership in this money management sector serve as an indication of how highly these streams of cash are valued.[2]

The implications of institutional domination of many financial markets is also highlighted in Chapter 6, where Hayes and Regan show how Rule 415 shelf registrations (a streamlined procedure by which large U.S. corporations can issue new securities) are a creature of an institutionalized market. Given the execution speed of shelf financings, the individual investor is typically not a viable target and therefore is shut out. In addition, the drastically shortened preparation for offering the securities allows for little meaningful due diligence to uncover information that would give additional protection to relatively unsophisticated individual investors. Further, the burgeoning medium-term note market, which depends on continuing dialogue between issuers and large investors, also consigns the retail investor to the role of spectator.

Private placements have long been the special preserve of institutional investors, and their rapid growth relative to public debt offerings during the 1980s represents still further subordination of the position of the individual investor in the capital markets. The inauguration and subsequent growth in use of Rule 144A, and creation of a secondary market for these institutionally placed securities, has assisted in attracting a wider group of both issuers and big investors. In short, Hayes and Regan conclude that the publicly issued and privately placed debt markets are steadily converging along regulatory, issuer, structural, and buyer dimensions—and all under institutional tutelage. Further, dominant institutional investors of the past continue their leading place in these markets.

An important element in these developments has been the desire of both investors and vendors for ready liquidity. For securities firms, liquidity was a prime impetus for the move into debt and equity principal trading. Today, principal positioning has yielded large profits (and losses!) for many securities firms. Just as strikingly, entirely new markets (such as asset-backed securities, futures, options, floating-rate paper, and the Euromarkets) and new processes (program trading, portfolio insurance, immunization, and optimization) have arisen to satisfy investor demands for liquidity. And institutional investors increasingly show no hesitation in sidestepping the vendor community

---

2. For example, Templeton Management and Van Kampen Merritt were sold by Xerox for $360 million, a gain of $100 million and 1.4 times book value.

in achieving liquidity through direct-dealing mechanisms such as Instinet and the ill-fated Capitalink.

In the equity markets, pressures to enhance the liquidity of secondary trading are perhaps most visible in the United States. American institutional investors have traditionally taken a passive, arm's-length approach to the governance of companies whose stock they own. When they grow disenchanted with results, their usual reaction has been to sell their holdings quickly and move on to something else. In the United States there is no mechanism to encourage long-term commitment and collaboration between companies and professional investors. In fact, many financial intermediaries are legally barred from holding shares in nonfinancial companies.

By contrast, Kester notes in Chapter 3 that major economic competitors of the United States fostered a collaborative atmosphere between private capital users and some large investors, notably financial institutions. In Japan and Germany, Kester points out, financial institutions are not only permitted to take long-term equity positions in their customers, but also are tacitly encouraged to take an active role in overseeing their operations. Thus, while the historical predisposition of U.S. institutional investors has been to "cut and run" from unattractive positions,[3] aided and abetted by a deep and liquid secondary market that is also presumed to be more "efficient," in other geographic secondary markets (such as Germany and Japan) the tendency is to hold investment positions and act like long-term owners. A number of observers believe such a pattern has significant advantages.

The preoccupation of American investors with liquidity and the mobility of capital certainly stimulated the securitization of financial assets and liabilities discussed at a number of points in this book. And we have observed that this phenomenon has its dark side. In Chapter 2, Baldwin and Esty show how many U.S. savings and loan operators used securitization to liquify dull but relatively stable home-mortgage portfolios in favor of higher-yielding but higher-risk asset classes: commercial loans, commercial real estate mortgages, junk bonds, and even equity investments in property developments. Certainly, dramatic trading losses have soured many sophisticated vendor firms on various forms of securitized exotica. Despite these hazards, other sectors of the global market are likely to embrace the U.S. brand of liquidity and capital mobility in the absence of explicit regulatory curbs or outright prohibitions. One hopes they will learn from mistakes in the United States.

---

3. The 1993 management and strategy changes at General Motors and Sears are indications that an era of institutional investor activism is in its early stage.

Capital Issuers

Just as there has been a power shift from financial services vendors to large investors, there has been an apparent power shift from the vendors to the corporations that provide the raw product material to sell to those investors. That trend is again more evident in the United States.

Crane and Eccles point out in Chapter 5 that the historically close ties between U.S. corporations and certain financial institutions have given way to a looser and less exclusive set of relationships. The importance and value of a client list—once the most prized possession of many investment and commercial banks—has declined. The increased financial sophistication of corporations and concerns about possible conflicts of interest with long-standing financial vendor-advisers have undoubtedly contributed to this loss of leverage. Corporate issuers initially cast a wandering eye in the 1970s, agitating for quicker, cheaper options for executing financing strategies. Some prominent U.S. investment banks further frayed corporate relationships in the 1980s when they shifted to more lucrative activities on behalf of their own accounts.

Even though financial vendors—particularly securities firms—seem to be regaining their appreciation for ongoing ties with corporations, Crane and Eccles predict that they are unlikely to recover all of their lost ground. They note that many U.S. corporations now appear to link vendor relationships with sharply priced financial transactions. A what-have-you-done-for-me-lately? attitude on the part of issuers reflects how greatly the balance of power has shifted in their direction.

Nevertheless, Kester argues in Chapter 3 that the apparent preference of U.S. corporate clients for a loose and almost ad hoc relationship with their financial vendors may not, in the long run, serve the interests of either party. He points to the enduring ties and a sense of common purpose that have benefited client and capital supplier in Japan and Germany, where the focus is more on long-term value maximization and less on quarterly earnings performance. It is difficult to be optimistic, however, about either the United States or Great Britain converting to the Japan-Germany model. Disintermediation of traditional vendors in favor of public market sources in the United States and Britain may be too far advanced to be reversed.

New Financing Techniques

The expanding array and sophistication of financial products and financing arrangements are yet another aspect of the contemporary marketplace explored in these pages. Baldwin and Esty point out in Chapter 2 that improvements in communications and information processing have brought much lower transaction costs and a vastly more efficient financial system—the ideal environment for fostering financial innovation (or in the case of the S&Ls, mischief!). Competition from off-shore sources of funds for capital issuers, particularly in the Euromarkets, made innovation necessary. The proliferation of shelf registrations, first in the United States and later in Japan, was a direct consequence of competition from the Euromarket's faster, less bureaucratic procedure for issuing debt securities.

All of this has helped accelerate the development of more specifically tailored financing arrangements in a variety of situations. The development of derivative securities has been greatly influenced by the growing liquidity of various financial assets and liabilities alluded to earlier and by new techniques for decoupling, evaluating, and reassembling specific features in financial contracts. This in turn has undermined any remaining cartel-like characteristics of financial market sectors. As Baldwin and Esty point out, innovation is a foe of cartelization. Hybrid securities and nontraditional financial contracts have made it possible for various players within the contemporary financial markets to circumvent artificial barriers erected either geographically or by financing product category. Similarly, the various competences offered by a vendor—credit, securities underwriting and distribution, financial advisory, M&A work, secondary market support—are increasingly seen as unbundled by the client, which often awards business discretely and expects it to be priced accordingly.

New Entrants

Both Vietor (Chapter 1) and Baldwin and Esty (Chapter 2) have chronicled how, in the wake of new regulations instituted in the 1930s, U.S. commercial banks and savings and loan associations occupied protected niches in the U.S. financial markets. With the recent turn toward deregulation, protective fences around these institutions were whittled away; today these vendors are adjusting to the rigors of a marketplace in which alternative and new competitors can undercut previous volume and profit margins. Mortgage bankers, money market mutual funds, discount brokers, consumer finance houses, auto finance subsidiaries, leasing companies, asset-based lenders, and diversified providers such as General Electric Capital threaten the market positions of conventional firms.

Probably no financial services sector is more price driven than the *reinsurance* industry, as Goodman points out in Chapter 4. Underwriting risks are "laid off" in a manner that epitomizes an arbitraged global market, yet the dominant vendors' economies of scale create quite effective barriers to new vendors' entry. The *non-life* insurance business offers a much different model. In his study of this market sector in Europe, Goodman concludes that where knowledge of local operating conditions, regulatory regimes, client cultures, and superior servicing count, incumbent vendors enjoy persistent barriers to entry, largely based on nonprice variables.

In another example of barriers to entry, Sirri and Tufano chronicle in Chapter 7 how U.S. mutual funds have capitalized on the individual investors' flight to safety. Phenomenal mutual fund growth in the United States has produced a bonanza for the funds' managers. While in theory there is relatively easy entry into the fund management business, the tendency of investors to stick with a particular fund or fund group once they have invested their money has worked to the advantage of existing funds and against new entrants. New entrants can, however, make market inroads if they have deep pockets, patience, and some kind of unique advantage. Vietor, for instance, shows the overhead advantages that the commercial banks could bring to bear in the distribution of both mutual funds and certain insurance products if the regulatory environment were amenable. Of course, even with regulatory approval, the exploitation of inherent advantages in a new market sector would remain a daunting challenge to management.

Vendor Organization

The array of financial market forces chronicled here has important implications for how vendors should organize themselves to compete effectively. The classic controversies over the merits of decentralized versus centralized management systems apply in equal measure in the financial services industry.

Any number of contemporary management books call for a basic rethinking of corporate organizational structure. Many conclude that large business organizations are inherently vulnerable to the problems of size and dysfunctional bureaucracies and suggest that responsibility should be decentralized and lodged at the level of the individual business unit. Certainly the chapters in this book have illustrated the importance of being able to respond rapidly to changing conditions in a product market or in a geographic location.

Goodman's study of European non-life insurance in Chapter 4 provides one example. The intensive local service critical to the successful delivery of non-life products presupposes an on-the-scene understanding of the market, the specific risk dimensions, and the idiosyncracies of the customer base. Moreover, it has been noted at various points in this book that corporate and institutional customers tend to "cherry pick" specific products and services from different financial vendors, depending on their special skills and unique market presence. Crane and Eccles draw attention in Chapter 5 to the importance of ad hoc coalition building within high-value-added corporate financial services organizations in winning and executing lucrative, complex assignments. This behavior pattern argues for maintaining decentralized organizational structures and incentives sufficient to encourage individual ingenuity. This can promote the kind of innovation and self-starting entrepreneurship that historically has yielded the most exciting new products and services and the highest profit margins.

Any slavish devotion to a minimalist central headquarters role in controlling the parts of a business has to be tempered, however, by the other realities of doing business. Maintaining adequate financial and managerial controls can be more vexing in financial services than in some other industries because of the fungibility of the product (money) and the potential for disaster to strike as a consequence of actions by one or a few individuals. In Chapter 8, Merton and Perold enumerate some particularly hair-raising examples of this malfeasance in the U.S. securities and money-management sectors. The thrust of their chapter suggests that, from the standpoint of risk exposure and capital management, a financial services organization should be viewed as a whole if pricing of services, deployment of capital, and measurement of capital adequacy are to be executed efficiently.

Management of Vendor Capital

The preoccupation with capital is almost universal among financial vendors, and almost every chapter in this volume has dealt with some aspect of it. Maintaining (or rebuilding) an adequate capital cushion has been difficult for many U.S. and off-shore lending institutions.

U.S. securities firms have operated with high levels of financial leverage. (Indeed, such "gearing" hastened the demise of E.F. Hutton and Drexel Burnham Lambert.) The issue of capital adequacy is all the more compelling for vendor firms servicing institutional investors that as already noted, expect vendors to provide liquidity for their portfolios.

Developing measures that ensure an adequate cushion for risk exposure while optimizing the use of risk capital over the long term is a major management preoccupation for securities firms. Kester argues that the imposition of rigid, uniform capital-to-asset ratios such as the BIS rules for commercial banks can be counterproductive. He asserts that the BIS rules have been instrumental in shutting down lending activity that could have been productively (and profitably) pursued.

These BIS rules, in Kester's opinion, were well intended but basically misguided (although Japanese commercial banks can be grateful that their rules prevented them from going further into risky loans than they did!)

Merton and Perold suggest flaws in conventional approaches to measuring the capital adequacy of financial services vendors. They note in Chapter 8 the essential opaqueness of a multidimensioned financial vendor's activities, which makes it difficult for outside capital suppliers to assess the net risk embedded in the vendor's business portfolio. They point out that it is not satisfactory to price out the capital exposure embedded in any particular *piece* of a firm's business portfolio. Merton and Perold argue persuasively for a distinction between cash capital, which is essentially riskless inventory financing, and risk capital, which is the equity buffer required to protect outside capital suppliers from erosion in the security of their loans and advances. Because of the cumulative portfolio effect of a vendor's total business activities, the marginal impact of an addition or subtraction of a line of business is unique to that particular organization and not easily measured by an outside capital supplier. The implications of this insight are obviously important for the management of a financial services firm. For one thing, it suggests that the firm will waste capital resources if it adopts the kind of piece-by-piece, disaggregated capital allocation that often characterizes a decentralized organization.

Another timely issue raised in these chapters is public ownership of financial vendors and the resulting pressure for near-term performance. The historically high equity returns of the U.S. securities industry are due in part to their high degree of financial leverage. Of course, high leverage is associated with high fluctuations in earnings because of such factors as volatility in interest rates and inventory values. Thus there is an inevitable preoccupation with market valuation of vendor performance and, quite possibly, a bias toward short-term earnings and away from long-term value building. Consequently Kester argues in Chapter 3 for a different complexion in financial firm ownership—one that downplays short-term results in favor of the benefits of long-term ownership. This new ownership status would in turn invest the financial firm with a longer-term approach to its own lines of business. For example, the short-term trading in a company's securities might be downgraded in favor of certain types of insider information that could enable the vendor to provide high-value-added *and* high-margin service based on an intimate knowledge of the client's business. Proposals such as Kester's inevitably cause regulatory warning lights to start flashing, so we now turn to this important variable in the competitive equation.

Implications for Regulation

Discussion of regulation in this book has focused mainly on the U.S. experience. Because American authorities catalyzed broad deregulation of financial services not just at home but overseas, this is perhaps an appropriate focus. Vietor describes in Chapter 1 the cartel-like regulation that made Bank of America prosperous but inefficient during much of the post–World War II period. Given this benign environment, it is not surprising that overcapacity developed in U.S. commercial banking. A similar situation existed in Europe and Japan during the same period.

The consequences of removing many of those regulatory props should not have been as surprising—or as costly to taxpayers—as they have proven to be. Baldwin and Esty highlight the danger of *half* measures in regulatory reform. In the American case, deregulation of the asset side of the balance sheet, and maintenance of the status quo in funding liabilities, created an imbalance in which moral hazard and adverse selection prevailed. These authors describe how the conversion of many S&Ls to stock ownership and new rules on how assets could be invested encouraged the new owners to pursue maximum profits with higher-risk strategies. With federal deposit insurance backing, their ill-conceived investments and fiscal disasters were almost inevitable.

The S&L experience raises the important issue of whether it is realistic in any complex economic society to rely on market forces to do most of the essential policing of its financial services sector. Vietor argues that regulatory intervention is very likely to distort so-called natural market forces and lead to serious inequities and dysfunctional behavior. But none of our authors would agree to let the marketplace act as sole arbiter of economic behavior; we live, after all, in a political world where the interests of multiple constituencies must be considered and ultimately reconciled. In the securities industry, prohibitions against insider trading and the maintenance of vendor-financed insurance funds such as SIPC have provided a measure of protection for both customers and the industry.

There is, of course, a very fine line between over- and underregulation, analogous to the tension between centralized and decentralized accountability in financial institutions discussed earlier. A marketplace as complex as the contemporary one does not lend itself to the regulation of the millions of individual transactions that occur each day. On the other hand, a completely laissez faire approach toward financial markets would very likely degenerate into abuse and lack of public confidence. Thus some level of regulatory intervention is both healthy and inevitable.

This being the case, the form in which that regulation takes place must be considered. Populist traditions in the United States have given it a fragmented superstructure at both federal and state levels. In Japan the Ministry of Finance has provided the sole oversight of the country's various financial activities since about 1878. Aside from the important issue of centralized versus decentralized regulatory machinery, there is the question of the units that will be overseen and regulated. A compelling argument can be made that it is better to regulate by *function* rather than by institutional entity. Earlier chapters have illustrated how financial markets and services have evolved over time, outpacing the institutional vendor frameworks that had grown up around them. It would be naive to think that a market system's traditional financial institutions would conveniently disappear when rendered obsolete by developments. Nevertheless, it would seem better to provide at least the basis for the orderly demise of institutions through a focus on functions rather than through a focus on the institutions that may be terminally ill.

Goodman, in Chapter 4, makes the important summary point that an increasingly integrated and interdependent global market for money sharply reduces the tolerance for asymmetries in national regulation. Inconsistencies among various national rules adversely affects the entire structure of competition and, therefore, highlights the need to negotiate common rules worldwide.

Looking Forward

Prognostication in an industry as dynamic as financial services is likely to be a fool's errand. Rapid change is what we have seen in the recent past, and rapid change is the likely course of the near and distant future. Just what shapes future change will take, however, is anyone's guess. Certainly few of us who have enjoyed long careers in this industry could have envisioned many of the financial products or the vendor/client practices commonplace in the 1990s. Still fewer of us can describe the products and practices that will prevail in the coming decades. Nevertheless, trends once established often persist, and the same might be said of powerful trends within the financial industry today.

As the introduction to this volume pointed out, the financial services industry is driven by information. Its forward momentum is sustained by information quality, speed of transmission, and the growing sophistication of information analysis. It is difficult to envision a scenario in which that forward movement will be interrupted or reversed. Similarly, in the area of regulation it is difficult to believe that the increasing interdependence of nations, their economies, and financial markets will lead to anything but a convergence in the nature of market regulation.

Still more difficult to envision is an economic climate in which the changing needs of investors and capital users will not provoke an innovative response in terms of new products and services. If it has done nothing else, the financial profession—going back to the early bankers of the Renaissance—has made its way in the world by applying creativity and skill to satisfy the financing/investing needs of those who lacked the ability or innovative insights to do it for themselves. This long tradition of creative response to changing needs will undoubtedly persist and will ultimately determine which firms will be successful in the years ahead.

For global financial services, the abiding *constant* is continual *change;* and for top managers, this fact has important implications. They must maintain organizations that are sufficiently stable to provide for continuity and sufficiently flexible to accommodate the changes that will inevitably invade their operating environments. And they must develop the internal competencies to deal with changes as they appear; these competencies may be in new-product development, distribution, information systems and analysis, customer service, and development of their own human resources.

Few industries have the capacity to rapidly "remake" themselves as times change. Unburdened by bricks and mortar, the financial services firm can, however, change itself as its surroundings change. Its building materials are not circuit boards or ingots of metal, but intangible ideas. Guiding the process of that continuous metamorphosis is the most important job of top management; this is at once the great challenge and the opportunity of managing in the financial services industry.

ABOUT THE CONTRIBUTORS

Carliss Y. Baldwin is the William L. White Professor of Business Administration at the Harvard Business School and teaches in the first-year program. She graduated from MIT in 1972 and received her M.B.A. and D.B.A. from Harvard in 1974 and 1977, respectively. Before joining the Harvard Business School, she was an assistant professor at the Sloan School of Management. Her research focuses on real capital decisions in corporations, and she is currently investigating the impact of capital budgeting systems on corporate competitiveness as well as financing practices of high-tech companies. Baldwin is the author of many papers, a director of the Federal Loan Bank of Boston, a member of the Advisory Board of the Earle Palmer Brown Companies, and a member of the Emerging Markets Advisory Committee of the SEC.

Dwight B. Crane is the George Gund Professor of Finance and Banking and Senior Associate Dean for Faculty Development at the Harvard Business School, where he teaches in the M.B.A. and executive programs. He is a graduate of MIT and received his M.B.A. from the University of Michigan and his Ph.D. in economics from Carnegie-Mellon. Before joining the Harvard Business School, Crane headed an economics research group at Mellon Bank in Pittsburgh. An active consultant, Crane has worked with several financial institutions and other organizations. He is a member of the board of directors of SLB Investment Portfolios Inc. and other mutual funds sponsored by Smith Barney Shearson. His research interests concern the strategy and structure of financial institutions. The author of papers, monographs, and books, his most recent volume is *Doing Deals: Investment Banks at Work*, which he co-authored with Robert G. Eccles.

Robert G. Eccles is professor of Business Administration and chairman of the Organizational Behavior/Human Resource Management area at the Harvard Business School. He received two S.B. degrees from

MIT (mathematics and humanities/social science) and a Ph.D. in sociology from Harvard University. For the past 20 years, his professional objective has been the development of a practical perspective on management that combines the useful contributions of different theories from the social sciences. More recently he has shifted his attention to the contribution that the humanities can make to the study, teaching, and practice of management.

Benjamin C. Esty is a doctoral student at the Harvard Business School. He received his bachelor's degree from Stanford University in 1985 and his M.B.A. from the Harvard Business School in 1991. Prior to joining the doctoral program, Esty was a financial services consultant at Bain and Company and financial manager at Commercial Mortgage Corporation, a startup company in Boston. His current research focuses on the incentive effects of different capital and ownership structures and how they affect firm performance.

John B. Goodman is an associate professor at the Harvard Business School. He received his bachelor's degree summa cum laude from Middlebury College and his master's and Ph.D. degrees from Harvard University. He is the author of *Monetary Sovereignty: The Politics of Central Banking in Westen Europe* (Cornell University Press, 1992), as well as a number of articles on European integration, financial deregulation, and privatization. His current research focuses on the changing pattern of business-government relations.

Samuel L. Hayes, III holds the Jacob H. Schiff Chair in Investment Banking at the Harvard Business School, where he has taught since 1971; before that he was a tenured member of the faculty at Columbia University's Graduate School of Business. He received a B.A. from Swarthmore, and an M.B.A. and a D.B.A. from the Harvard Business School. Hayes's research has focused on the capital markets and on the corporate interface with the securities markets. He has written numerous widely published papers and articles and has contributed chapters to a number of books. He is the co-editor or co-author of five books, including *Competition in the Investment Banking Industry, Investment Banking and Diligence,* and *Investment Banking: A Tale of Three Cities.* Hayes consults for a number of corporations, financial institutions, and government agencies. For twelve years he was Chairman of the Finance Advisory Board of the Commonwealth of Massachusetts and presently serves on the board of managers of Swarthmore College and the New England Conservatory of Music and on the boards of directors of the Eaton-Vance mutual funds and Tiffany & Co.

W. Carl Kester is professor of business administration at the Harvard Business School, where he teaches international finance. An economics graduate of Amherst College, Kester also holds an M.B.A. from the Harvard Business School, and a Ph.D. from Harvard University's Graduate School of Arts and Sciences, and an M.S.C. from the London School of Economics. He has written numerous articles for a wide variety of journals, case studies, and the volume *Japanese Takeovers: The Global Contest for Corporate Control*, research for which was supported by the 1987 O'Melveny & Myers Centennial Grant. He also serves as co-editor for two leading finance case books. The focus of his current research is the theory and practice of international finance.

Robert C. Merton is the George Fisher Baker Professor of Business Administration at the Harvard Business School. He received a B.S. in engineering mathematics from Columbia University in 1966, an M.S. in applied mathematics from California Institute of Technology in 1967, an honorary M.A. from Harvard in 1989, a Ph.D. in economics from MIT in 1970, and an LL.D. from the University of Chicago in 1991. Merton was an assistant professor, associate professor, professor, and J.C. Penney Professor of Management in the finance area at the Sloan School of Management. He joined the Harvard Business School faculty in 1988 and teaches finance in the doctoral program. He is the author of many papers and articles and of the book *Continuous-Time Finance*. He has served as president and director of the American Finance Association, won the Leo Melamed Prize from the University of Chicago, and twice received the first prize from the Institute of Quantitative Research in Finance in its Roger Murray Prize Competition. Merton also serves on the editorial and advisory boards of numerous journals.

André Perold is professor of business administration at the Harvard Business School, where he teaches the second-year Capital Markets course and is the faculty chair of the Corporate Financial Management executive education program. He holds a B.Sc. (Hons) from the University of the Witwatersrand, Johannesburg, and an M.S. in statistics and a Ph.D. in operations research, both from Stanford University. His recent research has investigated questions relating to risk management and capital allocation within principal financial firms, stock market efficiency and liquidity, dynamic portfolio decision rules, management of currency risk, and implementation costs within investment organizations. He is the developer of a widely used software package for portfolio construction. Perold serves on the editorial board of the *Financial Analysts Journal*. He is consultant to a number of financial institutions and investment organizations, and serves as a director/trustee of several Merrill Lynch mutual funds, The Common Fund, and Quantec Investment Technology.

Andrew D. Regan is Charles M. Williams Fellow at the Harvard Business School. He received his A.B. in Modern European History from Harvard, his M.Sc. in West European Politics from the London School of

Economics, and his M.B.A. from the Harvard Business School, where he was a Baker Scholar. Before returning to Harvard, he was a securities analyst for Donaldson, Lufkin and Jenrette. As a fellow, Mr. Regan has written chapters of books and case studies, and is currently collaborating on a major study of the leveraged buyout business.

Erik R. Sirri is an assistant professor at the Harvard Business School, where he teaches the second-year Capital Markets course. He received his B.S. in astronomy from the California Institute of Technology, an M.B.A. from the University of California, Irvine, and a Ph.D. in finance from the University of California, Los Angeles. Before joining the Harvard Business School, he worked at NASA and in the aerospace industry. He has also consulted for investment banks, brokerage houses, economic consulting firms, and mutual fund companies. His research concerns the design of financial markets—his most recent study examines the determinants of investor inflows into mutual fund complexes and distribution of investor capital among the funds in each complex.

Peter Tufano is an assistant professor of business administration at the Harvard Business School. He earned his A.B., M.B.A., and Ph.D. all from Harvard. Before receiving his doctorate, he was a management consultant at Booz-Allen & Hamilton and in real estate development in Boston and New York. His research focuses on the design of securities, especially by firms under financial stress, as well as on product-level competition among financial institutions. His research has appeared in several journals and as portions of several books. He is developing a new course on how corporations can utilize the range of products offered by the capital markets to manage financial risks and lower their costs of financing.

Richard H. K. Vietor is a professor at the Harvard Business School, where he teaches courses on the regulation of business, environmental management, and the international political economy. He received an economics degree from Union College and graduate degrees in history from Hofstra University and the University of Pittsburgh. Before coming to the Harvard Business School in 1978, he held faculty appointments at Virginia Polytechnic Institute and the University of Missouri.

Professor Vietor's research, which focuses on business-government relations, has been published in numerous journals and cases and several books, including *Energy Policy in America Since 1945* (1984), *Telecommunications in Transition* (1986), *Strategic Management in the Regulatory Environment* (1989), and most recently, *Contrived Competition: Regulation and Deregulation in America* (Harvard University Press, 1993). He serves on the editorial board of the *Business History Review* and is president of the Business History Conference.

INDEX